Faithful and Brave

Sponsors

As the team responsible for
the delivery of the new Campus,
we are delighted to be involved in
celebrating the past, present and future
of James Gillespie's High School.

Here's to the next chapter in
the school's history.

Faithful and Brave

A CELEBRATION OF
JAMES GILLESPIE'S
HIGH SCHOOL

John MacLeod

BIRLINN

First published in 2016 by
Birlinn Limited
West Newington House
10 Newington Road
Edinburgh
EH9 1QS

www.birlinn.co.uk

ISBN 978 1 78027 382 2

British Library Cataloguing-in-Publication Data
A catalogue record for this book is available
from the British Library

Designed by Mark Blackadder

Printed and bound by TJ International, Cornwall

for
Dr Patricia Thomas

and to the memory of
Alan McMurray
1966–2006
and
Rupert Ford
1968–2001

Contents

Foreword

I can still remember the day in June 1979 when I found out what class I was going to be in at James Gillespie's High School: 1R1. But the excitement soon turned to bewilderment. No one from my class at Bruntsfield Primary School was allocated the same class as me.

As I made my way home that day, I remember feeling gutted about the prospect of starting up at 'big school' after the summer all alone. That, however, changed when I bumped into my mate and neighbour, Paul Baur. He went to Sciennes Primary and, unbelievably, it turned out that not only was he going to Gillespie's too but he was going to be in 1R1 as well. My mind was put at rest and suddenly I was excited about heading to High School once again.

The ensuing years at James Gillespie's High School turned out to be six of the most important, fulfilling and entertaining years of my life.

If you'd told me then that, nearly forty years later, I'd be invited to write the Foreword to a book about the place, I'd have laughed out loud. As I'm sure Paul Baur would have. In fact, I know he did, because I told him just after John asked me to do it. Paul and I are still huge mates. As are most of the guys I formed close friendships with through our formative years at Gillespie's. Together we've been through marriages, divorces, births and – sadly – deaths together. But the common bond that was formed over those High School years is as strong now as it ever was.

I always viewed school as a place to daily interact with my mates first, and education second.

It's difficult to sum up what Gillespie's meant to me as it gave me so much. And I don't just mean the four O-Grades and two Highers I left with. My time off Whitehouse Loan gave me lessons, and not just from the language lab or the English block – but in life.

So many teachers left their mark on me. I'd like to take the opportunity here to highlight just two of them.

First: Miss Jean Clark, my Drama teacher. Miss Clark was a beautifully spoken, perfectly turned-out lady who always gave the impression that she loved what she was doing. I always felt she would have been much better served performing in some classic period piece at The Lyceum. However, teaching was her vocation and that was very much to my benefit.

I remember we were all really impressed as Miss Clark name-dropped the fact that she had been to drama college with MARY MARQUIS!!! Aye, her off the news!

I really took to Miss Clark and I'm so glad to say she took to me too. I was far from the perfect pupil, but she seemed to get my cheeky humour – and I guess she thought it was important to allow that to flow, given the subject she was teaching.

Drama was absolutely my favourite subject at school. It was the first after-school club I signed up for. Even though it meant that big trek across the Links to the Darroch Annexe, it was always worth it.

On occasion, my route to the Annexe meant passing by the King's Theatre. I can vividly remember looking in its big windows, staring at the production- shots of the show that week – and thinking, how cool would it be to do this drama thing for real on a stage like that? I've never forgotten that feeling. And still remember it every time I pass the front of the theatre on my way to the stage door.

I've been lucky enough to work there for a number of years now in the annual Panto. It still gives me a huge buzz to perform on that famous stage every Christmas. I don't know if Miss Clark ever came to see me at the King's before she died. I like to think she did.

And probably took notes to give me on my performance . . .

She saw me through my First and Second Year Drama classes and then my O-Level – as there wasn't O-Grade Drama back then, JGHS offered the English alternative.

But the biggest thing I learnt from her wasn't in the classroom. It came on the stage in the Main Hall, up at the High School.

As a budding young thesp, Gillepie's annual Christmas show, directed by Mr Stewart McDougall and orchestrated by Head of Music Mr Alistair Hair, was something I was desperate to be involved in. And, luckily, after making my debut as The Coroner Munchkin in *The Wizard of Oz* in Second Year, I auditioned for – and got the part of – Pepe in *Viva Mexico!* as a slightly more confident Third Year.

This was the main comic part and a huge deal for me. My sidekick was

David Treadgold who played Pablo. I think I'd learned the words within a week of getting the script. David and I even rehearsed our routines in the garage at my house, as I recall – such was our enthusiasm.

And it paid off. Without wanting to blow my own trumpet, we were a hit. For the three nights that the show ran, I felt like a superstar. Those three nights were probably the best three nights of my life up to that point, and I can still remember the huge downer when it was all over.

However, it just made me want to do it more.

And this is where the big lesson comes in. I let that very early success go to my head. Decided I knew it all. This acting lark was a breeze. Or so I thought . . .

A few months later, I was back at Drama Club having been trusted with the lead role in a farce with Miss Clark directing. Such was the size of my head at that time, I never really bothered with learning the lines. Even on the dress rehearsal I still had the script in my hand. Miss Clark was absolutely furious with me, and let rip in a rare display of anger. I told her it would be 'All right on the night', and indeed it was – but not as good as it could have been had I put in the effort.

My ego never really let the dressing-down from Miss Clark bother me. I thought it'd all be fine and she would just forget it.

It wasn't. And she didn't.

After the summer holidays, it was time to audition for the next big Gillespie's production. This time, however, there was a change at the top. Mr McDougall had stepped down as director and – yup, you've guessed it – Miss Clark had taken over.

The show was *Calamity Jane* and I immediately knew the part I wanted (and fully expected) to get. Francis Fryer was the comic role who ended up dressing up and singing as a girl – perfect, I thought. I swanned in for my audition and I actually thought I did a great job – of *course* I did!

This was right where Miss Clark saw her chance to teach me a lesson for stressing her out earlier in the year. Days later, the cast was announced on the notice board of the Music Department in Bruntsfield House. A bunch of us gathered round eagerly checking to see if our names were there. I immediately checked who was playing Francis Fryer.

And I'd to check twice because apparently Grant Stott hadn't been cast in the role – my mate Adam Foster had. I continued desperately to scan the list. I didn't see my name until the very bottom. I had secured the part of Rattlesnake the Coachdriver. No funny routines. No songs. No 'business'. Two lines. And that was it.

As delighted as I was for Adam, who went on and did a brilliant job in my part – sorry, *the* part – I'd been brought down to earth with a bump. A thud. An almighty clatter. And I've never forgotten that one. Enjoy the moment – but don't be a big idiot because of it.

Another teacher who went the extra mile for me was my English teacher, Mrs Harkness. She had me in her O-Grade English class and had a formidable reputation for not tolerating nonsense, but I really liked her.

She was tough, but I never minded that because she was a great teacher who had time for us all. I did well in her class and got great grades right up until actually sitting my O-Grade itself. For some reason I'd gone off the rails a bit, late in Fourth Year, and pretty much blew all my exams. My only passes were for Drama and Secretarial Studies. It was a disaster. My folks went mad.

Mrs Harkness was equally disappointed in my performance in English and immediately appealed the grade as my 'Prelim' marks were decent. It was declined, and prospects of re-studying O-Grade English in Fifth Year beckoned. But Mrs Harkness took me aside and said she felt I was capable of passing my Higher – and, against the wishes of the Principal Teacher, Mr Davidson, she'd take me in her class. She had stuck her neck out for me. She didn't need to – but she had.

The consequences of failing that Higher didn't bear thinking about. Mrs Harkness made that VERY clear.

I'm glad to say I worked hard, and with her help I got my Higher English along with every other exam I sat that year – and I believe that's down to her. I was just too scared to let down the faith she'd shown in me. And I was also just a wee bit desperate to prove Mr Davidson wrong.

I can still remember his face the day it was confirmed I had passed. As well as his reply. 'Yes, son,' he said, 'I believe miracles *do* happen . . .'

Gillespie's wasn't just the place where I was educated but the place where I learned so much. I had my first trips to France, London and Loch Tay in my time there and had great times with my mates that we still talk about today.

And talking of my school mates, I actually went on to marry one of them – Claire (Claire Ball, as was) and I got married in 1996 and both our children, Sam and Lori, went through James Gillespie's High School . . . so in many ways I feel I've never really left.

'Fidelis et Fortis' . . . and enjoy the book!

Grant Stott
May 2016
http://www.pantovillain.co.uk/

Preface

In April 1980, newly fourteen, a small and bespectacled Glasgow Highlander in the bewildering new world of Edinburgh, adjusting frantically to a city that then still boasted widespread coal fires and ambling horse-drawn milk floats, I remember once spending the best part of my lunch-break in the James Gillespie's High School library, browsing assorted copies of old school magazines I had unearthed from a low cupboard.

It was, within minutes, evident that the school, as an institution, was very old; that it had a rich and fascinating past; and that it had most recently come through dramatic change – from a selective, fee-paying 'Corporation Grammar' exclusively for girls, to a free, non-selective and co-educational area comprehensive.

I did hope vaguely, one day, to explore this intriguing history thoroughly and in depth. I am grateful to Donald J. Macdonald, Head Teacher, three decades later for offering me the opportunity; and to the enthusiastic and, on occasion, unforgettable interest of the James Gillespie's Trust, who agree to it. I am indebted, as ever, to the keen professionalism of Hugh Andrew, Andrew Simmons, Deborah Warner, James Hutcheson and all at Birlinn Ltd. In particular I would thank my editor, Barbara Simmons, for her unflagging, perennially cheerful work in the final preparation of the text for publication. I must thank the many individual subscribers – former pupils all – to this publication, and our sponsors, the team who have built the new school: Hub South East Scotland Ltd, Galliford Try, and Morrison Construction.

I owe a particular debt to Iona M. Cameron, Tom Johnson and Finlay Cunniffe for reading through chapters as I produced them, for alerting me to egregious errors or infelicitous turns of phrase and all the while lavishing interest, enthusiasm and encouragement. Both Miss Cameron and Mr

Johnson had the dubious pleasure of teaching me at Gillespie's, over three decades ago, and both have besides honoured me with their hospitality. Finlay is himself a recent pupil of the school, from August 2009 to June 2015, and with whom I share Hebridean background and Gaelic heritage. Between them, they have personally experienced half a century of Gillespie's history and their perspective has been invaluable. I myself, nevertheless, take sole responsibility for any inadvertent factual error.

I am besides indebted to Mr Macdonald, for his keen interest and the kettle ever aboil; for all members of staff, past and present, who chose to help – David Anderson, Douglas Burke, Janis Croll, Andrew Digance, Colin Finlayson, Hamish McDougall, Dr Patricia Thomas and Alex Wallace; to school contemporaries of my own who continue to feed memories and photographs to various Gillespie's-related Facebook pages; to Grant, for writing such a generous and engaging Foreword; to the estate of the late Dame Muriel Spark for permission to quote from various works; and to Edi Stark, for permission to use material from her poignant and outstanding 2003 BBC Radio Scotland documentary.

I must, though, single out Andrew Digance, master of Design Technology, a highly respected member of the school's staff, for all his hard work in recent months in taking so many of the photographs that appear in this volume, all in his own scant free time and without payment, often at my urgent request and with never a murmur of complaint. The splendid frontispiece of the new playground will disappoint no one familiar with Mr Digance's skill behind a lens, and at a vital, visual level this book is as much his achievement as mine.

I should make plain, too, that any opinions expressed here are my own, and only my own – not those of the Head Teacher, the school, the Trust, the City of Edinburgh Council or any of its officers. No doubt I have my prejudices. But, as the wise man once joked, to expect a historian to write without prejudice is like expecting a man to go courting without a girl.

A word on the title and the school motto. 'Fidelis et Fortis' was adopted by James Gillespie's only in 1927; the Headmaster of the day, Thomas J Burnett, was then enthusiastically rebranding his establishment. I translate it as 'Faithful and Brave' both because, by my time, that was what we were taught it meant – indeed, it is explicitly so rendered in the 1977 school magazine – and because I myself believe it is the correct interpretation of the Latin. This is not in any way to disrespect the very many former pupils, from pre-comprehensive days, who assert ardently that it means 'Faithful and Strong'. One does have sympathy with the earnest lad who confessed to Edi Stark, back in 2003, of 'Fidelis et Fortis' that 'I just thought the name was, like, Philadelphia or something – I thought it was, like, cheese . . .'

Few things in life are, for good and ill, as emotive as our schooldays, especially as we move so swiftly from the first glad morning of life to that stage, pushing fifty, when suddenly all seems autumnal, shortly after five in the evening, time for tea and the shadows lengthening on the lawn.

But we look forward, now, to new beginnings in splendid modern facilities and – in these days of austerity – the Scottish Government and the City of Edinburgh Council must be commending for delivering a new James Gillespie's High School on time and on budget.

It has been a privilege to pen this history of James Gillespie's High School before I am history myself; and the more so not just with wistful memories of certain vivid, inspirational and self-sacrificing teachers granted, it would seem, every gift save length of days – the late Ian Caddell, Miss Lindsay Hamilton, Allan Leslie, Ian Nicol, Thomas Laing-Reilly, Robert Mutter, Stewart R. McDougall, Douglas Scott – but those schoolfellows who, at the dawn of my sixth decade, I myself have in Providence somehow outlived. They walk and smile and serve and play, for always, and for many of us, in these recently demolished corridors now surviving but in the palace of our memories.

It is a strange truth that often, in the less gripping moments of a classroom day and grappling with a less favoured school subject, I would gaze out of a certain Bruntsfield House window and think of Lewis; and that, over thirty years later, amidst a sea of those school magazines and many other resources, I found myself toiling hard on that island while thinking fondly of Gillespie's.

Our schooldays, and their personalities, in such remembrance, remind us all poignantly that, while we can usually return to the 'where', we can never go back to the 'when'.

John MacLeod
Drover's Rest, Marybank, Isle of Lewis
jm.macleod@btinternet.com
October 2016

CHAPTER ONE

'Crème de la crème?'

It was the spring of 1977 – damp, chill, Scottish – and, in an elegant office in the sometime and stately dining room of a sixteenth-century manor house, a very tall woman was immersed in her latest and sensational discovery.

Occasionally the period bell rang. Outside, below, in a mishmash of maroon blazers, grey flannel and the odd, defiant blur of denim, teenagers scurried along, below covered walkways and between assorted classes in somewhat characterless, modern and already rather worn classroom blocks about this storied old Bruntsfield House, now an engine room of administration and music. Just two doors away, in what had once been a drawing room, children sang; from high floors above, down steep stony stairs, determined young fingers in some eerie little practice room attacked an aging piano; down below, sturdy ladies tapped their own, more bureaucratic rhythms onto reams of foolscap through clickety-tickety electric typewriters.

Dr Patricia Thomas, Head Teacher of James Gillespie's High School, very much in her prime and in the understated but elegant raiment, tasteful jewellery, subtly scented, soft-set hair ensemble of the Fifties that had made her and defined her, as many other women of her generation in their brilliant careers in a new post-war order, scribbled on. Occasionally she walked in her languid way the length of the room, pausing at another window as the adjacent primary school enjoyed its interval and very small children bounced ceaselessly about its grounds – 'just like little jumping-beans', a successor would muse four decades later.

Days and weeks passed. Was the lady of her interest really a hundred and two, as Anne Laird – herself a former pupil – believed? The birth certificate had to be ordered; an industrial chemist in her first career,

Thomas left nothing to chance. Another epistle winged its way, to a nursing home in Thetford, in distant Norfolk. Dr Thomas had no desire, she stressed, to cause the old woman any strain or excitement, but . . . Soothing words came in due course from Mrs Meek, Matron of the Priorsmead establishment, wherein the alert and serene Mrs Margaret Ashton resided. There followed fast letters, in a big and careful and characterful hand, from the lady herself. An idea took shape in Dr Thomas's head. She summoned her school captains. Linda Urquhart and Sheila Prestage, the Head and Deputy Head Girls, sat respectfully in her chamber, immaculate in uniform, accepting their brief . . . another letter shortly flew to Norfolk: could accommodation for them be arranged?

Thus, amidst the incessant interruptions of a Head Teacher's day, the regular meetings with staff, the occasional probing interview with a potential new recruit, the odd, brisk disciplinary encounter, the details of timetables and schemes of work and School Council diets and yet more memos of cool, sweet, aggressive reason to her Lothian Region purse-masters and the plans for the summer term and the latest, bonding jaunt of First Year pupils and the younger and more adventurous staff to Loch Tay, Dr Thomas laid her plans . . .

Hers was a splendid study and, really, a very Gillespie's room; the tall windows, the magnificent chimney-piece – with the practical electric fire set before; the neutral tones, the heavily detailed plasterwork of the ceiling, the grey-green carpet atop the parquet floor. It was also, manifestly, a woman's space. Pictures were hung just so. Assorted sculptures and *objets d'art* deftly drew the eye. Atop a tall cabinet sat a particular favourite, a stylised carved wooden owl. Two Adam Smith Thompson paintings and some copper etchings hallowed one wall. There were always flowers, and immaculately tended potted plants. And the room was furnished in careful zones and for different scales of drama – for, like all great teachers and the occasional queen, there was a distinct touch of the actress, even the impresario, to Dr Patricia Thomas BSc PhD ARIC.

There was the little desk, facing the wall, where she attended to correspondence. In a far corner, five chairs formed a semi-circle about a low coffee table, with yet more flowers; here, in state, she met with her immediate lieutenants: her shy and chilly Deputy Head, Emily Ferguson, and the Assistant Head Teachers, Douglas Burke and Iona Cameron, Stewart McDougall and Tony Merriman. In the corner opposite that – by the wall of the main doors and so placed that you had to step nervously right into the room, once bidden, before seeing it and her – was the main desk of state. Here she could chat with her secretary; from here, too, Dr

Thomas could wield the telephone like a broadsword. Across the desk, facing her, sat three chairs for more formal encounters: appropriately awed parents; a member of staff called to account or for compliment; certain favoured and honoured pupils. And, beside it – to her right, when seated – was just enough expanse of carpet for a scholar of less esteem to stand, sufficiently unnerved and respectful, when occasion called to discuss their proposed schedule of Highers or ask exactly why that Maths homework had not been done for Mrs Hoenkhe . . . and decades on, though you could remember little of what Dr Thomas had said, you could still remember how, with disconcertingly elusive eye contact and scant but pointed words in the softest of Yorkshire accents, she could make you feel . . .

And, though never on view and only for extremity – such as the time a lad had scurried rather too noisily down the stairs of this Bruntsfield House, rather too near her door and shouting with language Dr Thomas did not care to hear – there was, in her drawer, a two-tail, heavyweight Lochgelly tawse. Dr Thomas disliked corporal punishment, was determined soon to rid it from every corner of her realm, and kept close account of every instance, in the school and by certain incorrigible colleagues, when it was used . . . but she was by training and outlook a scientist and the belt had one lonely virtue: it saved time.

And shortly, when the trees were in blossom and the daffodils grew dusty, those two senior girls travelled south, stayed for two nights, met the redoubtable old lady, and duly wrote up their interview for that year's school magazine with Mrs Margaret Ashton, born at 9 Marchmont Street on 22 February 1875 and from 1880 to 1888 a pupil at Gillespie's School for Boys and Girls – comprehensive and co-educational, without distinction for class or hint of privilege, with neither uniform nor academic gowns and as for most of the great sweep of its history . . . save for a period Dr Patricia Thomas was very, very anxious to live down and for which purposes the clear and tenemented memories of the 102-year-old were now priceless ammunition.

Weeks later, in flaming June, photographed in appropriate regality and gazing into the much more interesting distance, Dr Thomas dictated her words for that same school magazine as if they were being carved in granite as she spoke.

Time passes swiftly and it is difficult to realise that I have already been at Gillespie's for just over two years.

The change to a comprehensive system is almost completed and this term has seen our first comprehensive pupils take SCE O-Grade examinations. The new CSE courses have proved successful and many pupils had excellent results in the recent external assessments. I would like to pay tribute to the staff who have had a difficult task over the past four years in establishing a new school. Many new and excellent courses have been provided for pupils of all abilities and academic standards have been maintained.

The most successful new venture is the provision of a residential week of outdoor education for all First Year pupils at Craggan on Loch Tay. During the past two years there has been a tremendous increase in the provision of extra-curricular activities and outdoor education in the school. This has only been possible because of the interest and enthusiasm of the staff concerned who have given so willingly of their own time.

The PTA is now fully established. A varied and interesting programme of meetings has been offered, throughout the session. In this connection I would also like to thank the parents for their unfailing support and encouragement over the past two years.

Pupils leaving school this session are entering a difficult and unpredictable world. I wish them success in all they do and hope their path is not too difficult.

And there, following humorous editorial, jolly-hockeysticks House reports, earnest little essays and diligent verses and scrawly art and hilarious reportage of Loch Tay, is that interview with Mrs Margaret Ashton: and there she sits, engaged and amused and looking a good deal younger than her weight of years, with the two earnest girls and their cassette recorder. Together, they link a long egalitarian past with a birthing egalitarian present, and all three eye the camera with that same Gillespie's smile – a smile of Edinburgh, and of the Enlightenment.

•　　•　　•

The burden that so exasperated Patricia Thomas weighs on her successors still. The history of Gillespie's is long, honourable and mildly complicated. Founded in 1803 – by the bequest of a childless bachelor who, with his late brother, had amassed a considerable fortune in the manufacture and sale of snuff – it has been, successively, James Gillespie's School; James Gillespie's Schools; James Gillespie's Higher Grade School; James Gillespie's Secondary School for Girls; James Gillespie's High School for Girls . . . and, since August 1973, James Gillespie's High School *simpliciter*.

14 *Eastern Evening News, Friday, April 22, 1977*

Girls get a glimpse of school life in the 1880s

Thetford centenarian Mrs. Margaret Ashton took a trip down memory lane yesterday to her schooldays in the reign of Queen Victoria.

For two lassies made the long trek from Scotland to Priorsmead old people's home in the town to talk with 102-year-old Mrs. Ashton about her life at the James Gillespie High School in Edinburgh.

The school's head girl, 17-year-old Linda Urquhart, and her deputy, Sheila Prestage (18), found Mrs. Ashton in a lively mood as she recounted her nine years at school which began in 1880.

In those days school lessons were held in one big hall and the children were punished with the tawse, a leather strap, if they talked.

"It's not so bad now, but the belt is still used," Miss Urquhart explained.

SCHOOL MOTTO

"We had no dinner hour. The baker used to come in with a large board on his head, full of buns and cakes," Mrs. Ashton remembered.

Though her school career ended nearly 90 years ago, Mrs. Ashton has obviously kept in mind her school motto, "Fidelis et Fortis," which means faithful and strong.

Miss Prestage and Mrs. Ashton also found one link apart from their school connection — they both celebrate their birthdays on February 2nd.

The girls, who were staying with friends in Gt. Ellingham, will write an article on Mrs. Ashton for the school magazine.

MRS. MARGARET ASHTON, aged 102, with her two Scottish schoolgirl interviewers, Linda Urquhart (left) and Sheila Prestage.

There have besides been related but separately led establishments – James Gillespie's Boys' School (from 1929 to 1973), James Gillespie's Primary School (since 1973), and James Gillespie's Nursery School. Though always in the same very small, pleasant corner of south-central Edinburgh – by one side or another of the Bruntsfield Links – the school has occupied four different buildings and made use besides, for annexe purposes, of two others. It has torn down the fourth, Lauderdale Street campus – the buildings, then scarcely forty years old and with all the shoddy character of a delusional age, were in 2009 quite properly condemned – and, in August 2016, took full possession of new buildings, if retaining Bruntsfield House as its heart. And it could well claim, cheekily, to be 'Scotland's comprehensive' – for the catchment area includes most of the University of Edinburgh, Edinburgh Castle, the Royal Mile, St Giles Cathedral, Greyfriars Kirk, the Cowgate, the Grassmarket, the General Assembly Hall

of the Church of Scotland, Princes Street Gardens, the former offices of
The Scotsman and even the Scottish Parliament.

Gillespie's was the first completely free school in Scotland and, since its
first flitting to the south side of Bruntsfield Links in 1914, has been –
geographically – the highest school in Edinburgh. It has spent the mass of
its history as a non-selective and co-educational academy. By October 2016
the school will have been a free, area-based co-ed comprehensive for a full
forty-three years. It has always had a tolerant, liberal outlook; a wry spirit
of 'nevertheless!' and open arms – in a most cosmopolitan part of the city,
noted for medicine, higher education, printing and publishing and
newspaper offices and characterful little bookshops – for pupils of any
creed, background or nationality. (At the time of writing, forty-seven
official languages – that is, tongues for which there is at least one dictionary
in print – are spoken in the school community.) Three decades ago, when
I was a Gillespie's pupil myself, we had several openly gay senior pupils and
at least two gay teachers. And no one batted an eyelid . . .

Many admirable Scottish secondary schools, with enviable results in
the public examinations, disgorge dozens of scholars each year into the
safe tramlines of respectable, remunerative but decidedly unadventurous
employment. This Edinburgh institution's academic standards stand up
with the pack of them.

Yet a high proportion of its alumni make a notable impact in public
life. From my own tight little Gillespie's generation – those who left in the
mid-1980s – I can count, without even checking the internet, such remarkable personalities as John Leslie, television presenter; his younger brother,
Grant Stott, long a star of local radio and King's Theatre pantomime and
these days an Edinburgh institution; Dr Ewen Stewart, one of Britain's
foremost and most respected authorities on the care of people with HIV
and Aids; journalists, like Moira Jeffrey and Ben McPherson – the latter,
lately, an acclaimed novelist; Finn McGrath, film director; Mark Munro,
of the BBC, senior in the production team behind *Mrs Brown's Boys* (not,
admittedly, everyone's cup of Earl Grey) and Robert Cavanah, the actor –
who for a session, when he was plain Robert Scott, sat beside me in
remedial O-Grade Maths and now, rather more glamorously, 'lives between
London and Los Angeles'.

In 2001, we mourned Rupert Ford, still only thirty-three years old,
brilliant scientist and meteorologist and as near to a genius as the school
ever produced. When, in March 2012, Bolton Wanderers player Fabrice
Muamba collapsed on the pitch and his heart, for dreadful moments,
stopped beating, the team who finally took charge of him at the London

Miss Gallacher's First Year registration class, August 1980.

Chest Hospital included eminent cardiologist Dr Sam Mohiddin: in 1988, Mohiddin was Head Boy at Gillespie's. That same school year besides produced the late Morag Siller, a gifted actor and special human being.

Just before our time, Linda Urquhart – the very lass sent hot-foot to Norfolk in 1977 as Our Reporter – has spent her entire career in Edinburgh, is Chairman and sometime Chief Executive of Morton Fraser Ltd, is one of Scotland's most astute and respected businesswomen, holds a rack of directorships, gives to the wider community as a member of the Development Board of the Prince's Trust Scotland and an Ambassador for Girl Guiding UK, and in 2012 was honoured with an OBE. Gillespie's, she murmured in a recent interview, raised her and defined her in one central life lesson, 'Work hard, and you'll do well'.

Looking back over the mist of decades, notable Gillespie's alumni (including that School for Boys) include the eminent Edwardian sculptor, Herbert Snell Gamley; the portrait painter, Henry Raeburn Dobson; the

Relaxation between classes – and heavy-handed policing – in the Sixth Year common room, 1970.

landscape artist Christopher Wood; star of stage and screen, Alastair Sim; the diminutive, late and much-loved comic, Ronnie Corbett; sometime leader of the Liberal Party, David Steel; the historical novelist Dorothy Dunnett; an unflappable Christian missionary, Irene Glass; broadcaster Edi Stark and – since my time – actor Michael Thomson, who attended Gillespie's in the 1990s and played the wry, lanky Jonnie Maconie in BBC hospital drama *Holby City*. And, to general Gillespie's delirium, in August 2016 we finally had an Olympic champion: cyclist Callum Skinner, a pupil from 2005 to 2011, returned from Rio de Janeiro with gold and silver medals.

This list is far from exhaustive and covers many notable achievers from unremarkable Edinburgh homes. And yet Gillespie's has been stalked for decades, and to this day, by a brutally undeserved reputation for privilege, exclusivity and the smuggest elitism – thanks to its really rather brief period as a girls-only 'Corporation Grammar School', from 1929 to 1973, when it charged but token fees and admitted pupils solely on their academic merit, without regard for class or wealth or religion. As recently as 1999 – when what remains, happily, the school's only serious scandal hit the headlines – *The Sun* sneered, absurdly, of 'posh James Gillespie's High in Edinburgh'; this of a school that had by then been an uncomplicated local comp for nearly three decades, had years earlier discarded uniform, is one glorious mix of ethnicity and draws pupils from some of the poorest quarters of

Still, for many, their abiding idea of James Gillespie's High School – prim, behatted, the sort of Edinburgh faces suggesting virtue is its own punishment. Dr Ethel Rennie, founder of Craigie College in Ayr and one of Scotland's greatest educationists, holds forth as guest of honour at Founder's Day in 1970. In the background, Robert Galt and Iona Cameron look suitably grave; to Dr Rennie's left, Provost Brechin tries to look interested and, on her far right, May Andrew seems never to have left.

the old city – at the time of writing, 11 per cent of all Gillespie's children are eligible for free school meals.

Yet it is dogged still by the sub-St Trinian's image of toffee-nosed little girls with Morningside accents, queuing in crocodiles at the school gates in silly little hats, trying to walk like Sybil Thorndike, holding their heads up, *up* . . .

It is the unintended, unlooked-for legacy of our most celebrated former pupil of all, one Muriel Camberg, born at 160 Bruntsfield Place in 1918, who attended Gillespie's from 1923 to 1935, and with distinction. Her parents lacked the means to send her to university, but the young woman took a course in 'commercial correspondence', acquired a husband – Sidney Oswald Spark – emigrated to what was then Southern Rhodesia, and in 1940 discarded the ghastly Mr Spark while astutely retaining his surname. By her death in April 2006, Dame Muriel Spark had been long thought the greatest living British novelist; and, though arguably not her greatest work, her most famous is her short, magical and very, very funny 1961 opus, drawing heavily from her own Edinburgh schooldays – *The Prime of Miss Jean Brodie*. Indeed, Miss Brodie is one of the few characters in our post-

The future Dame Muriel Spark in her upper Primary class about 1928. Muriel Camberg is fifth from left in the second, seated row.

war fiction to have become a household name, in all her charm, self-regard and final monstrosity.

This is not one of those tales of a clever young miss whose later success in letters would embarrass past, obtuse teachers. Muriel Camberg's precocious gifts as a poet were celebrated at Gillespie's at the time; the 1930 school magazine printed a full five of them, because 'they are so much out of the ordinary', when she was but twelve years old. Nor is it the tale – at least till much later – of an alumnus whose work embarrassed her old school. Through the Fifties and Sixties the same magazine regularly chronicled her achievements.

Nor is it even the story of a celebrity who turned her back on a humble past. Spark wrote often, and warmly, of Gillespie's, corresponded with Dr Thomas's successor, Colin Finlayson, and, near century's end, directed a large chunk of a substantial cash prize – a full £10,000 – to Gillespie's, long a comprehensive and not even in the same premises.

A certain tension set in, perhaps, after the 1968 cinematic release of *The Prime of Miss Jean Brodie*, from a script by Jay Presson Allen and drawing

40   GILLESPIE'S HIGH SCHOOL MAGAZINE

THE LEAVES.

" Come, little leaves," cried the wind one day,
" Oh ! please come over the meadows and play,
All of you, green and orange and red,
Oh, come with me just before going to bed."

So from the trees they came fluttering down
All orange and red and golden brown ;
And soon the wind with a mighty shout
Scattered those little leaves about.

Then the old trees all gnarled and bare
Stood sad and still in the Autumn air ;
But they look with joy to the coming year
When all their young leaves will reappear.
                    JEAN RITCHIE, 1 Sen. C.

✦ ✦ ✦ ✦

A GROUP OF POEMS.

It is very seldom that we print more than one contribution from any one author, but the work of Muriel Camberg, aged twelve (2 Sen. A). is so much out of the ordinary that we feel it worth while to give the following five of her poems :—

THE SEA.

Listen to the breakers as they dash against the cliffs,
Listen as they strike the pebbles grey !
The sea is but a lion in a temper and a rage !
And the ships upon its surface are its prey.

Oh, who would go a-riding on the billow-horse so strong ?
Oh, who would go a-riding on the foam ?
Now galloping, now trotting, now walking at a pace !
Now furious, but still a-rolling on.

THE LAND OF POETRY.

I sought the land to find a place,
A place where I could rest,
To fade away from hurrying pace
I tried with zeal and zest.

GILLESPIE'S HIGH SCHOOL MAGAZINE   41

I tried, I tried with all my might
To find a peaceful grove
Away from gaiety so bright,
Where quietly to rove.

My hopes, they seemed to be in vain,
For I sought far and wide,
I sought by hill and vale and plain,
I sought by river-side.

But lo ! at last I found retreat,
A garden fair to see,
Where I was far from hurrying feet.
The Land of Poetry.

✦ ✦ ✦

THE WINDING OF THE HORN.

I heard ten thousand mingled cries,
I heard the blood-hound's whine.
I heard the winding of the horn,
On a morning crisp and fine.
Oh, the winding of the horn I heard !
The winding of the horn,
To bring to bay
The timid deer,
Oh ! such a woeful morn !

I saw the horses paw the ground,
Impatient with the meet.
I saw them galloping, galloping off,
With hastening, hurrying feet.
And the winding of the horn I heard !
The winding of the horn,
To bring to bay
The timid deer,
Oh ! such a woeful morn !

I knew the hounds were on the scent,
For excited was the meet.
They had spotted the tender, timid deer,
And they hastened so swift and fleet.

heavily on her earlier stage treatment of the novel. Though it deservedly won an Oscar for Maggie Smith, the movie raised many an Edinburgh eyebrow at the time (several of Spark's sometime teachers eagerly attended the local première, and emerged shaken and distressed) and makes most uncomfortable viewing today, in an age much more aware of sexual predation on children. There followed shortly, from 1973, the traumatic recasting of Gillespie's as a comprehensive school and, just as Mary McIver and Dr Thomas had all but steered it home, Scottish Television aired their own adaptation of Spark's novel for the small screen, a seven-part and rather cosier series where Geraldine McEwan made the role her own – though it ended ambiguously and a second series was never commissioned.

Far more, inevitably, have been exposed to these productions than have troubled ever to read the enthralling but complex little book and – as so many former pupils can resignedly relate – you have only to mention 'Gillespie's' to invite raised eyebrows, incredulous cackles (especially if you are male) and then highly unoriginal queries as to whether one is in one's prime or, at least, of the 'crème de la crème'. Some of us, if only as defence mechanism, learned to plant our retaliation in first. In a lively 2002 article about the latest internet sensation of the time, that clunking and now deceased grandpappy of all social networking websites Friends Reunited, my sometime classmate James Nice archly declared, 'In 1982 I moved to Edinburgh and it transformed my life. I was enrolled by my father in a vastly superior school, James Gillespie's High, which Muriel Spark made infamous through *The Prime of Miss Jean Brodie*. By the time I arrived pupils were no longer required to pose naked for the art master, or run away to fight for Franco in Spain . . .'

By that point, in the wake of Smith's Technicolor histrionics and McEwan's incessant forsooths, both Miss Brodie and her creator and especially their 'girrrls' were practically campus swear words. The novel, as far as I can remember, was conspicuously absent from the school library. It was never a set English text. Once, early in my Higher English career with crisp little Miss Cuthbert (who might herself have stepped from Spark's pages, along with several other survivors from the Corporation Grammar) I asked timidly about the book and pointed out fatuously – and as if that remarkable mistress might not know – that its author had attended our school.

I was put in my place with a sardonic sigh, a sag of tiny shoulders and a few well-vinegared words; the subject of Spark was emphatically departed from, and our communal attention was instead directed anew to Dylan Thomas, and *Under Milk Wood*, and Llaregyb, and 'Alone until she dies, Bessie Bighead, hired help, born in the workhouse, smelling of the cowshed, snores bass and gruff on a couch of straw in a loft in Salt Lake Farm and picks a posy of daisies in Sunday Meadow to put on the grave of Gomer Owen who kissed her once by the pig-sty when she wasn't looking and never kissed her again although she was looking all the time . . .' – and Diarmid Ross, who may or may not have been later famous for sex, invited me *sotto voce* to pronounce Llaregyb backwards. (Only Miss Cuthbert, even in what would be the final year of a teaching career launched amidst the Second World War, could have taught from such an innuendo-clotted text to a bunch of 16-year-olds and yet maintained entire classroom order.)

By 1990, the whole 'I am in my prime!' thing bordered on open war.

'The Former Pupils' Association didn't want to know,' snapped Dr Thomas in an interview. 'I refused to pander to them . . .' Muriel Spark and Jean Brodie? 'That's simply not what we're about these days . . .'

Over three decades later, the context – and all its tensions – is more readily understood.

Gillespie's, long and then and for always, is a quintessentially Edinburgh school and has time and again suffered from quintessential Edinburgh problems.

One is a barnacled tradition of what has often seemed the worst, most mean-spirited and cheapskate municipal government in Scotland. It was over forty years after the Edinburgh International Festival had been established before the city fathers could bring themselves to erect an opera house. As recently as 1977, the 'Athens of the North' – cradle of Hutcheson and Hume, Ramsay and Raeburn, Adam Smith and Sir Walter Scott and Robert Louis Stevenson – still, almost in a spirit of bleak triumph, poured its raw untreated sewage straight into the sea.

Things have since improved. But there remains the scarcely less barnacled – and obsessive – love-in between the Edinburgh bourgeoisie and private education. For as long as anyone can remember, and even in the second decade of the twenty-first century, roughly a quarter of all Edinburgh children of secondary-school age have been despatched, often at considerable sacrifice by their parents, to the capital's goodly collection of independent schools. When we arrived as a family in the city in 1980, we were at once shocked – and diverted – by how often, outside church and so on, people pressed to know, 'What school do you go to?' (The same question is of course asked in Glasgow, but for very different reasons.)

It might, from afar, seem a good thing that so many parents, of their beneficence, relieve the public purse from the burden of converting their dribbling sprogs into literate and well-rounded citizens. It is a very bad one. It means that successive administrations have been held to unusually lenient public account as to how the city's state schools are administered – and, more, how generously they are funded. That is a particular concern when, like most Scottish local authorities, Edinburgh must maintain and run separate, highly regarded Roman Catholic schools within that system and from the same cash pot. A great many involved in directing the city's state schools, or with oversight over them, or with active power to do them harm, have no personal stake in them: assorted MPs, MSPs, local councillors and even some comprehensive teachers put their bairns to private schools, as do many of the city's senior journalists and most of its richest professionals.

That is hard to think on when you bring to mind too that, for as long as anyone can remember, Gillespie's – at both its Warrender Park Crescent and the later Bruntsfield House sites – has been overcrowded, cramped for space, has never enjoyed adjacent and adequate outdoor sports facilities and, for decades since the 1960s, endured incessant council budget cuts and straitened resources. (My interview-without-coffee with Dr Thomas, in March 1982, happened because my maths teacher had prescribed homework from a text the school was unable to supply – that was an especially grim year; the Labour-led Lothian Regional Council being then in full war with the Thatcher Government and, as usual, cynically cutting financial corners by clobbering its schools department – and which I had been too embarrassed to ask my cash-strapped parents to buy.)

And yet, through all this, and despite the loss from 1991 of much tradition – it is now the only state secondary in Edinburgh not to have a uniform – Gillespie's has turned in, regularly, some of the best exam results in Scotland, was twice in 2015 granted the accolade of the country's best state secondary school and (thanks to Muriel Spark) is known the world over. There is keen, longstanding parental competition for places and a waiting list at times sevenscore. And perhaps because of all this, and Miss Jean Brodie, there has long been a strange spite, in wider Edinburgh and in certain high places, against Gillespie's: it was true in Dr Thomas's pomp, from 1975 to 1991, and it is true still, and can make life most trying for its leadership.

The historian has to be careful not to view the past through the spectacles of the present. Schools are vulnerable to the demands of parents, the whims of central government, the antics of local politicians and – of course – the claw of the press, for we all tend to approach any given school (or the educational needs of our day) through the spectacles of the past. Few of us have entirely happy memories of our schooldays. Most of us rather envy teachers – all those holidays! – and have little idea of how hard, very hard, a conscientious teacher has to work. In the consumerist age in which, since the 1980s, we have generally lived – one marked, as Andrew Marr has deliciously put it, above all by the politics of shopping – we are more apt to treat those entrusted with the education of our children as if they were but a business who should be grateful for the honour of our custom. Any Head Teacher, in this new century, can attest to the incessant interruption of his day by the unheralded and urgent squawking of some parent – often most rudely, and with menaces, however often parents are told that the first point of contact should be with their child's Guidance teacher and that one ought only to trouble senior management with the gravest problems. The advent of email – in an age when many seem positively to idolise their offspring and tend to have the most unrealistic expectations of them – has made this pressure even worse.

Schools have besides become the more burdened through recent decades in a fast-changing society. The rapid secularisation of Scotland, from the 1960s – to the point where church-going is, apart from certain far corners of the Highlands, now considered great eccentricity – has left a pastoral vacuum our state schools have had increasingly to fill, from moral and social education to immediate support for a child in, say, a bereavement. Family breakdown has added new pressures, not least – in the worst instances – from a school's responsibility to protect a child in the custody of one parent from abduction by another. A growing and vocal atheistic lobby in modern Scotland, too, now puts schools at the risk of incandescent attack for such enormities as holding a carol service or inviting the local minister to address an assembly. (There is today little awareness that, in terms of the 1918 Education (Scotland) Act, which integrated Roman Catholic and Episcopalian schools into the state system, 'non-denominational' does not mean Humanist; it means Christian and Presbyterian.)

James Gillespie's High School is not, in some respects, a typical Scottish secondary. Its catchment area – which has been amended only once since 1973, ceding pleasant parts of Polwarth, Merchiston and North Morningside for less moneyed blocks to the east – remains broadly middle class. ('If you could combine Gillespie's with Liberton High School,' says the current Head Teacher – he should know, for he has led both – 'you'd have the perfect comprehensive.') It has also, as one would expect of an area with much employment in the media, higher education and the arts, an unusually liberal, socially aware, environmentally concerned and self-consciously high-minded parental base. Yet there remain corners of real poverty and deprivation – not least spiritually. Tollcross, Fountain Bridge and the West Port – victim to protracted 'planning blight' from the mid-1960s, followed by a great deal of demolition – is today home to very few young families. But there are still, elsewhere, pockets where some Gillespie's students make for school with their jotters in a plastic bag; head home of an evening with no better bed for a night's rest than the floor.

Part of that ongoing animus against Gillespie's, in certain quarters, is the caricature of its community as one earnest, Yummy Mummy set of humourless *Guardian*isti: so many Marchmont Bores against the Bomb.

But there have always been fractures and tensions. The school, far into the comprehensive era, was pilloried for its averred appeal to the sort of parents who really wanted private schooling for their offspring, but without the fees. But it has certainly been patronised – one was very conscious of it in the 1980s – by the sort of Left-leaning folk in distressed corduroy who could more than afford the fees for, say, George Heriot's, but think – as a matter of fixed principle – that private schools are wicked. Then, of course, there are the 'New Scots'; for some reason, a great many refugees and asylum seekers have long settled in south-central Edinburgh. The Sciennes area is historically the city's Jewish quarter; a little to the north, east of the University, has very many Asian families and, indeed, businesses. And, in the most hopeless closes and mini-tower blocks – as always, in one of Europe's most socially divided cities – are the poor, marginalised and broken.

Any Gillespie's Head Teacher of the last forty years – and Dr Thomas and her three successors are all still living – will attest wryly to an ongoing paradox: the failure of a small minority of parents to engage in any way with the school or take the slightest interest in their children's education – and the incessant waste of school time by just as small a minority who seem unable to think of anything else.

The school has a long, long history and at various points over these two centuries its succeeding generations have grated uneasily against each other. Though most of her time was dominated by urgent issues of fabric, overcrowding and resources, Dr Thomas tried determinedly to move on from the less attractive and obsolete features of the late James Gillespie's High School for Girls. Later leaders, in turn, almost overnight did away with every element of tradition – and have since proved apt to exaggerate the 'elitist' elements of the school they inherited . . . this after everything she and her staff did to raise social awareness, community engagement and multi-cultural tolerance. (A disturbing number of teachers most immediately involved in that endeavour died in harness and tragically young.)

In my day Gaelic was not on the school syllabus. Highland history was not taught either. My new classmates were genially bewildered by my thick accent. Welsh, perhaps, or Irish, or Pakistani? One recalls incidents of what might now be thought, at least by those who seriously need to get a life, anti-Highland racism. 'Two hundred years ago, John,' Miss Cuthbert once cooed, and to the joy unconfined of my classmates – she and I had a warm but spiky relationship, dotted by her occasional, determined offensives to keep me humble, matched by one or two outrages of my own – 'you'd have been padding through the glen to go to university, with your little sack of oatmeal in one hand and your little barrel of salt-herring in the other . . .' I could but smile wanly. Today, of course, Gillespie's is the reception-secondary for Edinburgh's Gaelic-medium primary; five members of secondary staff (including the Head Teacher) are native Gaelic speakers; several others are learning; several subjects are taught in Gaelic and Gaelic itself is taught to learners. As of August 2013, eighty-seven pupils – about 8 per cent of the entire school roll – were fluent in the language of Eden.

Nor does the old James Gillespie's High School for Girls emerge at all well in respect for its own past: in all its four decades, for instance, it never once commemorated or honoured the 'old boys' of Gillespie's School – at least forty-four of them – who had made the supreme sacrifice in the First World War. Nor were its traditions as venerable as all that – most were invented, by the remarkable Headmaster of the time, in the late 1920s; and the swelling chords, sobbing strings and slightly strained sentiments of the school song, 'Fidelis et Fortis', date only from 1945. Dr Thomas had older members of staff bridling when, from the first, she refused to wear her academic gown (save for the most solemn and high days), with the inevitable consequence that, by the time I arrived, no teachers wore it in the classroom at all. But until 1938, when May Andrew had imposed the garb on her academic colleagues, no Gillespie's teacher had ever sported it.

Such, in the round, is the fascinating, often awkward, occasionally difficult history of our school. This book is besides a celebration of Gillespie's, of its ethos and values, its personalities and excursions and good humour, times good and bad, as we turn the page in its third century to another new beginning – and in hope for the future, as well as respect for the past.

But it is time, now, we met the Merchant of Spylaw . . .

•   •   •

It's a moneyed, cosy, characterful place, Colinton, a sought-after enclave of greater Edinburgh, with big houses and fine cars, and which still – though suburbia crept out to it in the decades after the Great War – retains the atmosphere of a country village. Clustered either side of the peaty, burbling Water of Leith, it has besides an oddly Sicilian feel, for wherever you go seems to be very steep, be it down this road or up that lane or clattering down great flights of stone steps or along lofty pavements.

But let us make for the parish church, down Spylaw Street and over the stately bridge, and past the tender new sculpture of a boyish Robert Louis Stevenson with his dog (for here his grandfather was minister) and in the gates and past the great, sinister coffin-shaped shell of heavy iron – a 'mortsafe', which long ago, when it was a genuine problem anywhere near a medical school, you could inter over a loved one's coffin for a few months (and, of course, for a fee) until the remains, putting it delicately, were no longer of value to the infamous body-snatchers.

The sufficiently rich, though, were above such precautions, and if you steal past the front of the eighteenth-century kirk and round the corner, in this sonorous old graveyard, and by melancholy evergreens, you immediately meet a notable tomb – a 'stone structure with a double-pitched roof', drones the official record of Scotland's historic monuments; a 'rusticated and pedimented mausoleum . . . to the north of the church'.

For the privilege of annexing a chunk of the graveyard and erecting this structure, five years before his death, the deceased paid the kirk session £5 for the good of the local poor. He could well afford £5, for he had – by the standards of the day – an enormous fortune. And owned a great deal – including, almost casually, Colinton.

Autumn leaves always seem to have drifted into corners as you gaze through the redoubtable wrought-iron gate; but there, on the floor of encaustic tiles and above the dust of two brothers in the vault below, is recorded 'JAMES GILLESPIE'. And if you step back a pace and look up at the inscription outside and above, you are advised

WITHIN REST THE REMAINS OF

JAMES GILLESPIE OF SPYLAW

WHO BEQUEATHED THE BULK OF HIS FORTUNE

FOR THE ENDOWMENT OF A HOSPITAL IN THE CITY OF EDINBURGH

FOR THE MAINTENANCE OF AGED MEN AND WOMEN

AND OF A FREE SCHOOL FOR THE EDUCATION OF POOR BOYS

BOTH OF WHICH HAVE PROVED MOST USEFUL PUBLIC CHARITIES.

DIED 8TH APRIL 1797

Few stop by this sepulchre today, and the 'hospital' – in the sense, at that time, of what we would now call an eventide home – has long gone. But Gillespie's school, remarkably, endures, far bigger and more sophisticated than he could ever have imagined, and still within sight of its original stance. And Gillespie himself is still thought of kindly in Colinton and endures in the folk-memory of Edinburgh, for he was known by people of substance and men of letters and was, by every account, a droll and engaging and extremely kind man of unforgettable nutcracker profile, with its jutting jaw and enormous nose.

He was, we gather, a little touchy about the latter (there is an Edinburgh tradition that he offered John Kay money to repress, or at least adjust, his engaging caricature). But Gillespie had over the decades made a considerable fortune from the noses of others – for he innovatively made and sold ready-ground snuff; fine tobacco expertly dried, pulverised into the finest powder, snorted daintily for an immediate hit of nicotine, and surrounded – and shared – by all sorts of etiquette and manners. Well into the twentieth century the Gillespie tobacco shop was a High Street institution on the city's fabled Royal Mile, and 'Gillespie's' remained a popular brand of Scottish snuff.

For many years it was widely thought that James Gillespie was the elder of two brothers and had been born in Roslin, Midlothian, seven miles south of the modern city's boundaries. Indeed, for much of the twentieth century one of the school's four 'Houses' was named Roslin on that basis. The mistakes were made in the first, 1838, edition of John Kay's *Original Portraits and Character Etchings*, and inexplicably repeated in the third, published in 1877 – for the second, in 1842, had corrected them, after diligent checking of the city's parish registers.

There the record of Gillespie's baptism was soon found: 'Edinburgh, May 1, 1727. – James Gilespie, Indweller, and Elizabeth M'beath, his spous, A.S.N. [a son], James, W. [witness] Tho. Whytland, saidler, and George Gilespie, Tennent in Broughton, born 28th April last . . .' Broughton, now best known as Edinburgh's gay district, was then a humdrum village with a dark, past reputation for witchcraft.

He was the younger son of poor but upright parents – his brother John had arrived in 1724 – and there was also a sister, whose name is lost to us. And it was a religious home, James senior and Elizabeth being earnest 'Cameronians', who refused to worship in the Established Church as the terms of its final settlement after the Revolution of 1689 had ducked the obligations of the Solemn League and Covenant – the deal cut by Scots with Oliver Cromwell to establish a Presbyterian order over the whole island of Britain, of which the chief legacy is the Westminster Confession of Faith. But it was besides rooted in the awful persecution of the Covenanters after the Restoration of 1660 – Presbyterians who refused to submit to the Episcopalian order imposed by Charles II, very many of whom were tortured and killed. The atrocities of the period are well documented and incontestable. They include the murder of one David Steel – shot in cold blood before his own door, and indeed his wife and babe, after surrendering in good faith to an army officer who promised quarter and a fair trial, on 20 December 1786. Nearly three centuries later, one of his clan would be the school's Headmistress – and her possible relative, once a pupil of James Gillespie's Boys' School, would crown an eminent political career as the first Presiding Officer of the Scottish Parliament.

From these 'Killing Times', bitterness endured for decades to come, and they were almost as near to the infant Gillespie as the Falklands conflict is to us now. Even by 1726 there were no Cameronian ministers, and many services – conducted perforce by laymen – were still held in dank barns or even out of doors; there were, too, annual 'conventicles' on the sites of particularly awful battles. In 1745, though, two defecting ministers from the Kirk could at last establish a presbytery and ordain other ministers, and though the Reformed Presbyterian Church of Scotland now only holds the allegiance of perhaps three hundred Scots, the tradition has found rich soil overseas, producing such eminent men as evangelist Billy Graham and the astronaut John Glenn. Though, as laird of Spylaw and 'heritor' of the parish kirk in Colinton, James Gillespie felt obliged to worship there, he never repudiated his Reformed Presbyterian roots and attended the annual conventicle at Rullion Green till the infirmity of old age.

It took guts to be a Cameronian. The Gillespie boys grew up in an atmosphere of religious principle and daily piety but also, self-consciously, as outsiders. And they grew up on the breadline, there being nothing to suggest their father was much more than a common labourer. They lived to see enormous change in their city – and, well into manhood, amidst abiding public apprehension.

For the seventeenth century had been generally dreadful for Scotland; decades of civil war, tumult, occupation, tyranny and religious persecution. Though the Revolution brought stability and a measure of peace, King William took scant interest in his northern realm, never bothered to visit it, and viewed Scotland as little more than a potential back door for Jacobite revolt – first in the interests of his deposed father-in-law, the sulking James VII, and then his son, the 'Old Pretender'. The disastrous Darien venture all but beggared the land – it devoured at least a quarter of all Scotland's liquid capital – and there were successive awful harvests: in the late 1690s some 5 per cent of the entire population simply starved to death. The Union of 1707 was profoundly unpopular and there were ongoing attempts to restore the Stuarts – most seriously in 1715 and most spectacularly in 1745, when Charles Edward Stuart occupied Edinburgh with embarrass-ingly little difficulty and when James Gillespie was already an adult. Little in the Scotland he grew up in was sure or certain.

All their lives the Gillespie brothers were of sober character and the hardest of workers. James, in particular, would be remembered for his frugality – he is said to have coined the phrase, 'Waste not, want not' – but he was the brother of true business acumen. By around 1750 they had established themselves as tobacconists in Edinburgh and in 1759 acquired a mill by the Water of Leith, three miles west of Edinburgh in what is now Spylaw Park in the village of Colinton. Later, around 1777, he bought a second mill, in upper Spylaw and also powered by the Water of Leith; it had been built for the manufacture, of all things, of playing-cards, and the premises had subsequently seen service as a dubious inn, that enterprise ending suddenly after a mortifying Customs raid in 1776.

James continued to invest in land, acquiring the whole Spylaw estate in two instalments – in 1766 and 1768; and gaining adjacent ones, Bonaly and Fernielaw, in 1773.

Now a gentleman, he enjoyed rental income as well as the profits of the business – and, after the American Revolution sent the value of tobacco soaring, it became highly profitable indeed, Gillespie speculating in the stuff with great shrewdness. The money piled in and James was able to advance large secured loans at remunerative interest. We know, for instance, that he 'lent £500 in 1776 on security of house property at Leith, and in 1782, under the designation "James Gillespie of Spylaw", advanced £1,000 on a bond over the estate of Woodhall in his own neighbourhood . . .'

By the age of sixty he was an immensely wealthy man; a contented patriarchal figure who seldom left Colinton, supervised snuff production closely, day and night (he would pad about the mill in blanket and nightcap, to keep the snuff off his good clothes), and kept a canny eye on the books. His brother John was front-of-house, manning the High Street shop and a popular figure in his own right. In one shrewd business move they took down and rebuilt their shop, on more gracious lines; in another, they cannily gave their finest snuff out free, and on a regular basis, to some of Edinburgh's most notable (and influential) personalities, but all the while, as recorded in *Kay's Edinburgh Portraits*:

> James, or as he was styled, 'The Laird', constantly resided at Spylaw, a property which he purchased at Colinton . . . This pleasant residence is distant about four miles west of Edinburgh. It is situated on the banks of a small rivulet, at the head of the hollow or strath occupied by the village of Colinton. The house is of a somewhat antiquated form, but in excellent repair; and the courtyard and walks around are tastefully kept in order . . .

Neither of the brothers were ever married. Although frugal and industrious, they were by no means miserly. On the contrary, James, in particular, is described as one of the best and kindest of men; living amongst his domestics in the most homely and patriarchal manner. Many of the last century characters of Edinburgh were supplied with snuff gratis by the Messrs. Gillespie. Among others, Laird Robertson and Jean Cameron had their 'mulls' regularly filled. He invariably sat at the same table with his servants, indulging in familiar conversation, and entering with much spirit into their amusements. Newspapers were not so widely circulated at that period as they are now; and on the return of any of his domestics from the city, which one or other of them daily visited, he listened with great attention to 'the news', and enjoyed with much zest the narration of any jocular incident that had occurred.

Without family of his own, he made family of those in his employ – took an interest in them, gave good advice, impressed on them the importance of sobriety and industry. Yet he spared nothing for their own comfort.

The utmost abundance of every necessary, of the best quality, and at the command of all the inmates, was unscrupulously provided. Neither was his generosity confined to objects of his own species. It extended alike to every living creature about his establishment. From his horses to his poultry, all experienced the bounty of his hand; and wherever he went, in the fields, or about his own doors, he had difficulty in escaping from their affectionate gambols and joyous clamour. The almost companionable fondness, reciprocal betwixt the laird and his riding-horse, was altogether amusing. Well fed, and in excellent spirit and condition, it frequently indulged in a little restive curveting with its master, especially when the latter was about to get into the saddle. 'Come, come,' he would say on such occasions, addressing the animal in his usual quiet way, 'hae dune noo, for ye'll no like if I come across your lugs wi' the stick.' This 'terror to evil doers' he sometimes brandished, but was never known to 'come across the lugs' of any one . . .

He had never forgotten the poverty of his earliest years and is remembered as a 'peculiarly indulgent' landlord, his name even in the early twentieth century 'still green in the parish'. He had many small tenants, in this cottage or that indifferent little farm, and took a relaxed attitude to rent, accepting his dues as they found it convenient to pay it and happy with even a modest instalment. A young apprentice in the mill, Andrew Fraser, was often sent out in search of arrears. 'Well, laddie, hae ye gotten anything?' Gillespie would inquire easily on his return. More than once the boy could show only a shilling for the afternoon's endeavour. 'Weel, weel,' the merchant of Spylaw would chuckle, 'it's aye better than naething; but it's weel seen they're the lairds and no' me . . .'

He never took legal action. Some believe Andrew Fraser was briefly considered as his heir, but he seems to have been of loose habits and had a sad later life. There is no published evidence, despite claims in 2003, of one 'John Cotton' to whom Gillespie promised to leave everything if he would only change his surname to Gillespie.

The merchant afforded himself one indulgence – a big yellow carriage, but 'of the plainest description', its only grandiloquence being a sort of coat-of-arms on the doors, with his two initials. He is said once unwisely to have asked the Honourable Henry Erskine – a keen-brained fellow who would twice serve as Lord Advocate – if he might think up a good motto. In a flash, the wit replied

Wha would hae thocht it
That noses had bocht it?

Only in the last year of his life, though, would Gillespie take the coach to church – he thought it more seemly to walk. John had died in 1795 – he, too, lies in that vault in Colinton kirkyard – and James, now seventy and a very old man by the standards of the time, must have been devastated.

'The story of James Gillespie, Esq. of Spylaw is in many ways the most charming of all the merchants' histories,' Muriel Spark reflected two centuries later. 'He was so satisfactorily and completely an Edinburgh character . . .'

He was not, of course, the first Edinburgh eminence to endow a school: those established by the final disposals of George Heriot, George Watson, Daniel Stuart and Mary Erskine prosper still – in the private sector. And the Merchant Company of Edinburgh still hold, in their gracious Hanover Street premises, some Gillespie effects – his snuffbox, the original marble bust, his personal Bible (allegedly) and the key for his mausoleum. His shop sign is preserved in a Canongate museum and his home in Spylaw Park, too, survives; it has now been divided into private flats, after continued service as a snuff-mill and later use as a riding school and by youth organisations. Behind it, the tumbled foundations of his mill can still be seen.

There are, of course, in our day two grounds for unease, which may explain why, over the last three decades, the school nervously distanced itself from celebration of its founder. It is not immediately easy in our own day, when tobacco can no longer legally be advertised or even displayed openly in Scottish shops, to vaunt a dealer of snuff as a hero to children; still more sensitive in a multi-ethnic school, any trade of that nature, at that time – and certainly from the Americas – involved slaves and the slave trade. In that regard, as a child of his age, James Gillespie is certainly compromised; but no less certainly, there are aspects of our culture today that would appal him.

We have two portraits of the merchant of Spylaw. One is the charming engraving of the Gillespie brothers, in profile, neatly periwigged, by John Kay, who could remember them vividly. James stands at ease, his arm relaxed atop the wall before them; his brother is stiffer, arms folded, at once bristling and deferential.

In the other, an engaging study in oils by his neighbour, Sir James Foulis, Bt of Woodhall – now held in Edinburgh's City Art Centre – James Gillespie is an old man, sitting in the garden shade on a rustic seat, hands resting on a croquet stick. A mild and kindly figure, a self-made man – and with the serenity of one who has at last finalised his will; with that same smile, of Edinburgh, and of the Enlightenment.

CHAPTER TWO

'The hideous edifice'
1803–1874

——————

James Gillespie signed his last will and testament on 16 April 1796. We may presume it nullified earlier plans to leave the bulk of his estate to his brother, who had died the previous year. Besides detailed instructions for the care of his staff and servants, there were two huge bequests. All his lands, and what was then the vast sum of £12,000, were left, in the charge of Trustees from the Merchant Company of Edinburgh, 'for the special intent and purpose of founding and endowing a Hospital and charitable institution for the aliment and maintenance of old men and women; and which Hospital should always be called, denominated, and described, by the name of JAMES GILLESPIE'S HOSPITAL'.

And an additional £2,700 was bestowed to establish a 'charitable or free school within the city of Edinburgh or suburbs thereof' for the education of one hundred boys – and for the administration of both, and admission to either, the old man laid down strict rules, duly codified and published in 1802. Those concerning the care home start with particular splendour –

> The persons entitled to be admitted into, and maintained in, the Hospital, shall be, 1. Mr Gillespie's old servants, of whatever age they be. 2. Persons of the name of GILLESPIE, 55 years of age and upwards, whatever part of Scotland they may come from. 3. Persons belonging to Edinburgh and its suburbs, men and women, aged 55 years and upwards, belonging to Leith, Newhaven, and other parts of the county of Mid-Lothian. And, lastly, failing of applications from all these places, persons 55 years of age, coming from any part of Scotland; but none shall be admitted who are pensioners, or have an allowance from any other Charity. And seeing the intention of Mr Gillespie, in founding this Hospital, was to relieve the poor, none

Gillespie's Hospital as altered for school use around 1874, with a rebuilt roofline and a further storey either side of the clock tower.

are to be admitted until they shall produce satisfying evidence to the Governors, of their indigent circumstances; and the Governors are required to admit none, but such as are truly objects of this Charity: And it is hereby ordained and appointed, agreeably to the will and directions of Mr Gillespie, that none but decent, godly, and well behaved men and women, (whatever in other respects may be their claims), shall be admitted into the Hospital; and the number of persons to be constantly entertained, shall be so many as the revenue of the Hospital can conveniently maintain, after deduction of the charge of management, and of maintaining the fabric, and supporting and keeping up the clothing and furniture of the House; and the vacancies occasioned by death or dismission, shall be filled up by the Governors, at the Quarterly Meetings held on the Second Monday of January, and Second Monday of July, after such vacancies happen . . .

The Province of the Chaplain, or Household Governor, shall be, to inspect the manners and behaviour of all the persons in the Hospital, particularly of the men, and to report what he finds amiss to the Treasurer; to discourse with both men and women; counsel, advise, and reprove them, as occasion requires; to sit at the table, where the persons eat; to officiate as Chaplain in family worship, and in the duties of reading a portion of Scripture, singing of Psalms, and praying, both mornings and evenings; and, on the

evening of every Lord's day, at six o'clock, shall assemble the whole
members of the family in the Great Hall, and employ one hour, at
least. In expounding the doctrines and duties of our holy religion,
as contained in that excellent abridgement of them in the Assembly's
Shorter Catechism, in reading the Scriptures, and in prayer and
praise. He shall carefully attend the sick and the dying, and join with
them in suitable exercises of devotion; and shall, in all the duties of
his office, be subject to, and receive from the Governors, or their
Ordinary Committee, such directions as, from time to time, they
may deem to be necessary.

It is hard not to feel that the duties specified for the chaplain were very
much as Gillespie himself had lived among his servants and kept the
household Sabbath – and, sweetly, recall that the Shorter Catechism was
still being taught at Gillespie's within living memory. Writing of her school
days in 1991, Muriel Spark warmly remembered these lessons.

The 'Statutes and Rules of James Gillespie's Hospital and Free School'
seem paternalistic today – even patronising – in the extreme; for instance,
they imposed a strict night-time curfew, the 'great gate to be locked at 8
o'clock in Summer, and 6 o'clock in Winter; and none to be admitted into,
or allowed to go out of, the Home thereafter, without the express permission of the Chaplain or Mistress'. But there were generous terms for, for
instance, the provision of clothing and the supply of food and beer; there
were clear rules for accountability and to guard against embezzlement;
there had to be regular visits by governors, and a 'surgeon' – a doctor – was
to be appointed. Quite a number of positions are called for and each was
to be paid a given salary.

And the rules for the school are in a similar vein of righteousness and
rectitude, annual interest from the capital sum duly endowed to pay the
salaries of its master and his assistant, and the rest of it in 'purchasing
books, paper, pens and ink for the boys'. As for those staff –

The persons to be chosen by the Governors to be Master and
Assistant of said School, shall be of good and respectable characters,
qualified to explain the doctrines and duties of the Christian
religion, and capable of teaching the boys reading of English
grammatically, writing and arithmetic. The Rector shall have, in
name of salary, 70£. a year; and the Assistant, who shall be an
unmarried man, the foresaid sum of 30£. per annum; and the Rector
shall have the use of the upper storey of the School-house, for the

accommodation of himself and family; and there shall be in full of
every claim, either to the Rector or his Assistant: That the Master
and Assistant shall employ six hours in Summer, and five hours in
Winter, each day, Sabbath excepted, in teaching and instructing the
boys as aforesaid; also to meet the boys on Sunday evening, to
instruct them in the principles of the Christian religion, agreeably
to Mr Gillespie's will, immediately after their return from public
worship, especially the doctrines and duties of our holy religion,
according to the received standards of the Church of Scotland, and
to subscribe the formula prescribed by law, to all public teachers
within the realm of Scotland . . .

The pupils, too, were carefully to be screened.

There shall be chosen by the Governors, from the city of Edinburgh
and its suburbs, and admitted into the School, one hundred boys at
least, to be taught to read English, writing and arithmetic: And as
the intention of Mr Gillespie, in founding this School, was evidently
to relieve the poor, none are to be chosen, unless they produce and
lay before the Governors, certificates of their indigent circumstances, from the Minister of the Kirk-session of the parish where
they reside, or produce other evidence satisfying to the Governors;
and none shall be admitted under the age of Six, or above the age
of Twelve; and they shall be entitled to remain at school for three
years; and no boys shall be admitted, who are affected by any conta-
gious distemper: That the first election shall be as soon as the
School-house is ready; and every after election or meeting for that
purpose, shall be twice in the year, viz. on the first Monday of April,
and first Monday of October annually, and, except upon one or
other of these days, no boys shall be admitted.
   A Special Committee shall be annually chosen, to be called the
Education Committee, who are to have the immediate care and
inspection of the School, the attention of the teachers to their duty,
and the conduct and progress of the boys, with power to dismiss
from the School such boys as appear obstinate and incorrigible: That
a book be kept in the School, which shall contain, 1st, The names of
the boys: 2ndly, Their father's name and profession: 3rdly, Their age:
4thly, The state of their education at admission; 5thly, The date of
their leaving the School: and, 6thly, a space left blank for the report
of their progress, at the time of the examination by the Education

Committee, and such of the Governors as may please to attend; and that this public examination is to be held upon the day most convenient, immediately before the vacation granted to the School, which shall be for four weeks at the commencement of the Harvest, annually. Immediately after the list of the scholars, the Education Committee shall insert in the book, such remarks as may, from time to time, occur to them, upon the conduct of either Masters or Scholars; and a new list, according to the above form, shall be made out, of all the scholars, after every opening of the School after the vacation.

And a solemn oath of office 'by God, and as I shall answer to Him at the Great Day' was to be taken by every Governor, and in but slightly reduced form besides by the Treasurer, the Chaplain, and the Mistress.

The insistence on Sabbath evening instruction of the lads suggests strongly that in its early years, at least, Gillespie's was a residential school. The pupils were evidently hard worked, with no day completely free from lessons of some sort and only four weeks of holiday a year. The curriculum seems to us dreich and narrow; the discipline, no doubt, was ferocious. But they would be decently fed and accommodated and, three years later, enter society at least able to read, write and count. In an age when there was no state educational provision, and at a time when – not least with the colossal social change, and massive population drift to Scotland's cities, of the Industrial Revolution – the Church of Scotland was struggling to provide even the meanest parochial schooling, the first pupils of Gillespie's would leave with a signal advantage over thousands of their unfortunate peers in Scotland's ancient capital.

Unfortunately the Trustees – the Merchant Company – would make a single, colossal mistake that not only greatly weakened the school's funding but also dragged the entire enterprise – and even Gillespie's personal, posthumous reputation – into eminently avoidable trouble.

•   •   •

Land has always been at a premium in and around Edinburgh, and throughout its entire history Gillespie's has never had quite as much ground or accommodation or space as it really needs. Even at the time of writing, in the spring of 2016, with the surprisingly low 'capping' of pupil numbers at the new school at 1,150, rather than 1,350, the school already anticipates a struggle both to admit all the eligible pupils from its

Wrychtis Housis, or
Boroughmuir Castle.
The blithe demolition
of this medieval pile,
to clear a site for
Gillespie's Hospital,
infuriated the
aesthetes of Edinburgh.

catchment area and the annual intake of Gaelic-medium First Years from
Bun-sgoil Taobh na Pàirce; the more mortifying as the Gaelic language,
even today, has vocal and powerful enemies.

But the decision of the Trustees, about 1799, to buy Lord Bargenie's
venerable mansion in Bruntsfield – a fantastic, castellated building, dating
back to the fifteenth century, and clotted with sculptures and antiquities –
was a signal blunder. Whatever the pile was actually called – it was known
variously as Wrychtich Housis, Wrychtis Housis, Wrytes Houses, Bryntsfield
Castle, Boroughmuir Castle and Burganie Castle – it proved rapidly to be
quite beyond adaptation for use as a residential home and besides a school
and, worse, it was held in high, romantic esteem by Edinburgh's most self-
consciously cultured antiquarians and gentlemen. They were sniffy enough
about its acquisition for such proletarian purposes – and then,
compounding the error, instead of selling the castle on and looking for land
elsewhere, the Trustees decided to knock it down. As men in 1800 moved in
with hammers and crowbars, the *Edinburgh Magazine* had a tartan fit –

> How grateful must it have been to the inhabitants of Edinburgh to
> be able to point the attention of a prejudiced stranger to the
> towering and venerable fabric of Wrytes House, one existing
> memorial, among many others of the ancient power and greatness
> of Scotland, and of her early proficiency in the architecture and

sculpture formerly in repute. Will persons of taste in this country believe it? – will liberal and lettered Englishmen believe it? – this beautiful castle, in the environs of the capital, and the ornament of Bruntsfield Links, a public resort, is at this moment resounding to the blows of the hammers and axes of final demolition!

The manager of the late Mr. Gillespie's mortification having by reason, it is said, of the voracity of some greedy proprietor, been disappointed in their original intentions,

They spied this goodly castle,
Which choosing for their Hospital,
They thither marched

and who could have doubted that it might easily have been trans- formed into a most capacious and elegant hospital – a truly splendid abode for decayed Gillespies!

But down it must come, if it should be for the sake only of the timber, the slates, and the stones. Its fate is now irretrievable. A few weeks will leave scarcely a trace to tell where once it stood. Ten thousand pounds would not rear such another castle; and, if it did, still it would be modern.

But flattened it was, and with such little oversight or common sense that, for instance, scant effort was made to save the statuary and carved stones of Wrychtis Housis for posterity or even to sell them on the open market. The heads of assorted Caesars and many sculptures of varied figures from classical mythology were allowed to fall and smash – and the new building that rose in its stead, and at additional and enormous expense, was widely decried. A 'tasteless modern erection', lamented Daniel Wilson in 1848; and even in 1882 James Grant did not mince his words as he keened for Wrychtis Housis –

On the summit of the green slope now crowned by the hideous edifice known as Gillespie's Hospital, a picturesque mansion of very great antiquity, striking in outline with its Peel Tower, turrets, crow- stepped gables and gablets, encrusted with legends, dates and coats- of-arms, for ages formed one of the most important features of the Burgh Muir. This was the mansion of Wrychtis-Housis, belonging to an old baronial family named Napier. There were emblematic representations of the five senses. Emblems of the Virtues were

The site of Gillespie's Hospital today. Controversial as it was at the time, it was far more handsome than these modern flats. (Andrew Digance)

profusely carved on different parts of the building, and on one was a rude representation of our first parents with the distich,

Quken Adam delved and Eve span
Quhair war a' the gentles then?

'In 1800,' thundered Grant in conclusion, 'the building was demolished and Gillespie's Hospital, a tasteless edifice designed by Mr Burn, a builder, in that ridiculous castellated style called "Carpenter's Gothic", took its place.'

But it was Henry, Lord Cockburn – one of the most influential men in the city and whose memoirs and journals are still widely read – who really put the boot in.

'Gillespie's Hospital, for the shrouding of aged indigence,' he mewed, 'was commenced about this time, and completed in 1805. If I recollect right, this was the first of the public charities of this century by which Edinburgh has been blessed, or cursed. The founder was a snuff seller, who brought up an excellent young man as his heir, and then left death to disclose that, for the vanity of being remembered by a thing called after himself, he had all the while had a deed executed, by which this, his nearest relation, was disinherited.'

As put-downs go, 'a snuff seller' is no less dismissive than 'a builder'. But Cockburn thus begot the enduring myth that Gillespie had spitefully disinherited some relative or protégé. For this the evidence is thin indeed.

His surviving nephew, Richard Dick, was generously provided for – being left the shop, Gillespie's two townhouses, Spylaw House and the mill, on condition that he pay £10 annually to David Dick, perhaps a relative and certainly Gillespie's most esteemed servant. Two of the Trustees bore the Gillespie surname, and may have been cousins, and the will itself identified all his servants, and by name, as first entitled to take residence in the Hospital if they chose – 'First, Anne Bishop, John Whyte and his wife, and said Anne Mercer; John Black, an old servant; and Robert Ross, wright in Collington, also an old servant, with all others who have been or may be my hired servants, whatever their age may be.'

These are not the actions of a vindictive man and many people of wealth and achievement, through history, have left their families on comfortable terms but shrewdly bequeathed the bulk of their fortune elsewhere. The late Anita Roddick, of Body Shop fame, once bluntly described the very idea of leaving vast riches to your offspring as 'obscene', and in the last months of her life gave away her entire, remaining estate – some £51 million – to a range of charities and good causes.

Gillespie, then, has had mean treatment from such lounge-lizard histo-rians as Cockburn; but he was even more dreadfully let down by the Merchant Company, for the purchase of Wrychtis Housis, its subsequent demolition and then the erection of a huge new building bit deeply into the capital that was needed subsequently to earn interest and so fund the actual operation of the Hospital and School. What should have been handily covered by the £700 set aside for site and property ended up costing far more.

The debacle had consequences. Having wasted so much money building a Hospital with accommodation for sixty-six pensioners, the Governors were never able to support more than forty-two. And, when the School opened in 1803, it was for only sixty-five boys, not a hundred – and its first Headmaster, John Robertson, had to teach them all by himself, for they could not afford to pay an assistant. With so shaky a start, and among those aware of the precarious finances, few could have foreseen that the school would still be in business over two centuries later, in a very different Scotland and in a new millennium.

•   •   •

We know very little about the first James Gillespie's School. No photograph of the 'Free School', as it was remembered, survives. It was a detached, two-storey building at the southeast grounds of the Hospital and was demolished in 1874, for the tenements and shops erected soon after – and still standing – between 37 and 43 Bruntsfield Place.

We do know what the very first Headmaster looked like, for the Merchant Company – or, to give them their proper handle, The Company of Merchants of the City of Edinburgh – still hold a fine portrait of him, displayed on the stairs at the Merchants' Hall in Hanover Street. John Robertson looks like a patient, kindly man, and served a full forty years, from appointment in 1803 till his retirement in 1843 and on an annual salary of £65 – £1, it would appear, for each pupil.

Founded in 1681 and consolidated by two royal charters and two Acts of Parliament – over two centuries apart – the Merchant Company was established in order to protect trading rights in the city of Edinburgh. By Victorian times, though, it concerned itself much more with charitable and education endeavour, most notably with its 'hospital schools' – boarding institutions, like Gillespie's in these first decades, also set up by posthumous endowment. But, fatefully, these were even by the early 1800s much older, already rather grand, and self-consciously posh. They comprised the Merchant Maiden Hospital (now the Mary Erskine School), George Watson's Hospital (now George Watson's College) and Daniel Stewart's Hospital (now part of Stewart's Melville College.) All four, as we shall see, were dramatically reformed in the 1870s – and all, save Gillespie's (which by the Great War had been enthusiastically entrusted to the Corporation) are today private and distinctly expensive.

And, as Kathryn Thompkins details in her unpublished, handwritten 1960 history, school in early nineteenth-century Scotland – especially in a bleak place like the first Gillespie's, expected to make lads of humble background literate and numerate in just three years – was far less fun than it is now. The teaching philosophy was not to educate – in the true sense of 'drawing out', in stimulating a child's mind and helping him acquire the power to reason, the power to research, the power to think – but to cram; and in the culture of the times in a suffocatingly religious way –

> Education generally began with learning the alphabet which was usually found printed in large and small letters on the back of the Shorter Catechism. After mastering the alphabet the pupil began to learn to read, using the Bible or the Catechism as a text-book. The use of the Bible was very common to teach reading, spelling and grammar but changes were gradually coming about. Teachers were introducing a graduated series of school books which enabled the scholars to be classified more satisfactorily. There was one set of these

books published by command of the Commissioners of National Education in Ireland but another series compiled for the Scottish Schoolbook Association was rapidly becoming more popular.

One book used to teach arithmetic was called 'Elementary Arithmetic' by Rev. J.C. Wigram . . . nearly all the examples were taken from the Scriptures and the teacher was warned, in the preface, of the need of enforcing the serious attention of the children to the facts alluded to, and that the examples should be treated 'as all other Scriptural information should be treated'.

The following are random examples –

The children of Israel were sadly given to idolatry, notwithstanding all they knew of God. Moses was obliged to have three thousand men put to death for this grievous sin. What digits must you use to express the number?

Of Jacob's four wives, Leah had six sons, Rachel had two sons, Billah had two and Zillah also had two. How many sons had Jacob?

There are twenty-four chapters in the Gospel of Luke and twenty-eight chapters in the book of the Acts of the Apostles. What difference is there in the two?

When Moses dedicated the Tabernacle, each of the twelve priests of Israel made an offering to God of two oxen, five rams, five he-goats and five lambs. How many oxen did they offer? How many rams? How many goats and lambs together? And how many animals in all? . . .

The following is one of the first lessons in a work called The Infant Teacher's Assistant. The book was described by the Literary Gazette as one of the best of its kind and by the 1840s had already run to three editions –

SCRIPTURE ALPHABETS
A – is an angel who praises the Lord.
B – is for Bible, – Gods most holy Word.
C – is for Church, where the righteous resort.
D – is for Devil, who wishes our hurt.
. . .
U – is for Uzzah, who died for his sins.

V – is for Vashti, the hard-fated queen.
W – is for whale, which Jonah did dread.
X – is a cross, upon which Jesus bled.
Y – is a yoke, 'tis the badge of a slave.
Z – is for Zacchaeus, whom Jesus did save.

The authors gave this instruction for using the lesson –

A child is to stand in the rostrum, having twenty-six squares of
wood, on which are painted the letters of the alphabet, great and
small. The child then holding up the squares on which the letters
Aa are drawn calls aloud, 'A stands for angel, who praises the Lord,'
which the children – looking at the letter – repeat after him. He then
holds up Bb and so on throughout the whole twenty-six squares.
Thus the children become familiarised with the letters, and at the
same time their little minds are stored with Scripture truths which,
under the teaching of the Holy Spirit, may lead them to a knowledge
of Him whom to know is life eternal.

The children were also expected to learn by heart from this volume –

The names of all the books in the Old and New Testaments.
All the passages relating to the working of the Holy Spirit.
The parallels between Moses and Jesus.
The names of all the mountains mentioned in the Scriptures,
The principal prophecies relating to Christ.
Sins recorded in the Scriptures, with examples.
All that is said of No. 7 in Scripture.
All that is said of No. 40 in Scripture.
The offices of the angels.
Names given to Christ.

It was, of course, a religious age – indeed, arguably more so than the
broken, cynical Scotland of a century earlier, for in the final decades of the
1700s there had been repeated waves of Christian revival and the temper
of Scotland by 1840 was profoundly 'Evangelical'– that is, a Christianity
centred on the absolute authority of Scripture, the need for personal
Christian conversion and the obligation of Christian mission, at home and
overseas, both social and spiritual.
    The Evangelical movement was central to the most spectacular single

event in nineteenth-century Scotland – the Disruption of 1843, when a near-majority of the Kirk's ministers (and an absolute one of her people) quit the Established Church in protest over 'patronage' – the absolute power of a local laird to appoint the local minister, whatever the wishes of the congregation, a privilege in express breach of the Articles of Union in 1707 but which was upheld by the Court of Session in repeated judgements against local Presbyteries.

For the rest of Victoria's reign the huge, new Free Church of Scotland would be a mighty force in national life, its leaders latterly very close to the Liberal Party, and taking intense interest in education. Free Church schools would be built all over the country, and three theological colleges besides; and Free Churchmen like David Stowe would in time revolutionise teacher training itself. But the Free Church never subjected the temper of the times – hard, laissez-faire, free-market economics, with its wholesale exploitation and ensuing human misery – to any intelligent Christian critique. And by century's end it was increasingly alarmed by wholesale Irish immigration, rapidly transforming the religious character of Scotland and importing ancient hatreds this side of the North Channel. In 1800 there was very little anti-Roman Catholic sentiment in Edinburgh. After all, there were hardly

A steel-cut of Sir George Harvey's slightly treacly 1847 painting, 'Quitting the Manse'. The Disruption of 1843 transformed Scottish life in many ways, not least the schooling of our children.

any of them. By 1900, of course, there were tens of thousands; the Pope had in 1878 restored the Scottish hierarchy, and the issue of Irish home rule had split the Liberals and redefined Scotland's politics – even today, sectarian tensions linger among the less herbivorous communities of west-central Scotland.

All this in time had dramatic impact on Scotland's schools. Gravely weakened by the Disruption, the Established Church had rapidly to yield many of her traditional duties (not least the relief of paupers) to local government and the wider State. Those insistent that children be educated had to contend with parents (and farms, and factories) more interested in their potential as cheap labour. It became increasingly evident, as the arguments of social reformers began to prevail, that education should be compulsory; that the State itself would eventually have to provide it; and that in time it would also have to provide the schooling of a burgeoning Roman Catholic population – whatever the paranoia of the Protestant majority. It would be 1918 before any Government dared to furnish it.

We know little of Robertson's immediate successors as Headmaster, save that they were both ministers – or, more accurately, probationers; trained and qualified but never ordained to a pastoral charge. Far into the twentieth century such 'stickit ministers' had often to content themselves with a teaching career. Rev. R .T. Auld served for six years at Gillespie's, from 1843 to 1849, and Rev. D. Henderson thereafter until 1870. All the evidence suggests they were mediocre to incompetent.

Big change, though, was coming. The government of the day was increasingly anxious to rationalise school provision in Scotland, with a view at last to imposing compulsory education. This required a Royal Commission – a favourite device of politicians in a pickle; there had to be delicate negotiation with the churches, and there had to be a change in the law to free the endowed schools (like Gillespie's) from the more rigid demands of long-dead benefactors. The Merchant Company was in any event eager to consolidate its operations – and modernise its academies – and asked one Simon S. Laurie, Secretary of the Educational Committee of the Established Church, to write a report on its hospital schools. No doubt they hinted heavily as to what answer they wanted, and Mr Laurie duly obliged. 'If monasteries are bad for men who deliberately enter them after their characters are formed,' he declared sententiously, 'how much more hurtful must they be to boys whose characters they form.'

In a Scotland now very jumpy about renascent Roman Catholicism, monasteries were a touchy subject. But it is certainly striking that, as the rising classes in England took avidly to consigning their sons to boarding school, Scots – by and large – sharply moved in the opposite direction. There are still very few boarding schools in Scotland – with many pupils from south of the border – and something in our national character, perhaps the strong Presbyterian emphasis on personal, parental involvement in spiritual development, has never taken to them. The Merchant Company now had the excuse to turn Watson's and the rest into nine-to-four day schools and the law shortly gave it opportunity. The Endowment Institutions (Scotland) Act (1869) freed charities and trustees all over the country from the unhelpful or archaic terms laid down in assorted wills. Especially – in our case – James Gillespie's insistence that all pupils be taught for free.

The solution was ruthless and obvious. The free school would close, the pensioners would be turned out of the Hospital – and, in 1870, duly were, sent to stay with friends or family and given a money allowance for the rest of their lives. For several years the Hospital lay empty as the Merchant Company manoeuvred for moral and political cover.

On 12 May 1874 a special investigative committee of the Merchant Company made hard proposals. The Hospital was swiftly to be converted into a fee-paying junior school for both boys and girls. Bursaries could be provided to help children from the poorest homes attend Gillespie's, and help the ablest to continue their studies at the higher schools of the Merchant Company. The Free School would close and the site be sold – for these were now the years when lands all around central Edinburgh were being feued off by happy gentry for massive tenement development, and lucratively so. Motives need not necessarily have been pure.

'The number of foundationers [that is, the sixty-five pupils granted free places] should be maintained,' declared this committee, 'and with that view that vacancies should be duly advertised; that encroachments on the capital should be refunded by annual instalments; estimates of income and expenditure for the ensuing year should be prepared, previous to the issue of the school prospectus; and that, in admission to the school, preference should be given (first) to children and grandchildren of members and (second) to children of families connected with Edinburgh, Leith and their suburbs.'

So Gillespie's survived, though with a subtle tweak of the helm that, for the next century, would take it further and further away from the social vision of its founder – and make it a far better school. For the incompetence of its early masters and its blinkered teaching ethos had just been sensationally damned; the next forty years would see rapid and sparkling reform.

CHAPTER THREE

'Forward!'
1874–1908

In 1874, as James Gillespie's became a fee-paying primary school for both sexes, it had operated for seven dreich decades as an indifferent elementary school for boys of poor background, taught the rudiments of reading and writing and counting in the most mechanical fashion and with the constant and enthusiastic use of corporal punishment.

By 1915, now James Gillespie's Higher Grade School, it was a bright, flourishing Edinburgh institution, in new and spacious quarters on the other side of the Bruntsfield Links (and where Gillespie's would remain till 1966). There was a vigorous social life and a flourishing Former Pupils' Club. There were drill and song, art and dramatics. There were sports and athletics – Gillespie's pupils had a particularly vigorous appetite for swimming; on Thirlestane Road the Warrender Baths were already a local institution. And Montessori classes began for infants, the very first anywhere in Scotland and, like those of Fröbel and others, reflecting new pedagogy: that early education must begin in play, in the child's exploration of her own environment, in the little boy's lightly supervised endeavours to solve his own problems.

The school had at some point acquired a motto – 'Forward!' – and a keen sense of its own past, of ongoing heritage, as well as ambitions for the future, not least because demand for places had long outstripped supply. No other school in Edinburgh had produced so many candidates for the teaching profession and – though, until 1908, it was effectively the Preparatory Department of the Merchant Company schools – Gillespie's boys besides and for years had topped the bursary competition for places at Heriot's, the oldest school in the city, whose magnificent Jacobean premises threatened to eclipse the Palace of Holyrood House.

'In the sunny halls of Gillespie's,' enthused John Roy Stewart in 1921 –

The boys' swimming team, 1913. One hopes they all survived the Great War.

Though many notable athletes have emerged from Gillespie's – such as Damien Hoyland, recently capped for Scotland's national rugby side – no girl has yet eclipsed Ellen King (1909–1994), a brilliant swimmer who twice won silver at the Olympics, repeatedly held world records for her breast-stroke and back-stroke speeds, devoted her life to teaching the sport and swam well into her eighties. In 1928 she was described as 'one of the world's greatest all-round swimmers'.

and writing of what had by then been broadly true – 'the theory of auto-education had become a living reality. School has been robbed of its terrors for the child. It is a pleasure to see the little ones freely moving about their self-selected tasks, proudly solving their own problems, and exulting in their achievements. The indefeasible right of childhood is joy, and it is good to know that the three Rs (with other things added to them) can be acquired just as readily in the brighter atmosphere of Montessori as under the rigid and passive methods lingering still in too many infant rooms . . . Meanwhile the bright battalions that surge through the gates of Gillespie's are brought up in the pride of its name and fame. Many of them are grand-children of citizens who tell of their own gambols in the now silent corridors across the Links, and have passed on the watchword and the spirit of the school to generations following.'

Everything in the early school magazines – the first appeared in 1910 – suggests an urbane humour, a liberal outlook and smiling tolerance, by then long established, and that have never since left James Gillespie's.

It had not always been so.

·   ·   ·

The first reports of Her Majesty's Inspectorate for Schools on Gillespie's, from 1874 and for some years thereafter, paint a depressing picture of what then still generally passed for the education of Scotland's children. Gillespie's was no worse than most, but for its boys and girls it must have been tedious in the extreme, and we had better give the grim Inspector a long shake of his sorry head:

> The most common fault in reading is that it is mechanical and monotonous, the natural result of the children only very partially understanding what they read. Many teachers seem to know nothing of the advantage of never letting a child read a passage till by some means or other it has mastered all the hard words in it. The large size of the class prevents the children reading more than two or three lines at a time each, and if a child is to learn to read well it must read a good quantity consecutively – half a page or more.
>
> The defective articulation which characterises much of the reading in Stands 1 and 2 results from careless and inefficient instruction. I frequently find that these classes are handed over to junior pupil-teachers or monitors, as if the forming of habits of good reading were a matter too easy to be entrusted to the senior members of the staff.
>
> The great fault in the teaching of grammar is that it almost overlooks the true end of grammar. Composition has been neglected more than any other branch of education and, when taught, it has been taught, as a rule, in a perfunctory and unsystematic manner.
>
> The prevalent fault in most schools has been the want of good oral instruction and the practice of allowing the scholars to learn, by rote, definitions from text books without intelligent study. One of the weakest points in elementary education is its mechanical character – the use of mechanical methods to effect a pass result in the quickest and easiest way.

THIS IS HOW ONE FEELS
ON THE FIRST DAY
AT SCHOOL

AND THIS — ON THE LAST.
(BY ONE WHO HAS EXPERIENCED IT.)

In geography and history in many cases, I should perhaps say in every case, the answers of the scholars show 'cram' and nothing else. The text-books seem in most cases to have been almost entirely committed to memory, verbatim.

The powerlessness on the part of the scholars to apply their accurate knowledge of the plain rules of arithmetic betokens great want of method in their instruction. I am of the opinion that the frequent inability of the higher standards even to attempt an arithmetical problem is more often due to deficiency of teaching than of learning powers. I am convinced that the fault in this case does not lie with the children, but that the failure comes from the way in which they are taught to deal with subjects. They are taught to work a question by a mere mechanical process requiring a knowledge of how to do their work and accuracy in its performance, but not with any accompanying understanding of the steps of the process. This latter way of working the examples takes more time than the former, but it requires the assent of the reasoning faculty at each step, and teaches a child to think about what he is doing. It is, perhaps, needless to say that few teachers adopt the better method. They cannot give the time required and its value is not paid for as a result.

The resignation of Robert Foulis as Headmaster in 1876 – he had been appointed in 1870 – was probably in response to such assessments. But the recollections of 102-year-old former pupil Mrs Margaret Ashton, interviewed in 1977 for the school magazine by Linda Urquhart and Sheila Prestage, suggest scant improvement even in the 1880s – if there were pleasures to be had elsewhere. Sadly, the tape recording of that encounter has been lost, but the subsequent article is instructive.

Mrs Ashton was born in February 1875, Margaret Carruthers, one of eleven children. Her parents owned a dairy at 5 Gillespie Place (now a boot repair shop) and she lived in Marchmont Steet. She started her education at the Normal School beside the Castle and then went on to Gillespie's. At that time, 1880, the school was in Gillespie Crescent – buildings now owned by the Blind Asylum.

Classes were held in one large hall, partitioned off by curtains, were in tiers, similar to our [Darroch] Annexe classrooms. Boys sat on one side and girls on the other. They never mixed and were punished with the 'tawse' or belt if they so much as spoke in class.

Both girls and boys were called by their surnames by staff. Female teachers took the children till they were nine when they were taught by men. In the infants' [class] Mrs Ashton remembers using slates to write on and then progressing to pencil and paper. Her first lessons in writing came early when she had to copy sayings in a book.

The school had no library at that time although the Central Library at George IV Bridge had just opened. School seems to have been very hard work at that time as they had only one break during the whole day and this was for lunch. Also they had no physical education or subjects like art or cookery. The children had no uniform and staff had no gowns so everyone just wore their day-to-day clothes. Mrs Ashton, though, remembers one trendy teacher who wore red cotton wool in her ears to match her red dress.

Mrs Ashton left Gillespie's at thirteen but her mother considered her too small to leave school so she was then sent to Warrender Park School from where she went on to Heriot Watt College to study art.

As there were no games at school the children made up their own which they played in the Links. They would also play golf on the Meadows short-hole course.

She also remembers going on pleasure-boat trips, which cost 6d, under the Forth Rail Bridge. Mrs Ashton even saw Queen Victoria when she visited Edinburgh to open an exhibition.

There were no school dinners, Mrs Ashton besides recalled of her time at Gillespie's, but, with the wistful memory of her inner little girl, 'the baker used to come in with a large board on his head, full of cakes and buns . . .'

The dry and dusty education she recalled reflected, really, two problems: a general shortage of teachers in Scotland (which would remain the case as recently as the 1970s) and the low standards of teacher training. From the Disruption of 1843 these began steadily to rise: in October 1846, for instance, the new Free Church acquired Moray House and its grounds for an Edinburgh school – and not just a 'sessional' school, under the direct oversight of a kirk session and for the children of that parish, but a 'Normal School', where able pupils were identified and expressly trained to be teachers. Moray House College of Education, as things turned out, would be training many of Scotland's best teachers till the last gasp of the twentieth century: in 1998 it was subsumed by the University of Edinburgh and is now, as Moray House School of Education, its educational faculty, within the College of Humanities and Social Science.

Yet 'monitorial' teaching and the deployment of exhausted and ill-waged pupil-teachers would endure to the end of the nineteenth century and beyond – and the system was far from ideal, as Moray House's own website details:

Monitorial systems developed at the end of the 18th century in response to a shortage of teachers and the increasing number of pupils in school classes. In England Dr Andrew Bell and Joseph Lancaster initially developed these systems. Both involved the selection from the older and more able children who could undertake the role of monitor. These children would receive additional instruction from the schoolmaster and in turn they would instruct a group of children: ten in the Lancaster method and up to thirty in the Bell system. The first to apply these techniques in Scotland in 1810 was James Pillans, Rector of the Royal High School in Edinburgh. He used a combination of class and group teaching, with monitors instructing groups of ten boys. Lancaster visited Edinburgh in 1812 and the Leith Wynd Sessional School, opened in 1812/3, at first followed his principles. In this school the desks were arranged around the walls of the schoolroom. The remainder of the space was empty except for the schoolmaster's desk.

The classes on the floor were arranged in groups facing the schoolmaster with a monitor keeping order over each group. At the end of an hour those at the desks would change over with those on the floor. Writing would be carried out on slates, although the older children might use paper.

Whilst monitorial systems overcame the teacher shortages and were inexpensive to run they had major drawbacks. They were regimented and involved rote learning and repetition. No child was 'oot o' the Bible' when studying reading and writing and children were unlikely to develop an enthusiasm for reading later in life. The mechanical routines of instruction also prevented an understanding of words and language.

The Free Church, though, had been quietly slipped £3,000 of public money for its acquisition and adaptation of Moray House – all the more remarkably, as it was just three years after a Disruption so fiercely deplored by the government of the day and Queen Victoria herself. For the state was now reluctantly but inexorably being drawn in to the provision of Scottish education, as Moray House's historians continue:

The increasing role of the government in teacher training is reflected in the Council of Education's Minutes for 1846, introducing a national pupil-teacher scheme. Schools could select from their most promising thirteen-year-old students those most likely to be able to undertake an apprenticeship of up to five years' duration. During the day they would follow the school's curriculum and then receive additional instruction outside school hours on the art of teaching from staff appointed for this purpose. The most able students, selected through a competitive examination, were awarded a Queen's Scholarship. Successful male students were awarded a grant of £25 and female students two thirds of this. These grants supported their maintenance at the Normal School. The school's curriculum at this time was a broad one and included subjects such as drawing and music. At the end of their course the students would take an examination in both general and professional subjects conducted by Her Majesty's Inspectors. The achievement of a Leaving Certificate carried with it an enhanced salary funded by the government.

Whilst not initially welcomed ('it assumed a child could do two exacting things at once'), the pupil-teacher scheme, especially for elementary school teachers, was an improvement on the previous monitorial model, guaranteeing a minimum level of personal knowledge and achievement of recognised teaching skills. Certificated teachers were able to organise and teach the large number of children in sessional and subscription schools.

The Normal Schools were funded by the government for the number of teachers they produced and the Free Church Normal Schools, in particular, responded positively to the increasing need for more teachers at this time. By 1857 the number of students in Scottish Training Colleges (Normal Schools) had increased to over 500, with a third of these women. A positive HMI Report on the Free Church Normal College at Moray House in 1858 noted that two large lecture rooms and the three class rooms had recently been opened to accommodate this increase in student numbers.

The success of students in their final examinations depended in part on the knowledge and skills of the teaching staff. In 1853 the government introduced payments to those Normal School lecturers who could pass an examination in a designated subject. On passing they would be paid an additional £100 on top of their £150 salary. There was some concern that 'lecturer' implied a concentration on academic work rather than on the practical training. However, James Sime, Rector of the Edinburgh Normal School (1855–1864), reassured doubters, 'Lecturers lecture and also show students how to impart knowledge.'

In 1858 the regular curriculum of the Normal Schools was extended to two years by regulation, with training ending in December instead of June. To qualify for their 'parchment' students, in addition to their Leaving Certificate, had to undertake a further two years of work teaching in a school. The final grade obtained depended on both their examination performance and the report of the HMI on their schoolwork.

This new system of teacher training began to have a major effect on Scottish education. Newly qualified and certificated teachers were sought after and reasonably well paid. Their training gave them a wider knowledge than many parish schoolteachers previously and this in turn enabled them to teach a broader curriculum to children. The link with the churches was also lessening with increased government funding and the abolition of the need for teachers to sign the Confession of Faith.

The Church of Scotland, too, opened a 'Normal School' in Edinburgh – that at Johnston Terrace, which Mrs Ashton had first attended, and subsequently augmented by additional premises on Chamber Street; and, in broad parallel, Scotland's two biggest denominations retained control of teacher training until 1907, when the Kirk and the United Free Church (as the Free Church majority had in 1900 become) voluntarily handed over their colleges and assets in Scotland to assorted Provincial Committees, with some local authority input but ultimately accountable to the Secretary for Scotland and the Crown.

The pupil-teacher system should not immediately be dismissed – two of the greatest Gillespie's Headmasters, as we shall see, thus first entered the profession – but it took decades for a new educational order, and, indeed, a whole new vision of education, to hit Gillespie's; and that was primarily the achievement of three men.

•   •   •

In 1876 the Merchant Company put William W. Dunlop MA in charge of Gillespie's, and though tribute paid to him in the school magazine in 1911 is more effulgent than detailed (he had just been elected a city councillor),

Though headmaster for just six years, decades before this 1911 photograph, William W. Dunlop's arts of cold leadership transformed what, today, we would call a failing school.

and his service was not that long, it was evidently marked by the brisk, reforming vigour of a new broom. A brief but vital pontificate that turned the fortunes of Gillespie's around, much as Bill Bedborough's short but determined reign would do for Glasgow's Jordanhill School in the 1990s and after broadly comparable crises.

It will doubtless be a pleasure to our readers – particularly to those whose memory of school life dates back to the early 'eighties' – to see in our pages the portrait of the Headmaster of those days. At the present time, it is specially appropriate that we should make reference to Mr Dunlop's connection with Gillespie's School. Though the period of his Headmastership of the School was of brief duration – six years in all – it is noteworthy as the time when the foundations of that reputation were laid, which his subsequent career did so much to justify and enhance. Appointed at a time when educational problems of a crucial kind had to be faced and dealt

with, Mr Dunlop overcame the difficulties of the situation with a
vigour and promptitude which at once inspired confidence and
ensured success; and, before his transference to Daniel Stewart's
College in 1882, he had already given evidence of the possession of
those characteristic qualities which were designed to bring to him
recognition as an educational authority and expert. He had, as
Headmaster, shown a clear and almost intuitive perception of the
best means by which improvements might be introduced; the power
of accurately discriminating between essentials and non-essentials,
and of keeping these in their due perspective; the art of lucidly
setting forth in his teaching and writings any subject with which he
was called upon to deal; and, what is perhaps of greater importance
in these days of restless change, he had, throughout his administrative work, combined a readiness to devise and adopt new methods
with a determination to keep permanent principles always in view,
and to conserve carefully whatever had been proved valuable by the
test of experience.

His connection with Gillespie's School did not cease with his
transference to Daniel Stewart's College. The Higher Grade Department of Gillespie's School had not at that time developed, and many
Gillespie boys who wished to continue their education beyond the
'Standards' were attracted to Daniel Stewart's College; and among
Mr Dunlop's warmest admirers may be still numbered many of
these Gillespie-Stewartonians. For many years Mr Dunlop's interest
in the School continued to be manifested by the annual presentation
of two handsome book prizes bearing the donor's name – one
awarded to the Dux in Latin, the other to the Dux in French. We
heartily congratulate Mr Dunlop on his recent election as one of
our City Councillors, and would express the earnest hope that he
may be long spared to enjoy municipal honours.

A former pupil never forgot Mr Dunlop. 'The first thing I remember, while
yet a child, was being taken to the school by my father, and ushered into
the presence of the headmaster, Mr Dunlop, to pass an examination,
written and oral, in my scholastic attainments. I was not very big at the
time, and the great tall man bending over me seemed the personification
of order and dignity, combined with a certain degree of sternness. I was to
make an acquaintance with this trait of his character later on through the
application of the "tawse" . . . One day, not long after I had entered the
School – it was at the lunch hour, too – we youngsters thought we could

use a little more liberty than usual by chasing one another up one stair, along the corridor, and down the other. The clatter of twelve tacketty boots on the stone stairs broke in on the quietude of the headmaster's sanctum, and he strode out majestically, just in time to seize one of the enemy and that one, unfortunately, myself. What could I say in defence? Of course, boy-like, we were prepared to run the risk of a few "palmies" for the sake of a little mild horse-play. And Mr Dunlop was not the one to disappoint us either. Like the spider with the fly he swooped down upon me and bore me in triumph to his den, where I was treated to a homily on the dignity of correct behaviour in school and out of it, enforced at the end of his tawse. And even yet I have lively recollection of the tawses's stinging properties. Thus was I made the scapegoat of the noisy troop; but the lesson went home, and the treatment did not require repetition . . .'

Dunlop, in charge for a mere six if decisive years, did not hang around Gillespie's long enough to see the fruit of his reforms – which do not appear to have been evident to Mrs Ashton either – but what he had begun was brought to fast and full glory by his successor, William T. Jenkins MA FEIS, Headmaster from 1882 to 1908 – an impressive run of twenty-six years, and who by character and in achievement ranks with Thomas Burnett and Patricia Thomas as one of the school's great defining commanders.

Jenkins was a man from the north. He was born in Burghead, Moray, the son of a fisherman in essentially a town of fisherfolk, who from boyhood took enthusiastically to the briny. And, but for a curious providence, he might have remained a mariner all his days. 'Few men,' reflected his obituarist, 'manifested greater pleasure or skill than he did in handling a boat, and nothing more excited his interest than the tale of some sea adventure, or the story of a voyage of exploration and discovery. He was not, however, designed for the sea. By one of those strange accidents, which often change a whole life-history, his thoughts and ambitions were, when he was but a boy, turned in another direction. A casual meeting with the Headmaster of a North Country school led him to think of becoming a teacher . . .'

Jenkins, following what was now the customary course into the profession, became a pupil-teacher in Aberdeen, and then proceeded to the Edinburgh Training College. He briefly held a situation in Pitlochry, suggesting, tantalisingly, he had at least some Gaelic; but the rest of his career would be in Edinburgh. He served as 'resident master' at John Watson's Institution, in Dean Village, while simultaneously studying for his university degree, and upon graduation was appointed to George Watson's College, where he spent twelve years as principal teacher of

He might well have spent his entire life as a fisherman, had not a chance encounter opened his eyes to the possibilities of teaching. In charge of Gillespie's for over a quarter of a century, the gentle William T. Jenkins was one of its best commanders.

English. As, in 1882, the Governors of the Merchant Company now transferred William Dunlop from Gillespie's to Stewart's, they simultaneously identified William Jenkins as his successor. He proved an inspired choice: physically robust, highly intelligent, genial and wily, genuinely modest and with a keen sense of humour, he was the ideal captain of the ship through decades of turbulent change in Scottish schools and at times of direct threat to Gillespie's itself, as his obituary in the school magazine makes clear –

> During the long period of his headmastership, many severe tests were, both directly and indirectly, applied to the School, threatening occasionally to affect, not just its vitality, but its very existence. Education was being, in many respects, completely revolutionised, and public opinion itself was undergoing a radical change as to the very first principles of education. Many of these changes, incidental to a time of transition – such as the general introduction of free education into the Board Schools of Edinburgh – were of such a nature as to require most tactful and judicious handling, but under the skilful management of the Headmaster the School more than

held its own. The two Departments of which, at that time, it consisted, grew and flourished, and an Advanced Department sprang into existence, ultimately developing into what is now a large and well-equipped Higher Grade School. The School building had to be repeatedly enlarged, and was, even after these extensions were made, crowded to its utmost capacity. The calls necessarily made upon the energies and powers of the Headmaster naturally increased. The School really became two schools, each with its own staff, its own methods and organisation, its own peculiarities and problems. All these changes involved an amount of work, worry, and anxiety which an outsider could neither realise nor appreciate. Throughout all these years the success of the School was attested not only by a great influx of pupils, many of them from a distance, but by the annual Official Reports on the work, which were uniformly gratifying, and, very frequently, of a most flattering kind.

The prosperity of the School was not accidental. It was in a large measure due to the personality of the Headmaster – to his resourcefulness and ability. Strong physically and mentally, he was also strong in character, possessing qualities that inspired confidence and would have ensured success in any sphere of life. He combined many characteristics not often found in conjunction. Energetic and resolute, he was, at the same time, very cautious, and deliberated long and carefully before taking any important step. When he did resolve upon a course of action the decision was clear, fixed and final. Naturally, he was a man of great versatility, as those who knew him most intimately would readily testify, but it was evident that he had firmly resolved to restrict his work within certain well-defined limits, to direct his energies into certain channels, and under no pretext or temptation to go beyond these. With his wide knowledge and experience of educational work, he might well have contributed liberally and effectively to educational literature; but such an idea, if ever it presented itself to him, was immediately set aside. His thorough acquaintance with the varying and intricate problems of modern school work would have entitled him to speak with authority and weight at Congresses and Conferences, but he was seldom, if ever, seen at such meetings.

Jenkins was himself a first-rate classroom teacher, and seems always to have 'kept his hand in', not true of some modern successors. He was as assured with an infant class on 'Fun Friday' – chortling with the little ones and

Opposite.
The frontispiece of
Mr Jenkins's high-end
school prospectus in
1906, with a daunting
view of the 'Burn
Bust' of Mr Gillespie
himself. Seriously
creepy – it may well
have been made from
a death mask – the
sculpture can still be
seen at the Merchant
Hall on Hanover
Street, Edinburgh.

encouraging them to find pennies he had hidden about the room – as he was addressing a gracious and sophisticated adult audience, or exhorting a senior class on the English language in all its beauty and subtlety. Everything suggests a decent, upright man. Jenkins never boasted of his own attainments. He never spoke unkindly of other people. He dealt with difficult or tedious colleagues – and in every school there will always be difficult or tedious colleagues – with profound patience and the utmost tact.

Though a devout man (he was for many years an elder of St Oswald's Parish Church) he had one indulgence: golf, serving as captain of the Baberton Golf Club in 1906. And when, in 1907, he attained a quarter-century as Headmaster of Gillespie's and due fuss was duly made, Jenkins 'was presented by the pupils of the School with a handsome service of silver-plate, and by the staff with an illuminated address in album form. A proof of his popularity, even more significant, was the presence, on that occasion, of many former teachers of the School, some of them from a considerable distance.'

The scale of Jenkins's achievement can be seen from a surviving, 1906 prospectus for the Infant Department of 'James Gillespie's Schools for Boys and Girls'. What is staggering about this publication is its sheer quality – richly embossed cover, thick silky pages, tasteful and striking illustration. In fact, it is almost entirely an album of photographs, with only a page and a half of quiet and authoritative information for prospective parents, as detailed by the Headmaster himself.

James Gillespie's Schools for Boys and Girls

ELEMENTARY DEPARTMENT
There is in connection with these Schools a very large and fully equipped Elementary Department, where Pupils [are] admitted from the age of 4 years; and the Governors desire to draw special attention of Parents and Guardians to its many advantages.

SCHOOL HOURS
The School Hours are from 9.15 A.M. to 2.30 P.M., and suitable intervals are given for Luncheon and Recreation in the Playground. During the cold months of the year arrangements are made for providing Hot Cocoa and Milk for Lunch at the nominal charge of 2D. per week.

JAMES GILLESPIE

JAMES GILLESPIE'S SCHOOLS
FOR BOYS AND GIRLS

HEAD MASTER
Mr WILLIAM JENKINS, M.A., F.E.I.S

BANKS & CO., EDINBURGH.

SEWING ROOM AND ORDINARY CLASS ROOM.

CLASS ROOMS

The accommodation provided for the Elementary Pupils consists of a spacious Infant Hall, – well lighted, comfortably seated, and containing a Gallery capable of seating at one time 400 children. Part of this Hall can be readily partitioned off into Class Rooms identified for Writing, Drawing, and Kindergarten Work. There are in addition four smaller Class Rooms on the ground floor of the building. Heating, illumination and wall decoration receive every attention with the view of making the Class Rooms comfortable, interesting, and attractive.

PLAYGROUND

The Playground is, undoubtedly, one of the best in the City. It is large, well arranged, and completely shut off from street traffic – thus, there is absolute freedom from street dangers. The younger children may be brought to School in the mornings by guardians or older brothers and sisters, and need not leave the premises until they are taken charge of by their friends.

COURSE OF STUDY

The Course of Instruction is varied and interesting. It embraces: – Religious Knowledge, Reading, Spelling, Recitation, Arithmetic, Elements of Grammar and Geography, Stories in History, Writing, Drawing, Object Lessons, Lessons in Form and Colour, Kindergarten Work, Sewing, Children's Games and Occupations, Singing, Musical Drill, and Gallery Exercises.

CLASSIFICATION

The entire Department is under the charge of a Head Infant Mistress, with 4 Certificated Teachers, 1 Ex-Pupil Teacher and 4 Pupil Teachers. There are 2 Divisions – Upper and Lower, that is, Standard 1 and Infants. The former is sub-divided into 3 classes, and the latter into 5 classes. These are carefully graded, and the number in each Class limited, so that Pupils may receive individual attention.

HOME LESSONS

In all the Classes Pupils are assisted in the preparation of Lessons. The work for next day is always gone over and difficulties explained – thus, very little Home Work is required.

Opposite.
You sense a most ordered environment in these Gillespie's classes of the Edwardian era – not least in the segregation of boys and girls – but, with all those engaged and serene young faces, by no means an unhappy one.

FEES
Fees payable Quarterly, and in advance.

LOWER DIVISION OR INFANTS – 4/6 per quarter

UPPER DIVISION OR STANDARD 1 – 5/6

NOTE – All School Books and School Materials necessary for Writing, Kindergarten, and Drawing, may, in the option of Parents, be obtained at School on payment of a Quarterly Charge of –

INFANTS – 4d Per Quarter   STANDARD 1 – 6D Per Quarter

INSPECTION OF CLASSES
The whole School is under Government Inspection, and all the Classes are annually examined and reported upon by one of H.M. Inspectors.

The following is the report for last Session on this Department –

'The Infant Department makes a distinct advance even on the highly satisfactory appearance of last year. Discipline is of the same thorough character as formerly, the teaching of Arithmetic is extremely intelligent, and Reading has considerably improved. I have seldom seen more effective Object Lessons given. The Children show a full and accurate knowledge of a considerable range of subjects, and their answers were extremely thoughtful and well expressed. Drill is admirable, and Kindergarten Work on good lines is receiving increased attention.'

ENROLMENT OF NEW PUPILS
The Headmaster will enrol pupils daily up to 27th July, and from Thursday, 13th September to Saturday, 15th inclusive, between 10 A.M. and 2 P.M.

PIANOFORTE INSTRUCTION
Instruction in Pianoforte is given to Boys and Girls. This subject is optional. The Fee is 10/6 per Quarter of 11 weeks, 2 Lessons per Week. The Session is 3 ½ Quarters.

This instruction is conducted by Mr HOBKIRK and Miss BELL, assisted by Miss RUSSELL and Miss M'Intyre. Pupils are received from all ages. Special attention is given to Beginners.

DANCING AND DEPORTMENT
These subjects are under the Tuition of Mr and Mrs LOWE, with Assistant.

FEE – 7/6 Per Quarter.
Only 2 Quarters per Session.
The Quarter Days for next Session are:-

| 1st Quarter, 18th September. | 3rd Quarter, 18th February |
| 2nd Quarter, 3rd December | 4th Quarter, 6th May. |

William Jenkins, M.A., F.E.I.S
Headmaster

Nervous pupils prepare to play their duets for the watchful music master, 1906. Classmates stand by to turn the page.

His words, the photographs, the production standards, the sheer authority of this prospectus and the sophistication of the education proffered (one cannot readily forget classes in 'Dancing and Deportment') assure us of a school that, at this height of the Edwardian summer, had no less assuredly arrived.

An anonymous former pupil recalled Jenkins warmly for the July 1915 number of the school magazine, that after Dunlop had departed for Daniel Stewart's College in 1882 –

> then Mr Jenkins took up the reins, and I need not tell you how well he filled the position, and how he was universally loved by both staff and pupils. My memories of him are of the pleasantest nature.
>
> I remember how he explained the word 'obviously'; it was a poser for most of us. He said, 'Now, if I told you the man was *obviously* drunk, what would you understand by that?' And then he assumed the gait of the bibulous gentleman and staggered up and down the class-room, much to the amusement of the pupils, in which also the teacher readily participated. That was the natural way of explaining it; the Latin root meaning and the prefix had no further interest for us. With such a demonstration, the answer was forthcoming from a round dozen eager scholars all at once.
>
> Before I leave Mr Jenkins, I must recount the following incident in which he was the principal figure. It well reveals his great good nature.
>
> It was winter time and, according to his usual custom, he came into the room to hear us at our lessons. What the subject was I cannot remember now; however, 'tis immaterial, and for a few minutes he listened. Then, taking the book from the teacher, he launched forth into the subject, and, all unconsciously, sat down on the fire-guard. Now there was a blazing fire roaring merrily up the chimney, but still the Headmaster held forth with his discourse. Then the sickly odour of singeing wool pervaded the atmosphere of the room; a faint struggling of the shoulders and a smothered groan; and Mr Jenkins bounded into the middle of the room with an agility that would have done credit to a seven-year-old.
>
> The scholars, ever ready to find an occasion for hilarity, thought the opportunity too good to be missed. The boys started sniggering, and some of the girls giggled, and finally, most ungraciously, all exploded in a general laugh at his plight. He joined in the laughter himself – what else could he do? – it was such a dramatic and abrupt

termination to an interesting subject. Then, gravely handing the text-book to the teacher, he left the room. It was a matter of great speculation for some time afterwards, the extent of the damage to his nether garments, but we remain in ignorance to this present day.

There was another type of question, calculated to stimulate our reasoning faculties, which was a favourite one of his, and I cannot refrain from noting one example. During the history lesson some reference had been made to the Chelsea Hospital in London. As was his wont, Mr Jenkins had been asking us whom should we find there. 'Old pensioners.' 'How should we find them?' 'In a disabled state.' 'And what is disabled?' 'A person wanting a limb, or maimed.' 'Correct; and now tell me if there are any old soldiers there wanting their heads?' This nonplussed the class for a minute or two; then a smile flitted from one row of anxious faces to another, quickly followed by a broad grin. And all doubts were set at rest by the truth dawning on someone, and answering boldly, 'No, sir!' And the class heaved a grand, united sigh of relief when it was certain that there were no headless defenders of the Empire in Chelsea.

Mention must also be made of Thomas Robertson, who would finally retire in 1921 after over forty-five years of service at Gillespie's, latterly as First Assistant and Deputy Headmaster and through many changes. He was under successive Headmasters the most loyal of lieutenants, he encouraged many in his classes to enter teaching, he was something of an authority on the life and works of Robert Louis Stevenson, and he was exceedingly fond of cricket. He besides designed the school badge that, until the wholesale changes under Thomas Burnett, adorned caps, hats and drill-costumes of the pupils, and survived with little modification on the cover of the school magazine into the 1950s. 'To the many new ideas in the method and subjects of teaching which he encountered in the course of his long career,' recorded a colleague, 'he always held an open mind and was ever ready to support their adoption if desirable, but he never lost sight of the fact that there is an irreducible minimum which must always be taught and which no ideas can remove.'

But, well before the Great War, Gillespie's was already buckling under the weight of its own success, and the former Hospital was no longer big enough to accommodate staff and pupils comfortably. Yet further classrooms were needed and what remained of Mr Gillespie's original endowment could not now fund such works. After quiet negotiation, and with professed reluctance, the Merchant Company handed operation of

Though little
remembered today,
Thomas Robertson
ended his Gillespie's
career as Deputy
Headmaster and was
highly regarded.

the School to the Edinburgh School Board in 1908. There was never any danger of Gillespie's simply closing down. But there was genuine doubt as to whether the Merchant Company would long allow it to continue trading, so to speak, under its founder's name – especially if, as seemed increasingly likely, the authorities chose to rehome the school elsewhere. For several years they were loath even to sell the building to the Edinburgh School Board.

None of this would be William Jenkins's concern. He stepped down that same year, in 1908, and – though he continued to attend school functions and reunions and so on – his retirement was scant. He died in February 1912, after sudden illness and a few days of great suffering, and is buried in Morningside Cemetery.

CHAPTER FOUR

'The School on the Links'
1908–1937

William Jenkins was succeeded by Alexander Blacklaws, BA (Lond). Apart from his disconcerting resemblance to the Kaiser – his portrait appears in the 1913 school magazine – we know surprisingly little about the gentleman. Blacklaws served for just eight years before moving on to a further command, at Broughton Higher Grade Centre. Every Head of Gillespie's since has held the post till retirement. The school magazine, launched in 1910, had not begun at the time of the Blacklaws appointment and, with the exigencies of the Great War, the 1915 issue was the last till 1919, so no

Though Alexander Blacklaws put in eight years as headmaster, we know very little about him – only that he dressed immaculately, and that pupils dubbed him 'Black-Legs'.

COURT TAILOR ✸ **S I M** ✸ HABIT MAKER

96 and 98 LOTHIAN ROAD

Ladies' and Gentlemen's Department.				
MADE TO ORDER.				
Dress Suits	-	-	-	from £4 4 0
Frock Coat Suits	-	-	„ 4 4 0
Sac Suits	-	-	-	„ 3 3 0
Overcoats	-	-	-	„ 2 2 0
Costumes	-	-	-	„ 3 10 0

Ladies' **Ready-to-Wear** Dresses and Costumes from 30/-

Ladies' **Ready-to-Wear** Ulsters and Rainproof Coats from **21/-**

"Our Girls" Department.

Dresses, Gostumes, Wraps, Coats, etc.

Latest Designs and Shades at Extraordinary Moderate Prices. For example—

Maids' Hard-wearing Blue Serge Dresses, - at 10/6
Maids' Stylish Cosy Wrap Coats - -from 10/6
Maids' Tweed Costumes - - - „ **17/6**

P.S.—Please note that we make a Speciality of Gymnastic Gostumes (Tunic, Girdle, and Knickers), from 8/6.

Elegant Edwardian apparel as advertised in the school magazine, 1913 – and even for your servants. Perhaps Sim's furnished Mr Blacklaws's frock coat.

biographical detail can be garnered from his departure either. There are but the platitudinous compliments of the 1913 number. 'We have much pleasure in reproducing in this issue the photograph of our esteemed headmaster, Mr Blacklaws. The coming of Mr Blacklaws to James Gillespie's School marked the beginning of a new era in the history of the school. It is now five years since that time, and during those years Mr Blacklaws has come to be loved and respected by both staff and pupils. To many pupils who have left, Mr Blacklaws, as Headmaster and man, needs no introduction; to many more of an earlier day, his photograph will serve to introduce a gentleman who worthily fills his place in a noble heritage.' For those of us a century later, the photograph is pretty well all we have, apart from reflections by a former pupil during the Second World War on how splendidly he dressed – frock coat and top hat; gold pocket-watch on its chain.

Yet the Blacklaws reign saw some important developments. It was at his decision, for instance, that the first Montessori class began at Gillespie's in 1914. A second would be launched in 1917; they were operated separately from the regular infant classes and directly accountable to the Headmaster.

Meanwhile, the school made final, uneasy parting of the ways with the

Merchant Company. For several years its campus – the old Hospital, and the three acres of land wherein it sat – was rented by Edinburgh School Board, at the surprisingly high annual charge of £655. The Merchant Company was loath to sell the building, and declined the Board's offer of £10,000. They besides declared they would no longer award bursaries. Amidst this ongoing stand-off, 'All the teachers except for two of the more elderly were retained,' writes Kathryn Thompkins, 'together with furniture which was not actually connected with Gillespie. There were 1,580 pupils at that time, all of whom paid fees and bought books and writing materials, until forty bursaries providing free education for one year were instituted.' And the Merchant Company held firmly onto their Gillespie memorabilia – the old gentleman's snuffbox, the spooky Burn bust, Gillespie's personal Bible and even the key to his sepulchre.

Morale was low, salaries had fallen behind those of other Edinburgh School Board establishments, and vacancies were not filled. The building itself was in increasingly dilapidated condition. The gallery in one classroom, one night and without any fuss, collapsed entirely – a victim to advancing dry rot. There was an urgent need for new premises, but would the Merchant Company then permit the uprooted if continuing school to retain Mr Gillespie's name? Many feared – and there is some evidence for this, for the Board advertised places at the two schools together and there were some shared classes – that an entire merger with Boroughmuir School was contemplated.

Amidst such uncertainty, life went on. In 1909 the dinner break was lengthened to an entire hour. Prizes were introduced for the first time – 'silver watches for the Dux boy and girl and merit prizes for all classes, to the total value of not more than £50'. Eight children between eight and thirteen were to receive bursaries valid for one year. That year, too, the Inspector called –

Infant Department – Excellent work despite difficulties of equipment. One of the most ill-adapted infant schools in Edinburgh.
Junior Department – Excellent with carefully graded classes.
Senior Department – Geography is not as good as in the lower
divisions. Vast accumulations of knowledge are attained without
any conception of the world as a whole. Reading and Recitation are
of a high standard. There is very sensible instruction in Grammar
and History and accuracy of results in Arithmetic. The Writing is
neat and accurate and the pupils have facility in English composition.

English – A varied programme is taught with representative literature which is well known. Good essays full of information are
written. Word formation is accurately understood and co-related to
French.

Latin – There is much skill in the teaching. The pupils translate well
though written exercises are less good. The grammar is thoroughly
learnt but pronunciation is poor.

French – Reading is not very fluent but the children grasp the
meaning and recite well. Although the grammar is well learnt there
is insufficient conversation for accent.

Science – There is much improvement.

Drawing – There are insufficient models and light.

Religious Instruction – The same course is followed as in the other
Board schools without the use of the Shorter Catechism.

In 1910 one element of uncertainty was finally resolved. The Edinburgh
School Board decided to build a new Boroughmuir Secondary School at
Viewforth, and to transfer the staff and pupils of Gillespie's to the really
rather new premises Boroughmuir had occupied for some years at
Warrender Park Crescent, on the southern height overlooking Bruntsfield
Links. The Merchant Company finally agreed terms of sale for the
Hospital building – the Edinburgh School Board was naturally reluctant
to maintain and repair premises it did not own – and, in November 1913,
at last agreed besides that the noble name of Gillespie could be retained,
even in what we would now call the public sector. The flitting finally took
place in the summer of 1914 and, as a parting gift, and after some negotiation of the wording with the School Board, the Merchant Company
presented a large wooden plaque with this immaculately painted inscription –

> This tablet was erected by the MERCHANT COMPANY OF
> EDINBURGH in memory of JAMES GILLESPIE OF SPYLAW,
> Merchant in Edinburgh, who bequeathed to the Company the
> bulk of his fortune to endow a Hospital and found a School.
> The School was opened in 1803 in a building erected at the
> north-east [sic] corner of the Hospital grounds next to the
> turnpike road, now Bruntsfield Place. Here, in 1908, it was
> taken over by the SCHOOL BOARD OF EDINBURGH and in
> 1914 Staff and Scholars were transferred to this building now
> known as JAMES GILLESPIE'S SCHOOL.

This Tablet was erected by
THE MERCHANT COMPANY
OF EDINBURGH
in memory of
JAMES GILLESPIE
OF SPYLAW
Merchant in Edinburgh,
who bequeathed to the Company
the bulk of his fortune to endow an
Hospital and found a School.
The School was opened in 1803 in a
building erected at the north-east
corner of the Hospital grounds,
next the turnpike road now
Bruntsfield Place. In 1870 it was
transferred to the Hospital building.
Here in 1908 it was taken over by the
SCHOOL BOARD OF EDINBURGH,
and in 1914 Staff and Scholars
were transferred to this building
now known as
JAMES GILLESPIE'S SCHOOL.

An elegant farewell from the Merchant Company, though the original school was actually at the southeast corner of the Gillespie's Hospital policies.

The plaque has been on prominent display at the school ever since, though from June 2013 spent some time in Edinburgh City Council storage as the 1966 campus at Lauderdale Street was readied for demolition.

Completed only in 1904, the Warrender Park Crescent building was high, handsome and imposing, built in good pink Dumfries stone, with high ceilings and tall windows and, thus, abundant light, gazing over the links and the Meadows to the Royal Infirmary, the University, and the

skyline of the old city, commanded as always by Edinburgh Castle. From
the highest windows, staff and pupils could even see Fife. And there was
another change. The former Warrender Park School, at the junction of
Marchmont Road and Marchmont Crescent, was now adopted as a
separate school for junior boys, and the infant and primary boys were now
accommodated there and, in time, under completely detached command
from the main school. It was only then, in 1929, it was formally named
James Gillespie's Boys' School, as the rest of Gillespie's took dramatic new
direction.

To this day many old 'Gillespie Girls' keenly regret the 1966 vacation of
'the School on the Links', and in 1921 John Roy Stewart enthused in the
school magazine of

> the splendid structure dominating the heights of Bruntsfield and
> looking across the spacious undulations of the Meadows to the
> bastions and spires of the historic ridge. The ordinary playground
> utilised in evening hours for tennis courts is supplemented by the
> natural playground of the Links, and scholars of Gillespie's are
> prescriptive members of the oldest golf course in Scotland, sharing
> their privilege with the leisured veterans (some of them Gillespie
> pensioners) who haunt the putting greens on summer days. The
> open-air class movement, in recent years encouraged by the
> Education Authority, naturally finds particular favour in the
> beautiful surroundings of the school. Interior features are the lofty
> corridors, the ample staircases, and the two great halls devoted to
> drill and song and academic and festal functions.

Looking back on the flitting in the July 1914 school magazine – that fabled,
glorious summer of 1914 – one master took a more mordant view:

> When we assembled in the old building in September to commence
> the year's labours, it was with the consciousness that we were not to
> finish them amid the same surroundings. And I can imagine a
> comparison of notes taking place twenty years hence between two
> old pupils who can fix a kind of common denominator of school
> experience by remembering where they were at the time of saying
> 'Goodbye' to 'old' Gillespie's.
>
> Much has already been said and printed regarding the change of
> residence; its necessity has been mourned and criticised, or
> welcomed and praised; some have been jealous enough to envy us

Third Year classes in the 1913–14 session, the last in the Gillespie's Hospital premises.

the new home and question our right to tenant it; others – including the small shop-keepers – are glad we have gone to a building worthy of our traditions and best future. With all these things we have at present nothing whatever to do. We confess to a feeling of sorrow when we saw the stream of young pupils make its way down the playground, and some of us plead guilty to a twinge of regret at parting with old associations; but, much though we cherish the comfort and texture of old clothes, dire necessity makes us capitulate, and, like our neighbours, we feel respectable when the new apparel is donned. So we are grateful for the new building, of which we mean to be worthy and in which we hope to expand. Some other pen may indite a eulogy of the edifice; for the present my space does not suffice; but we cannot help admitting that, while we enjoy the clean, airy lobbies, and admire unfolded at our feet the splendid city as Marmion saw it, we miss the mice of the old school. They were such kindly wee fellows, and very busy after the mid-day interval when they emerged from their family apartments and examined the wastepaper baskets. My heart goes out to them now, and were it not that some energetic policeman might misunderstand my motive, I should, on some grey evening, be found with a loaf, entering by a back window to renew an old friendship over a frugal supper . . .

One feature of school experience which will certainly charac- terise specially this session is the fact that the Closing Concert is no longer to be a function free and open to all. A Government official has ruled such expenses as are involved therein to be illegal; and so, with courage in both hands, the Headmaster and Choir have invited all parents, friends, old pupils and others to meet them in the Usher Hall, at a nominal charge, on the 13th July, to enjoy as delightful a programme of music as has ever been given by the School, and meet us all again in that pleasant capacity.

Now the weeks draw us on to holiday and rest, some to return to us for further industry and development, others to wider pastures and larger spheres. For the former we have every happy desire; to the latter we could say much by way of advice and well-wishing. One thought they ought to cherish if they forget all others, viz., that while many mistakes may happen in a school career, the great and eminent good remains in that all the effort and industry on the part of teacher and taught must make for permanent and living gain. Their next aspirations will be outside the schoolroom; let them maintain in this wider horizon the honour of their school and obey its watchword, 'Forward!'

Days earlier, in Sarajevo, Gavrilo Princip had fired a gun . . .

•   •   •

The First World War impacted immediately on Gillespie's. The school magazines of 1915 and 1919 – none appeared in between – are strikingly short of levity. Hundreds of former pupils, of course, fought for King and Country in assorted services, and at least forty-four died. (No memorial on the campus has ever been erected to them; perhaps the school may one day attend to this.) Thirteen who served (including two young women) were decorated. A number of staff, of course, volunteered for the Forces, and from 1917, as the national emergency deepened, still more were conscripted.

Pupils toiled for the Red Cross; sponsored beds in military hospitals; entertained wounded men with little concerts through the winter of 1917–

Died on Service.

Dulce et decorum est pro patria mori.

ANDERSON, GEORGE	5th Royal Scots.
BINNIE, ROBERT	9th Royal Scots.
BLACK, WALTER C.	London Scottish.
BROOKS, ALEXANDER	1st Lowland, R.F.A.
BROOKS, ROBERT	12th Royal Scots.
BRUCE, W. A.	Lothian and Border Horse.
CARMICHAEL, DAVID	4th Royal Scots.
CLOW, DAVID J.	Border Regiment.
CLOW, OSWALD W.	1st Lowland, R.F.A.
CLOW, THOMAS H.	4th Royal Scots.
COUSTON, ALEXANDER	9th Royal Scots.
COUTTS, JOHN	15th Royal Scots.
COWNIE, JOHN B.	Welsh Regiment.
DENHOLM, WILLIAM	Machine Gun Corps.
DOWNIE, GEORGE U. R.	5th Royal Scots.
ELLIOT, THOMAS S.	7th Cameron Highlanders.
GALLOWAY, HUGH S.	5th Royal Scots.
GEMMELL, ALEXANDER	Anti-Gas Dept., London.
GILMOUR, WALTER	Royal Garrison Artillery.
HASTINGS, JOSEPH E.	11th Black Watch.
HEGGIE, D. A.	15th Royal Scots.
JACK, THOMAS	9th Royal Scots.
LITTLEJOHN, ERIC	5th Royal Scots.
LOWE, ROBERT	5th Canadian Royal Highrs.

Died on Service—*continued.*

M'LAREN, JOHN F.	4th Cameron Highlanders.
MUIR, CHRISTISON	King's Own Scot. Borderers.
NIVEN, WILLIAM	9th Royal Scots.
RIDDELL, SIDNEY	Yorks. and Lancs. Regt.
RITCHIE, WILLIAM J.	5th Royal Scots.
ROSS, PETER	16th Royal Scots.
SCLATER, CHARLES M.	1st Royal Dragoons.
SHANKIE, ROY	9th Royal Scots.
SHANKIE, THOMAS	9th Royal Scots.
SHIRLAW, NINIAN F.	8th Argyle and Suth. Highs.
SIM, CHARLES	Royal Scots.
SPENCE, DAVID	Royal Field Artillery.
STEWART, JOHN	9th Royal Scots.
THOMSON, ROBERT	South African Force.
WALLACE, JOHN H. D.	5th Royal Scots.
WALLACE, WILLIAM	9th Royal Scots.
WALTER, CLEMENT	King's Own Scot. Borderers.
WALTER, RICHARD	American Army.
YOUNG, DAVID G.	10th Scottish Rifles.

Captain ALEX. GEMMELL, D.Sc., Analytical Chemist, a former pupil, for some time in command of Edinburgh University O.T.C., and latterly of the Anti-Gas Department, University College, London, died in January of this year as a result of experiments to discover efficient protection for the troops against poison gas.

1918, and raised a prodigious sum – almost £4,500 – for the War Savings Association. Everyone waged war on waste, the infants especially being exhorted as to the depravity of throwing away so much as the crust of a loaf. There was no room, now, for witticisms about mice.

The magazine's 'School Notes' for the autumn of 1915 give some idea of the atmosphere –

> Session 1915–16 is now well under way, and finds the School with a full roll of pupils, which, if room permitted, could be greatly enlarged. The First Term Examination is happily over and in a few weeks the Christmas vacation will afford a short respite deserved by all who have worked hard for it.

Mr Richard G. B. Prescott, Dux Boy 1911–12, who lately passed

Old Boys lost in the Great War, as bleakly recorded in the 1919 school magazine.

the Civil Service Examination for the Indian Police, has sailed to take up his duties in Farther India.

The Cookery Classes, which were for a time delayed, are now resumed. Miss Graham's services were given to teaching Cookery, first to soldiers at Peebles and then in Edinburgh. Her labours at both places were much appreciated and she was made the recipient of gifts when she left to resume her duties there.

It was with feelings of deep gratitude that his many friends among pupils and staff learned of the safety of Mr Callander, after his tragic experience on board HMS *Royal Edward* in August. [She was torpedoed in the Aegean on 13 August 1915; of some 1,600 men on board, only 600 survived.] From his latest letters we learn that he is well and fit in south-eastern Europe.

Sergeant Tait, writing from Flanders in the best of spirits, reports himself well and comfortable and appreciates highly the letters and gifts he is receiving.

Private W. Brown, 6th King's Own Scottish Borders, visited the school on furlough after being wounded at the battle of Loos, and gave us a soldier's plain tale of that desperate advance.

Among the names of former pupils whose names are now sacred to the cause of right and freedom we find these of three Old Boys – Captain Maclaren, 4th Cameron Highlanders; Lieutenant Christison Muir, 1st King's Own Scottish Borderers; 2nd Lieutenant David A Heggie, 1st Royal Scots Fusiliers. The first, who was Dux of School, was killed in the advance at Loos in October and in him we lost one whose future seemed full of success and reward. From the pen of Lieutenant Muir we have printed a short poem which has now a deeply pathetic interest . . .

The Sentry

Oh! It's weary, weary waitin' for the sun that doesn't rise,
While I'm standin' on the firin'-step a-watchin' at the skies;
An' my pals is still a-sleepin' with their bay'nits gleamin' bright,
For it's still an hour to daybreak – an' the longest of the night.

I can see the Turkish trenches, in the dimness o' the morn,
Just a low, long line o' sandbags lookin' dismal and forlorn;
'Cept the flash and crack o' snipers to remind you they're awake –
Oh! it's weary, I can tell ye, waitin' for the day to break.

I can hear our fellers diggin' and a-diggin' out ahead;
It's a buryin' party workin' – all a-buryin' o' the dead;
And beyon' the Turkish watch-dogs with their eerie, whiny bark,
An' the moanin' bay o' bloodhounds comin' floatin' through the
dark.

But the stars is still a-glintin' though the moon has long since gone,
And the Turks, they does their fightin' in the hour before the dawn,
And although yer eyes is sleepy, still ye've got to keep awake –
Oh! it's weary – mak's ye wonder if the day will never break.

Christison Muir subsequently died of wounds received on 27 October in
that infamous Gallipoli campaign. We could fill page upon page with the
Great War as it bore pitilessly on school life – the regular news of bereavement, the strains of food rationing, the frantic fund-raising endeavours
and knitting drives and all manner of good works (in July 1918, for instance,
a merry gang of 14-year-old Gillespie's boys spent a month at a forestry
camp in Aberfeldy, stripping up to 160 trees a day) . . . or, indeed, the terri-
fying night when a Zeppelin floated by the school, watched in dark wonder
by a little Lauderdale Street girl called Alison Laidlaw, and dropped a bomb
on Marchmont Crescent that plunged down a tenement stairwell and
mercifully failed to detonate . . . but it is almost all unutterably depressing.
The biggest change the war wrought, though, would fast and soon alter
the school all together – the infinite new possibilities now opening, for the
first time, for women.

'After a lapse of nearly four years,' ran the editorial in July 1919, 'we again
present to our readers an issue of *Gillespie's School Magazine*. There is no
need to apologise for these four years. Everybody knows how difficult it
was during these stirring times to carry on the necessary vocations of life,
and the surplus energies of the School were directed to those activities
which engaged, not only us of James Gillespie's School, but the whole
nation.'

And among the blithe stories of fairyland, and the photographs of
prefects and hockey teams and the rugby 1st XV, was almost casually
announced the new Headmaster, appointed three years earlier in 1916.

•   •   •

Thomas J. Burnett MA FEIS is among the greatest of Gillespie's captains.
He served for two decades and presided over signal change and noted

A Gillespie's primary class, the year after the Great War.

reforms. It was under his watch that it became, in 1923, first a full secondary school, able to send pupils straight to university; and then – from the summer of 1929 – exclusively the famous girls-only 'Corporation Grammar', recruiting pupils by special examination from all over the city. He was by all accounts a humble and humane man; in certain respects a very modernising one – an Edwardian, really, with that decade's sense of change and possibilities, rather than the set Victorian ways of his predecessors. He was an educationist, too, of such standing that a book he wrote – *Essentials of Teaching* – is still in print; and he had that extraordinary British genius for inventing ancient tradition: the school colours, crest and motto, even today in the twenty-first century, are all of his devising. Yet, though Burnett appears in dozens of school magazine photographs through these years, not one of them shows him smiling.

A son of Lasswade in Midlothian, Burnett attended the village school and put in four years as a pupil-teacher. He studied further at the Church of Scotland Training College in Edinburgh, and won his degree at the city's

Right. Pawky, correct, and rather shy – but Thomas Burnett, Headmaster from 1916 to 1937, was among our greatest leaders.

Below. Mr Burnett with supporting clergy and the handsome new H.F. Gamley bust, on Founder's Day, 1932. Only Gillespie musters a smile.

University, graduating in 1896 with a clutter of prizes and expressly qualified as an English teacher. He spent his entire career in or around the city, teaching first at Fisherrow School, and then successively at North Merchiston, Portobello, and Broughton Secondary School. For eight years, from 1908 to 1916, he was besides Master of Method in charge of student teachers at Broughton and Boroughmuir.

'He thus came to his new post in Gillespie's with a good record of varied experience behind him,' one observed at his retirement in 1937. 'To succeed an able and experienced head like his predecessor Mr Blacklaws was no easy task, but Mr Burnett ably and well carried on the great tradition of the school. He took up his new position in September 1916, during the Great War, a particularly difficult period, when staffs were depleted and the ordinary routine of school work was much disturbed.' His dearest friend, Rev. W.A. Guthrie – eventually minister of Fountainbridge United Free Church; the two men had graduated on the same day – remarked, after Burnett's death, 'He was one of that diminishing proportion of the teaching profession who entered through the hardest gate of all – through the gate of pupil-teachership, in which for four years a lad had both to study and to do a full day's teaching. That was an experience from which the present generation has been mercifully saved, but it made teachers, and it made him.'

Mr Burnett's leadership was defined by four aspects of his personality.

First, he was an exceptionally shrewd judge of ability and character, and some of the most gifted, memorable teachers in the history of the modern school were appointed by him – Alison Foster, Margaret Napier, Mabel Marr, John Brash, Agnes L. Anderson and Charlotte McLean among them, defining Gillespie's as an institution into the 1960s (indeed, Miss Marr endured till 1972) and whose voices yet resound in the ears of untold former pupils.

Second, like many effective leaders, Burnett had a romantic – even theatrical – streak. For one, almost single-handedly he revived interest in James Gillespie himself. In June 1926 he instituted an annual Founder's Day ceremony. The fortunate pupils were addressed by Rev. James Fergusson, Vice-Chairman of what was now the Edinburgh Education Authority, and addressed additionally by Sir Samuel Chapman Bt, Unionist MP for Edinburgh South. And Mr Burnett personally thought up rites which, within years, fast seemed lost in the mists of 1803 – the presentation of a snuffbox to the guest of honour by the most poised (or at least the prettiest) little mite from the youngest infant class; the solemn passing about of a snuff-mull among the platform party for a ritual snort (often

with highly diverting consequences for the pupils) and a vote of thanks
from a pupil – Margaret Moore, on this occasion, senior prefect: this always
concluded with an appeal for a holiday *simpliciter*, which was almost always
granted. If the Merchant Company had basely kept the Burn bust of our
great founder to themselves, Mr Burnett was unruffled; he simply commissioned an esteemed former pupil of the school, H.F. Gamley (among the
greatest sculptors of his day) to make a new one. It was duly unveiled by
Lord Provost Stevenson in the Founder's Day ceremony of June 1927 that,
panted *The Scotsman*, included former Headmaster William Dunlop
among the guests –

> The Lord Provost said he congratulated the Education Authority on
> the progress the School had made, and the headmaster on the
> responsibility he had in presiding over such a great school. Here they
> were, 130 years after the death of James Gillespie, met to unveil that
> memorial bust and so keep ever green his memory in that school
> which bore his name. He hoped that to every boy and girl that bust
> would be a permanent incentive to have high ideals. It seemed to
> him that the one lesson they could always take from the life of James
> Gillespie was that he had a high ideal, not only of citizenship but of
> the responsibility of wealth. All over the city today they had young
> men and women taking their places as citizens. It was to him one of
> the regrets of his life to see that today responsible citizens took so
> little interest in their incomparable city. He hoped that every boy
> and girl, when they looked at James Gillespie's bust, would feel that
> what one could do, he or she could do. There was always a great field
> open in the world's work for that man or woman imbued with the
> truly Scottish characteristics of industry and thrift. It seemed to him
> that there was a lesson also for the merchant princes of today. It was
> true that the City of Edinburgh had been generously endowed by
> men whose names they held in reverence. There was still more to
> be done He could imagine nothing more gratifying, nothing more
> satisfying to any man who had made money in that city than to feel
> he could do something for the boys and girls of tomorrow.
> (Applause.)
>   Sir Samuel Chapman, MP, said those of them who were not
> citizens of Edinburgh but took a great interest in public life were
> deeply moved by that ceremony. The boys and girls had in their
> hands and hearts the fortunes of the future of that great city. They
> had a noble heritage, and great examples had been set them. He had

faith in the future of their city. He thought the young people would do the right thing at the right time, and would be a credit to that great school and the City of Edinburgh. (Applause.)

Mr T.J. Burnett, the headmaster, thanked the pupils, former pupils, parents and well-wishers of Gillespie's for their generosity in contributing to the cost of the memorial.

Annie P. Coates, the senior prefect of the school, in proposing votes of thanks to the Lord Provost and the chairman, said James Gillespie had been to them merely a name. Now that they were privileged to see his likeness every day, they would come to look on him as a great friend, to whom they owed more than they could ever repay. They would always remember that day, but there was one particular method of enshrining the occasion in their hearts, which never failed. She wondered if she dared ask that Monday be made a holiday. (Laughter and applause.)

Bailie Alan announced amid applause that Monday would be a holiday, and the proceedings closed with the singing of the National Anthem.

A more benign view of Mr Gillespie than the Burn sculpture, the school has retained the bust ever since: from 2013 to 2016, Mr Gillespie was even pleased to reside at the Darroch Annexe, atop a cabinet by the main hall and unruffled by passing, exuberant senior pupils. But he was left a little shaken at the end of the session in June 2016, after the school had had to accommodate some Craigmount High School classes at Darroch and the wee tykes knocked him off his perch. Happily undamaged, the bust was borne to safety in the medical room.

Thomas Burnett also introduced uniform, in new and warm school colours – a rubyish maroon, golden-yellow – and imposed a new motto, 'Fidelis et Fortis', which means – debate continues – 'faithful and brave', or, for many old girls, 'faithful and strong'. He simply adapted it from the traditional one he found with the Gillespie crest in some gazetteer or other, 'Fidelis et in bello fortis' – 'faithful and in war brave' – which was not quite the line for a consciously post-war school. And Burnett liked the crest – a unicorn's head – so picked that as the school's motif. It soon appeared on hat and blazer badges though – oddly – not, for decades to come, in the school magazine, which retained an image of the old Hospital school on its frontispiece until 1953, and (slightly adapted) Thomas Robertson's cipher of the school initials on its cover.

With like élan Burnett besides divided the pupils into four competitive

The slightly less scary 1927 bust of James Gillespie by H. F. Gamley. (Andrew Digance)

'Houses', each named after districts associated with the school's immediate district or by report with Gillespie himself – Gilmour, Roslin, Spylaw and Warrender. And, by the Headmaster's direction, the school acquired a House Shield for which these chapters could compete each year. For the first time, too, he created school prefects, with which beings of vast importance he sat annually for a formal photograph.

More practically, Mr Burnett also introduced – and for the first time – school dinners, for both pupils and staff. And he took an intense and paternal interest in every aspect of the school community, as was wistfully noted after his death –

The School Magazine in its present form is largely Mr Burnett's idea. He considered that the School Magazine was the pupils' own magazine and should be produced by themselves for themselves. He presented to the editors the idea, then novel, that at least one contribution from each class in the school should be printed. He also advised the inclusion of the prize lists as a regular feature of each issue . . .

The Literary Society, the Science Association, the Former Pupil's Club, the opera productions, the school journeys, had his blessing and on occasion his attendance and active help. The athletics of the school had his warm support. He always knew when the First XI had won an important hockey match, and remembered the many outstanding achievements of our swimmers. The Athletic Fund which has done much in the past year to further the athletic activities of the school was primarily due to Mr Burnett's inspiration.

As a headmaster he was loved and respected by the pupils, some of the smallest children looking on him as a kind of 'Daddy.' Of his staff he was most considerate, believing that the teacher in the classroom should be interfered with as little as possible. Many of his colleagues remember with gratitude his ready sympathy in times of illness or trouble. His impromptu readiness of speech and pawkiness of phrase enlivened educational meetings and school social functions, and the gleam and smile, gradually breaking forth just before the humorous anecdote, is a reminiscence which will remain with many.

The school magazine through the Burnett years still reads with extraordinary brio, under the light stewardship of Alison Foster, and would never be quite the same after he retired, his successor being a much more controlling personality. To have an article published in its pages was a thrilling achievement. Reports of excursions far and wide – to the Wembley Exhibition, to Paris, to London again – are accompanied by jolly snapshots of happy boys and girls. There are tantalising glimpses of what could have been a thriving co-educational school, receiving infants at one end and delivering them to university or the professions at the other – but it was not what the temper of the times in Edinburgh called for or what Gillespie parents demanded.

By the autumn term of 1923 it was a true secondary school, having at last been granted an 'Intermediate' Department for the teaching of senior pupils. But two trends were now well under way. For one, clamour was growing – not least in that reliable weathercock of Edinburgh obsessions, the letters page of *The Scotsman* – for establishing Gillespie's as exclusively a school for girls. That was only accelerated by the growing reluctance of parents at the Warrender Park premises to send their sons up into the Gillespie's Secondary Department. They were increasingly inclined to try for Watson's or Heriot's instead. The city already had a 'Corporation

Smartly dressed
Gillespie's boys and
girls in London, 1924.

Grammar' for boys, the Royal High School, rather on the lines of the 'city academies' in today's England and accepting boys from all over Edinburgh by special examination, in addition to such local co-ed grammar schools as Boroughmuir. The Education Authority was besides confounded by the enormous popularity of Gillespie's – a fee-paying school within the public sector with a long, long waiting list for places. And, inflaming demand further, in post-war conditions the city's Merchant Company and other independent schools had considerably hiked their fees.

Some newspaper correspondence of the time shows the drift of things, and an Edinburgh *Evening News* article about Gillespie's in 1921 (the parental campaign for full secondary provision was then in full clamour) concluded –

EDUCATING THE GIRLS

Apart from any consideration of a particular scheme, the question arises as to the necessity of making ample provision in Edinburgh for the higher education of girls. Before 1914 there was a widespread

The school's rugby
side, 1922. How short
and slight the boys
seem by today's
standards.

agitation for the improved education of women. Now that some
millions of women have votes, there is a pressing necessity for
training the best intellects of the sex for guidance and leadership. The
clever daughter of the artisan or of the middle-class professional man
must now have an equal chance with her brother, who has been so
favoured in the past. The war has given an immense impetus to the
desire on the part of girls for continued education. It has opened up
new vistas of opportunity for service – in social work, in medicine,
teaching, law, and in many of the occupations that used to be considered exclusively the domain of the male. The census returns show
that the proportion of boys in Edinburgh between the ages of 14 and
18 is, roughly, three to two. How do the facilities for higher education
compare? There are six fee-paying [i.e. private] secondary schools
for boys and (including St George's) three for girls. The congested
state of the existing secondary schools and the economic difficulties
caused by high fees clearly make out a case for the establishment of

a new type of secondary school for girls where an education of an advanced kind may be obtained at a moderate cost.

Mr Burnett with prefects, 1929. There is just a hint of a smile; but the girls-only era was upon him.

The debate rumbled on, and the 1922 school magazine has two engaging articles on 'Co-Education' from the perspectives of a girl and a boy. 'A boy of the "mixed" school is considerate and even gentle,' purred Miriam Harris of Form 3 HGA. 'In the presence of girls he is not at all awkward and embarrassed; his manners in all ways are toned down – not in the least like those of the boy not educated under the co-education system.' 'This system of educating boys and girls together may seem to those who have never borne its yoke, but who have made a superficial examination of it, all that can be desired – I cannot say,' grumbled her classmate Donald Stewart. 'Its male victims hardly regard it in that light, unless one or two are excepted who are under the spell of some gay young creatures. Most boys find education irksome enough without having to endure girls as well . . . '

He – or at least his droll misogyny – would have his wish. The pressure for change was inexorable and, from the summer of 1929, it was James Gillespie's Secondary School for Girls. The following year it was more pleasingly renamed James Gillespie's High School for Girls – and would be thus till August 1973. That same year, 1930, Burnett introduced a Commercial class – teaching in typing, accounting, and basic office skills for aspiring 'Gillespie Girls'. And from 1934, in his last significant reform, he laid on Episcopalian religious instruction for pupils of that faith – a telling hint that Gillespie's was already climbing socially.

•   •   •

We have three warm glimpses of the school in this interwar period – two by pupils, and one by a visitor, Miss Margaret Wilkins from Buffalo, New York, and on bold teacher-exchange with Miss Margaret Napier. In the July 1932 school magazine, Miss Wilkins duly gave her impressions of the Scottish establishment –

> I have always wanted to spend a year in Great Britain, but it was beyond my wildest dream that I could actually take part in the life of a city such as Edinburgh. If you ever become a teacher and want an interesting experience, even adventure, do go on an exchange to some other country. You will find an exchange in one of the Dominions quite as interesting as one in a country out of the Empire. I have met a lot of overseas teachers this year, from the Dominions as well as the United States, and they all remark on my good fortune to be in Edinburgh. I quite agree with them, as I do with people in the city who tell me how fortunate I am to be in James Gillespie's. In addition to the obvious beauties and advantages of the capital of Scotland, which you who live here take so much for granted, many small things have made a great impression on me. Some of these are: – the very friendly look about a street when all the houses have gay beds of flowers in front of them, how much shorter the winter seems when the grass is green all the time and doesn't get brown and dry, the ease with which one can go into the country for walks, and the many beautiful walks that one can take there. No discussion of Edinburgh is complete without some reference to the weather. I will admit that I came with the feeling that there was always an atmosphere of dampness and mist in Scotland. As a matter of fact, I believe that you have more sunny days than we do in Buffalo, so that impression has been quite changed.

Invariably the first question I am asked is, 'How many gangsters do you know?' This is usually followed by, 'How do the schoolgirls in Scotland compare with those in America?' I am afraid my answer to the second question is as unsatisfactory as my prompt 'none' to the first. (I shall advise all prospective exchanges to do their utmost to get acquainted with a gangster.) I have found no startling differences. I know that there are differences, but they are the kind that are much more apparent in the home and in the use of time out of school than they are from nine to three-fifteen, five days a week. I think that Scottish girls are more natural and unaffected than American girls of the same age, but otherwise they are much the same. The girls at Gillespie's have been most kind and interested in anything that I could tell them about my country, even to the point of being willing to sacrifice a geometry period to it. Surprising, isn't it?

I shall remember with a great deal of pleasure the very friendly way the staff and pupils have combined to make me feel at home in James Gillespie's. More lasting even than my impressions of the beauties of Edinburgh will be my appreciation of the hospitality and friendliness I received there.

In that still drier Edinburgh humour that has long characterised the school, a pupil seven years earlier in the 1925 issue had sought to immortalise her own class.

FROM THE TRUMPETER'S HORN

Little is really known about our Form. In fact its light has been hidden under a bushel too long – so long that it is time the bushel was lifted. I shall endeavour to do the lifting, and dare to dazzle your eyes with the brilliancy of this hidden light.

Our little community consists of four-and-twenty fair maidens, each endowed with beauty and talents. A visitor to the school recently remarked, 'How is it, Mr Burnett, that Gillespie's girls are so good-looking?' That is our beauty testimonial. Let us pass on to the talents. In our Form we have talent in every direction. To prove this I shall enumerate a few at random.

Here sits a certain shingled maiden, who holds a singing scholarship. Nearby is another maiden, who, by her prowess with the violin, covered herself in glory at the past Musical Festival; while

The hockey 1st XI, 1926, with the redoubtable Miss Agnes L. 'Allie' Anderson (centre, back row), Principal Teacher of PE from 1922 to 1961. A composed Alison Laidlaw stands at the left end of the back row.

there reclines a stately damsel who came home first in a musical competition in the winter term. That will do for an illustration of our musical side – we shall now proceed to sport.

Dotted here and there at various desks and in various attitudes repose members of the Hockey 1st XI. In a prominent position in the front row is our Olympic swimmer; while a distinguished runner is to be found somewhere about the middle of the class. There are one or two promising golfers also, and on Wednesdays may be seen some star tennis-players. But these are accomplishments, I can hear you say. Well, in the academic line, we can produce an ex-school Dux, and we have our scholarship holders too. But there are times when we show ennui. What talent has to do with this? say you. Well, a little maiden with sandy-coloured hair has this talent, and in my opinion it is the gem of the collection. Her good-natured banter and caustic comments cause the most solemn to smile, while her witticisms and droll mimicry convulse her audience at any time. Needless to say we are never bored for long. May she stay with us always!

To catalogue every talent like this takes time and space, both of which are valuable; so in closing I should like to say that the fair maidens in our Form constitute a bevy of damsels unrivalled throughout the whole school.

Alison Laidlaw, Form IV

Miss Laidlaw's association with the school, as pupil and subsequently as a teacher and into great old age a sparkling institution, would endure into the twenty-first century.

But the school's most famous former pupil, Dame Muriel Spark, née

The future Muriel Spark in her final primary class, 1930, with their teacher, Miss Kay. Muriel Camberg is second from the right in the third row. Christina Kay (1878–1951), who taught at Gillespie's for over forty years, inspired the author's iconic Miss Jean Brodie, being – as Spark cracked in 1991 – 'a character in search of an author'. She resigned in 1942 after sustained complaints from parents about her defiant regard for Mussolini.

Camberg, left us with still more vivid memories in an autobiographical essay for the *New Yorker* magazine in 1991, later incorporated into her 1993 *Curriculum Vitae* autobiography. Born in 1918, in Bruntsfield Place –

> This was the school that it fell to my happy lot to attend. Gillespie's endowment allowed for parents of high aspirations and slender means, like my own, to pay moderate fees in return for educational services far beyond what they were paying for. When I first attended, at the age of five, it was co-educational, but after some years we lost our little boys and we were James Gillespie's High School for Girls . . .
>
> The official religion of James Gillespie's was Presbyterian of the Church of Scotland; much later, this rule was expanded to include Episcopalian doctrines. But in my day Tolerance was decidedly the prevailing religion, always with a puritanical slant. Nothing can be more puritanical in application than the virtues. To inquire into the differences between the professed religions around us might have been construed as Intolerance. Many religious persuasions were represented among the pupils. There were Jewish girls in practically every class. I remember one Hindu Indian, named Coti, whom we made much of. There were lots of Catholics. Some students were of mixed faiths – mother Protestant, father Jewish; Irish Catholic mother, Episcopalian father. It meant very little in practical terms to us. The Bible appeared to cover all these faiths, for I don't remember any segregation during our religious teaching, although in other classes some pupils may have sat apart, simply 'listening in'.
>
> Scotland was historically rich in sects. James Gillespie himself was an admirer of the Covenanters, those worthy bearers of Bible and sword who rebelled against the imposition of the English liturgy on the Scots in the seventeenth century. The Covenanters could be said to be reformers of the Reformation. But James Gillespie went further than that. He inclined towards a stricter sect, the Cameronians – a section of the Scottish Covenanters named after their chief exponent, Richard Cameron. In 1743 [*sic*], during James Gillespie's lifetime, they became the Reformed Presbyterians. Politically, they strongly opposed the union of England and Scotland.
>
> On Founder's Day, Friday, June 12, 1931, after the ceremony, twenty-five Gillespie's girls set off for the Covenanters' Grave in

the Pentland Hills to sing the Scottish paraphrase of the Twenty-First Psalm [*sic*] in Mr James Gillespie's honour –

I to the hills will lift mine eyes,
from whence doth come mine aid.
My safety cometh from the Lord,
who heav'n and earth hath made.

The school building had been built in 1904 for another school, Boroughmuir. But Gillespie's took over in 1914. It was an Edwardian building, and, for those days, modern inside, with large classrooms, and big windows that looked over the leafy trees, the skies, and the swooping gulls of Bruntsfield Links. From where I lived, the school was a ten-minute walk through avenues of tall trees. Leading away from the school was another avenue – of hawthorns, flowering dark pink in May. We called these 'may blossoms'. The school was surrounded by the large public moorland [*sic*] of the Links. A very attractive cottage (which had belonged to a fashionable photographer, Swan Watson) was attached to the school, but shortly after my arrival, to our mixed sorrow and delight, it was pulled down to make way for an extension that comprised a wonderful science room, a spacious gymnasium, and a totally new infants' department.

Of the infant school I remember comparatively little. My home life was still of the first importance, and remains imprinted in memories that I can still share with my brother, Philip. But of those early years at school I retain an impression of Plasticine modelling, carol singing, and reading aloud (which I did well). A medal was circulated every week. One week, I won it for a crayon drawing of a tomato. I remember my big red tomato on the dark-brown drawing-paper background; I couldn't see anything very special about it. I played the triangle in the percussion band. All I had to do was bang it rhythmically – something that would have driven my parents mad at home. I also played a milkmaid in a tableau.

There were always flowers in the classrooms, on the windowsills and on the teachers' tables, all through my school days. The girls or their parents usually provided these, but the teachers were always tending plants. Some of them would lift the vases each morning to see if the cleaners had cleaned properly underneath. We had hyacinths in the spring. My mother sometimes put a bunch of daffodils in my hands to take to school in the afternoon.

The furnaces for the central heating were stoked by Jannie (the janitor – an ex-policeman, whose real name was John Bremner). Jannie it was who, with his ally, Parkie (the park keeper) kept an eye on the leafy meadows surrounding the school so that no potential molesters or peeping men in mackintoshes ever got near us. All the same, we were cautioned not to turn somersaults on the low iron railings that lined the pathways, lest 'passing men might see your underwear'. Alas, those iron railings went, like so much other civic ironwork, to make armaments in wartime, never to be replaced . . .

I continued to enjoy a certain fame as the school's poet. I should describe at this point the curious and ambiguous experience I had after leaving Miss Kay's class when we all moved to the Higher Grade, as the senior school department was called. It was 1932, the year of the centenary of the death of Sir Walter Scott. A poetry competition was launched among the schools of Edinburgh by the Heather Club, a men's club founded in 1823 (for what purpose I do not know, except that it was very Scottish). I won first prize with my poem about Sir Walter Scott, and another girl at Gillespie's got third prize. The school was doubly jubilant; everyone was delighted. So delighted that I hadn't the heart, I couldn't possibly explain about the prize itself. Partly, it was a number of books, and that pleased me. But partly it was a coronet, with which I was to be crowned Queen of Poetry at some public Scott-centenary celebration. My mother was overjoyed, as was nearly everyone else, in school and out of school. I felt like the Dairy Queen of Dumfries, but I endured the experience and survived it. A star actress, Esther Ralston, did the crowning. It was a mystery to me what she had to do with poetry or Sir Walter Scott. The coronet itself was cheap-looking, I thought. The only person who openly agreed with my point of view was our reserved and usually silent headmaster, T. J. Burnett. He knew I had to go through with it now that I had won the prize, but he showed a sense of the unsuitable nature of this coronet affair. He was essentially an administrator, a man of very few words. 'Tinsel,' he said quietly to me, and then he made a congratulatory speech in front of the school. According to his daughter, Maida, he remarked at home, 'That lassie can write.' I know he was indignant for me.

Thomas Burnett gave nearly twenty-one years of service to Gillespie's and had taken the school further and higher than anyone during the dark days of the Great War would have thought possible. But the toil and anxiety and responsibility for so conscientious and taciturn a man wrought high personal cost. At his retiral in December 1936, off work by then for some months, he was already too ill to attend a formal presentation of gifts – a bureau, a card table and a fountain pen from pupils; a pair of armchairs from the staff and assorted books from former pupils. Within the year, in November 1937, he was dead, as a queen took firm possession of his throne.

CHAPTER FIVE

'She walked the corridors in a procession of one'
1937–1956

No Head of Gillespie's looms larger, six decades after her retirement and three after her death, than the poised and determined May Andrew, and none is more lionised by 'Gillespie Girls'. She was a sufficiently big personality in Edinburgh itself for her personal life to be of interest to the press (she once all but physically threw out of her office a reporter who dared to approach her as to unfounded rumours of romantic involvement with the then-Lord Provost, Sir William Young Darling); for her remarks at Founder's Day, prize-giving and so on to be reported in the evening papers. Miss Andrew's influence could be felt far into the 1980s; her portrait in oils still hangs in the school foyer and her immediate successors, Mary D. Steel and Mary G. McIver, visibly struggled (and failed) to escape her shadow – for their formidable predecessor, though no longer in post, proved loath, till her ninth decade, entirely to quit the stage. Only Patricia Thomas, from the late 1970s, proved wholly her own woman; and not till Donald J. Macdonald did Gillespie's have a head of comparable presence and force of personality: the same wide-set eyes and an air of danger.

'Well, girls, we are at war with Germany,' former pupil Margaret Wood, née Richardson, remembered in February 2008 from Miss Andrew's brisk address in September 1939. 'There is no Hitler going to change Gillespie's. We are going to carry on as if there is no war. There is not going to be any disruption. We are going to carry on as before and the standard is going to remain as high as it ever did. We are not going to lower our standards – school uniform, everything, remains the same. Teaching will remain the same . . .' On another occasion, Christine Matheson recalled, the Headmistress was so frustrated by frequent lateness from one corner of the city that she at last proclaimed, 'There will be no more excuses for Blackhall girls!'

May Andrew, at her appointment as Head-mistress, of commanding countenance and dangerous eyes. An imaginative and fearless leader, she took Gillespie's to unprecedented academic heights.

In recent years, in a very different Scotland, where the notions of selective entry, streamed classes and a girls-only academy sound to most both arcane and faintly ridiculous, too many have been tempted to carica-ture this remarkable woman, commander of Gillespie's from 1937 to 1956. May Andrew 'walked the corridors, I'm told, in a procession of one', pronounced Edi Stark in her controversial but moving 2003 BBC Radio Scotland documentary, *Crème de la Crème*, 'parting pupils like the Red Sea. She was a woman who demanded total conformity . . .'

'The only time I was in front of the formidable Miss Andrew,' grated Elizabeth Percival in the same programme, and whose memories of her schooldays seemed generally sour, 'was when a prefect reported me for standing in front of a shop-window putting on my hat. And I was called to Miss Andrew's room – '

'Were you punished by her?'

'Oh, *no*, just a . . . dressing-down, to make you feel like a *worm*. That's the only time I ever met the woman face-to-face. And if you saw the hats – like a sharpened-edge cottage-loaf and set squarely on the head . . .'

'Miss Andrew,' chuckled another Gillespie Girl, Liz Roberts, 'was like something out of Central Casting for the dignified headmistress – a bit of Alastair Sim there, but never mind. Grey hair beautifully waved; flowing black gown. One day, I can remember, I was sent out of a classroom on some errand and I walked along past the part of the school where Miss

Andrew's room was, with a little carpet outside, and she was standing there. She obviously didn't see me coming, and she wasn't wearing her gown – I think she was probably going out – and she was fixing a suspender. I nearly died. A *leg* . . . '

And we chuckle politely. But to reduce May Andrew – an extraordinarily able woman, haunted by the Great War, sincerely if unstuffily religious, most socially aware and convinced there should be no ceiling of any kind on a girl's ambition – to a manly-featured harridan obsessed with hats and hems is as foolish as it is unjust.

•   •   •

May Andrew was the first woman ever appointed Head of one of Edinburgh's municipal secondary schools. Born in Forfar in 1895, and schooled in Dundee, she 'always speaks with admiration of her early teachers', observed a colleague in 1956 –

> Of her life there one gathers that it was industrious, purposeful and happy. At the University of St Andrews she read English, in which she won the inevitable distinguished First. She also enjoyed speaking at the University Societies, and acting. She made rapid progress in what she later often happily referred to as 'good companionship'. Among her fellow-students were Edwin and Willa Muir, and Professor James Stewart. She also often spoke from a heavy heart of the men in her own class who were almost all wiped out in 1914. Self-sacrifice is a very real thing to Miss Andrew.
>
> Her teaching career at the beginning seems to have been a savouring of distant systems. It took her to Edinburgh, and the Lakes. Then she came back to Dundee and, as earlier as a schoolgirl, her spirit seized its native power. Many distinguished men and women in all walks of life who came under her influence in these formative years speak of her drive, enthusiasm, and fire. Some of her favourite authors in these days still retain her loyalty. When recently an opportunity arose for her to take the Sixth, it was Browning she chose. One, knowing Miss Andrew, can be in no doubt why: she likes certainty, she possesses it, and she likes others to possess it too. She believes ultimately in the spiritual values of life.
>
> On her first entry into the classroom her pupils must have been aware of what must strike anyone meeting Miss Andrew for the first

time. Her presence has every recommendation. Her head possesses leonine power. The eyes temper it with understanding, and when need be, gentleness. But there is never any trifling when it comes to fundamentals. Irked by some instruction of which one did not know enough to see the value, one would go to her room, pretty sure of a grievance, to make a case. Then with a slightly perceptible toss of her head, the blue eyes looking fearlessly at yours, 'Why not?' she would say. And the carapace of one's argument suddenly became an eggshell.

Miss Andrew, as a teacher, was an amazing judge of character. She looked people shrewdly in the eye, seized their personality in their face, and possessed herself of what was basic in their character before they were more than a minute or two in her room. Those of the staff who knew girls well over a period of years were often amazed at the shrewdness of these momentary assessments. She rarely forgot a face, and she never forgot a personality. That was because she was interested in people. Nothing gave her greater pleasure than to hear of the success of girls either at school, or who had left. It was disturbing at first to deal with a Headmistress who was not satisfied with your best. But you soon found that when she was keeping an eye on you – as she always was – you did better than your best. That was one of the main factors in the academic and other successes that have come the way of Gillespie girls.

Miss Andrew possesses a rare fund of humour, and tells stories with great felicity. She takes delight in doing what she must know she does incomparably well. Coming into a classroom unexpectedly, she would on occasion illuminate a point under discussion with a priceless anecdote, often from Dundee days, but Norway, London, America, dozens of places in her richly-packed experience, provided it just as well.

Her grasp of administration and detail was prodigious. There was not a department in Gillespie's that she did not know more about than did the Principal Teacher. That made her control informed, and to the solution of the many tricky problems of school life she brought to bear a perception which must have been unique.

Willa Muir, be it remembered, was one of Scotland's earliest and most articulate feminists, profiled in one episode of the 2016 BBC Scotland documentary, *Promised Land*. And a 'former pupil of the Twenties' – almost certainly Sir William Murrie, by 1956 Head of the Scottish Education

Department – wrote warmly, on her retirement, of the woman he had sat
under in his own Tayside schooldays.

> Ben Jonson noted that a good poet is made as well as born.
> Doubtless this is equally true of a good teacher. But so also is the
> converse; and while May Andrew had the advantage of all that goes
> to the making of a good teacher – a school and a University of
> character, quality and distinction – her success is fundamentally due
> to the fact that she was born one. She has the gift of communicating
> her own knowledge, her own interest, her own point of view, almost
> without letting the pupil know that she is doing so. She has the
> greater gift of taking it for granted that the pupil wants to receive
> what she has to give, and of making the assumption a reality.
>
> It is difficult to believe that it is now over thirty years since I first
> encountered these unusual qualities . . . For a young woman, with
> little teaching experience behind her, to tackle the teaching of
> English and History to the senior classes of a mixed school in the
> Dundee of the early Twenties can be seen in retrospect to have been
> more of an undertaking than it appeared at the time. She succeeded,
> I believe, because she did not so regard it; because she had been born
> a teacher as well as trained to teach. The problems which made some
> of her colleagues old before their time, the resistance to learning
> which they encountered every hour and which broke their tempers
> if not their spirits – these were things she did not recognise because
> she did not meet them. English and History were good for you;
> English and History were fun; English and History were things that,
> of course, you wanted to know about. And, strangely, it was so –
> with her, but not with some of the others . . .
>
> That was long ago, and she has since travelled far. The infectious
> qualities of the teacher have, I am sure, remained. But those of the
> headmistress have been revealed in equal abundance. I suppose
> someone may have tried to define what makes a good headmistress;
> but I suspect that, whatever it is, she too is born. She must obviously
> have the gift of leadership – of leading both her pupils and her staff
> in the directions she wants them to follow. We sometimes, as we get
> older and more absorbed in our daily work, forget how much the
> direction our life has taken was determined by our school; which
> means that it was determined by those who taught us and by those
> – especially the head of the school – who influenced both them and
> us . . . the ideals of Scottish education, the belief that the young have

the stuff of life in them no less in times present than in times past, the conviction that the talents entrusted to them will be duly multiplied in times to come – these things, like all good stewards of the tradition of Scottish teaching, she believes in deeply.

Miss Andrew's reign at Gillespie's was certainly marked by discipline, centred on three things – punctuality; neatness of appearance; and safe pupil movement around so large a building. It seems to have been she who, with thoughts of the latter, early and sensibly decreed that the girls stay in a given form-room all day (save, of course, for physical education and practical subjects) and that, instead, it was the teachers who flitted from classroom to classroom. She besides laid down a strict penal code, linked to the competitive 'House' system. An 'order-mark' for some infraction meant points off your house; three order-marks meant a 'conduct' – and three conducts meant expulsion. With such competitive entry for Gillespie's, and anxious parental commitment, no one seems ever to have been expelled. (The belt had been banished with the boys, though there was abundant smacking in junior school and a fair bit of ruler-on-the-knuckles everywhere and, as recently as 1970, Iona Cameron recalls, the ferocious Miss Marr slapped one girl across the face for the enormity of entering the school, on a day of heavy snow, in winter boots.)

The uniform has long been decried in hindsight. But it was less fussy, and arguably smarter, than those of quite a few other Edinburgh schools. Girls in mid-century wore navy-blue pinafores with a white blouse and school tie and sensible laced or strapped shoes and, of course, the maroon blazer with its unicorn badge. (By the mid-Sixties older girls wore a navy box-pleated skirt instead of the pinafore, with a navy pullover in colder months.) An appropriate navy overcoat was prescribed for winter. In summer, light green tussore dresses (which creased pitilessly) were donned instead, under the blazer. The hat – 'like an inverted strawberry punnet' – was a most vexing item, especially as it was never worn in class itself. But it had to be worn on travel to and from the school, and from the moment you left the house to the moment you returned, and to be seen hatless at any point by an alert mistress or a spiteful prefect meant trouble – an order-mark aside, you were then compelled to wear it at school all day, shrieking your shame before all. Primary girls besides had a panama hat, for the cool bright days of an Edinburgh summer.

'She was a strict disciplinarian,' a pupil recalled of Miss Andrew, 'but her object was to teach us to discipline ourselves. When the occasion merited she could be devastating and there were few second offenders; yet

she had a remarkably short memory for such things, and as the old physician would say, wrote her wrongs in ashes. Her reverent regard for life and confidence in the future have stimulated, and encouraged, all who have known her. She had a composure which nothing could disturb; a genuine interest in each one of us, and in our work; a sense of humour which could lighten the saddest of occasions and make the most of an amusing one . . . She taught that study had a purpose beyond the gaining of academic honours; that there was a strange alchemy in endeavour which could transmute apparent failure into a metal more precious than success; that to win or lose was nothing; to strive, all.'

Margaret Wood, née Richardson, a pupil of the school from 1930 to

Opposite and left. The outfitting market for Edinburgh school girls was lucrative. For decades, tireless traders advertised in Gillespie's magazine.

1943, recalled some minor emergency that compelled Miss Andrew to take her class one day, and the Headmistress gave them a gentle pep talk. 'I had not been any good at art,' May Andrew said, 'but I always used to try, and so I got a pass-mark. There is no such word as "can't" in the English language. You try, try try . . .'

Andrew besides saw herself not just as commander, but as high priest, placing great emphasis on morning prayers and conducting them with matchless authority. 'Of the daily part she played in the life of the school I suppose the ceremony that made the greatest impact on the minds and subsequent lives of her hearers was the morning service,' remembered one teacher. 'Deeply religious herself, she holds strongly that religious belief

May Andrew (front row, centre) and her staff at James Gillespie's High School, at the start of her final session in 1955. Emily Ferguson (fourth from right, fourth row) and Alexander Dall (fourth from right, front row) would serve into the 1980s. Notably, this group-photograph was taken in front of the archway by Bruntsfield House, not at the main campus on Warrender Park Crescent – and practically everyone is begowned.

should animate the whole life of the school. For her conduct of the service one feels gratitude and admiration. She had an unerring instinct for occasion. Her scorn for the trivial and the insincere was very great.'

But she had a pastoral heart. She took every First Form class, herself, for one period a week – partly to ease the girls into the life of the High School but also, shrewdly, giving her a chance to know them and to remember their names in her phenomenal memory. May Andrew besides took eager interest in the school environment, seeking out every opportunity to beautify and to decorate, to bring colour and style into dreich corners, flowers and pleasant garden areas in the wider grounds – even agreeing terms with the Corporation to have great paintings borrowed from dusty gallery storage and hung in its halls. Napkins and napkin rings suddenly appeared at school dinners. 'One of Miss Andrew's great qualities,' Margaret Napier declared, 'is her knowledge of, and interest in, the individual. A girl has had polio – Miss Andrew sets about to find her a

means of transport to school. A girl has had a bereavement – Miss Andrew finds some means of pecuniary aid.'

Her primary thrust, though, was academic. The original vision for the girls-only Gillespie's was one that would produce a well turned-out modern miss – secretaries and typists and bank tellers and assistants for the posher shops, bright little careers till the final life achievement of landing a husband and retiring to raise babies.

Andrew had bigger dreams; sought serious university material – women in the professions; women even in public life. The advent, in 1979, of a female Prime Minister must have thrilled her. And she strained every sinew (and those of everyone else) to raise standards and achievements and the general Gillespie's tone. In a shrewd and early move of re-branding, from the start of the 1938 school session all staff were required to wear academic gowns (augmented with colourful hoods for such occasions as Founder's Day – or, as it was dubbed from 1944, Commemoration Day). In a still more practical step, she instituted something long overdue – a school library, finding fast and permanent home in the former Crafts Room. Modern books were stocked from the Edinburgh Public Library, sixty-two volumes were bought during the 1937–38 session alone, girls leaving school were exhorted to give a book by way of memorial – and Miss Andrew donated a good many volumes herself.

Throughout her rule the number of girls presented annually (and successfully) for Leaving Certificate examinations rose steadily; more and more poured each year into the University of Edinburgh. There were only thirty-five presentations for Leaving Certificate in the year of her arrival. There were, annually, near 140 by her retirement. When, in 1946, Marguerite Myles made school history by achieving First Place (equal) in the Edinburgh University Bursary Competition, the ecstatic May Andrew declared a full day's holiday. She kept in keen touch with her overlords – especially Dr George Reith, the city's Director of Education, to whom she was also (in Gillespie's mythology) romantically linked – and fought for the interests of her school, the advancement of her ambition, at every tireless opportunity.

Andrew has been scorned for the 'streaming' system, into which girls were channelled by early secondary performance. In fact, she had inherited it. 'A-classes would be lawyers and doctors,' one has observed, 'B, teachers and civil servants; C, secretaries . . .' and down to the ignominy of E, girls to which May Andrew said (or, rather, is said to have said) 'You're fit to be nothing but mothers!' But such streaming was widespread in Scotland's high schools into the 1980s and was born, in truth, not so much from disparate pupil ability as from wildly ranging skills among teachers, few until very recent decades enjoying proper training in mixed-ability, core-and-extension classroom work – a big factor in the panicked flight of so many staff in Gillespie's when, at such short notice, it became an area comprehensive in 1973. Yet two of Miss Andrew's own appointments, Emily Ferguson and Alexander Dall, would endure serenely into the 1980s.

What slightly bewilders one today was how entirely, even by 1940, boys had been utterly forgotten at James Gillespie's High School. Reading old numbers of the school magazine, it was as if they had never crossed the door of the 'School on the Links'. A list of fifty former pupils in the services, carried in 1943, was exclusively female and 'Gillespie Girl' was already an Edinburgh catchphrase.

With so large a school and in such cramped premises, there was one great hope for the future. In 1935, the Corporation had acquired Bruntsfield House and its policies from the Warrender family trust and, in 1939, agreed

From the 1943 school magazine. Many past Gillespie boys must also have served – and died.

*   *   *   *

FORMER PUPILS IN THE SERVICES.

A large number of Former Pupils are now serving in the various Women's Services. The following are the names which have reached the Editor, who will be glad to receive others for insertion in next year's Magazine :—

A.T.S.:—Nan Cochrane, Rhoda Dickson,* Christina Durie, Margaret Ede, Glenys Edenborough, Ann Ferguson, Joan Fisher, Christine Jobson, Betty Lochore, Barbara Lowe, Helen Mackenzie, Clementine McIntyre, Sandra Mort, Helen Stewart, Iris Tait, Margaret Welsh.

W.R.N.S.:—Jean Deas, Renée Hall, Mabel Holland, Jean Littlejohn.

W.A.A.F.:—Jeanne Bauchope, Jessie Begrie, Maria Buchanan, Nyasa Burn, Isobel Dickson, Victoria Gillanders, Dorothy Lorimer, Betty MacDonald, Jessie McLean, Elma McPherson, Betty Martin, Sheila Mather, Muriel Newlands, Belly Sheed, Ann Storrar, Marjory Storrar, Laura Watt, Pauline Wood.

C.W.A.C.:—Patricia Mortimer, Pearl Mortimer.

W.L.A.:—Mabel Douglas, Helen Forbes, Alice Johnston, May Lammie, Winifred Morrison, Margaret Reid.

V.A.D.:—Muriel Edenborough, Patricia Hamilton,* Winifred Hamilton, Catherine Simpson.

*Serving abroad.

PRO PATRIA.

We have to record, with deep regret, the death on active service of Jean D. Scougall, A.T.S. Our warmest sympathy goes out to her parents.

---

*   *   *   *

in principle to the erection of a completely new school within these grounds, incorporating its sixteenth-century mansion. This did allow, with the completion of supposedly temporary huts of prefabricated steel in 1948, the transfer of almost the whole Primary Department (which would still be in them even in 1990). It would be 1958, though, before detailed plans were drawn up for the new High School; 1964 before its construction even began.

•   •   •

The Edinburgh Corporation prospectus for the 1938–39 session paints a proud picture of things as they then stood, with a fine photograph of the Warrender Park Crescent building and Miss Andrew's name prominent on the cover:

'The Education Committee desire to call attention to the excellent opportunities for a sound education provided in James Gillespie's High School for Girls. The School occupies a splendid and safe situation beside

Bruntsfield Links, and in addition to numerous excellent Class Rooms, contains a large Assembly Hall, a modern Gymnasium, and well-equipped Science Laboratories, up-to-date Art Studios, and a Department of Domestic Science which includes a Kitchen and Laundry as well as Needle-work rooms.

'The organisation provides for a Primary and a Secondary Course, and the curriculum is designed to meet the requirements of all pupils up to the stage of education necessary for obtaining the Leaving Certificate of the Scottish Education Department. The schemes of instruction are modern and well-balanced, the whole staff has been selected with great care, and the pupils are well grounded in all branches of education suitable to their age.'

Fees ranged from £3 3s per session for Infant School to £7 10s for the Post-Intermediate Division; what we would now call Fourth, Fifth and Sixth Year. Pupils were required to provide themselves with textbooks and there was an additional, modest 'Matriculation Fee' – one shilling per session for infants, half a crown for everyone else – to pay for stationery. The High School day was from 08.55 to 11.50; 12.35 to 15.20. There were still no morning or afternoon intervals. A two-course hot lunch was provided daily at a cost of £1 for the session, paid in advance.

'The curriculum of the Secondary Division is planned to provide a sound general education for the first three years of the Course before specialisation is begun,' the prospectus continues. 'The full Secondary Course extends over five or six sessions, and prepares for the Leaving Certificate of the Scottish Education Department. To suit the varying capacities and requirements of the post-intermediate pupils, in Forms IV, V, and VI, optional courses are arranged, and a choice of curricula suitable for different careers is open to the girls. English, Mathematics, Science, Modern and Classical Languages, Art and Music are included in the various courses designed as a preparation for the professions. Girls who do not intend to proceed to the University may from the fourth year of the Secondary division take the special Course of Secretarial Training or the practical Course in Domestic Science, including these subjects in the Higher Leaving Certificate Course. All pupils take Religious Instruction and Physical Education unless specifically excused.

'Instruction in Singing and in Musical Appreciation is given throughout the school. Outside of regular School hours, facilities are given to all who desire to have individual lessons in Pianoforte (Fee, payable in advance, is £1, 1s. a term – two lessons per week), and in Violin and 'Cello playing (by arrangement). A School Orchestra has been formed, and pupils are urged to join.'

SCHOOL SPORTS, 1938.

INTER-HOUSE RELAY RACE WINNERS.
Senior—Warrender.   Junior—Roslin.

BARBARA GRUBB.
Sports Champion.

Dancing classes were optional; school games – in the gymnasium, and hockey, tennis and cricket at Meggetland – were not. And the rules at James Gillespie's bore the unmistakable stamp of Miss Andrew –

School Regulations

1. Pupils must be punctual and regular in attendance from the first day until the last day of each term. A written excuse, signed by Parent or Guardian, in explanation of absence, lateness or non-preparation of homework is required from pupils. <u>All letters should bear the name of pupil's class.</u>

2. No explanation of absence save illness is regarded as satisfactory unless special leave of absence has been previously obtained from the Headmistress. Permission to leave School for part of a day can be obtained only by a written request stating the reason, and signed by the Parent or Guardian. This request must be sent to the Headmistress for approval at least one day in advance. Leave of absence for social engagements is not granted.

3. Parents or Guardians must give immediate intimation to the Headmistress if Infectious Disease occurs in the house, and all pupils affected thereby must at once be withdrawn from attendance. Resumption of attendance will be permitted only on production of a Medical Certificate clearing the pupil of any danger of infection.

4. No Class-teacher may be interviewed in the School by any Parent or Guardian without the previous sanction of the Headmistress.

5. No letters, postcards, etc., for pupils may be addressed to the School. Telephone calls for pupils in School are not received.

6. Parents are requested to examine, sign and return pupils' Term Reports, which are issued in the Primary and Secondary Divisions to show the results of the three Class Examinations held in the course of the year.

7. Hats, coats, shoes, and all property brought to the School or the playing field must bear the name of the owner.

8. No property or books may be left in School overnight, nor may money or valuables be left in pockets of coats, etc., in cloakrooms except at owner's risk. No responsibility is accepted for Bicycles brought to the School.

9. No modification of the School Hours can be made except for pupils holding Medical Certificates or for those travelling by train.

NOTE:- The Headmistress will be pleased to interview Parents or Guardians on Wednesdays during School Hours, or on other days by appointment.

Improvements to the fabric continued. In September 1938 girls 'returned to a building which showed not a few improvements; the most important innovation was the covered corridor which now connects the main building with the Gymnasium and Infant School, and which proves a real blessing in cold or wet weather. In the Demonstration Room wood

panelling has replaced the cold white tiles; the Middle Hall has been redec-
orated in cheerful yellow and furnished with an enlarged platform; half
the rooms in the school have been supplied with new desks; but the most
important of the minor alterations is certainly the installation of primrose-
yellow "blackboards" on which bright blue chalk is used. An addition to
the amenities of the school is the handsome natural oak lectern, table and
chair presented by the Swimming Club for use at morning assembly and
all services.' (These survive, though in recent decades have lived in the Head
Teacher's office.)

But the near-outbreak of war in August 1938, averted only by the
infamous Munich Agreement, had rattled everyone. 'Hardly had the work
of the session well begun when the grim days of the September "Crisis"
were upon us, and the school was closed for two days for distribution of
gas-masks. Rarely can pupils or teachers have returned so willingly to the
normality of school as after that unexpected holiday. Throughout the
session the Staff and at least the older pupils, like all thinking people, have
been conscious of an ever-present tension; the Current Events classes have
had an almost painful relevance; and one realises with thankfulness and
almost with surprise that a normal and satisfactory year's programme of
school activities has been carried through. Most of the Staff have trained
in A.R.P [air raid precautions] or First Aid work, and Gillespie's has its
share in the plans for evacuation in the event of the "emergency" which
we so earnestly hope may not arise.'

At Founder's Day Service, that last session of peace –

The school had the unique honour of welcoming as speaker the
Right Reverend Archibald Main, DD, Moderator of the Church of
Scotland, whose traditional lace ruffles and knee-breeches lent a
touch of unfamiliar pageantry. For the occasion the corridors and
hall were lavishly decorated with palms and pink hydrangeas. A
platform party of about forty included the Heads of several distinguished Edinburgh schools, as well as representatives of Edinburgh
Education Committee, the Education Offices, and the Inspectorate.
The Chairman was Dr J.B. Clark, CBE, late Headmaster of George
Heriot's School. The Moderator, whose genial humour delighted
the pupils, in recalling James Gillespie's generosity hoped that we
today had not lost 'the romance of benefaction,' and from the
Moderatorial ring with its engraving of the St Andrew's Cross and
the Burning Bush drew lessons of loyalty to our country and our
church. The Senior Prefect, Nancy Paterson, thanked the Moderator

Gillespie girls evidently enjoying proceedings at Founder's Day in 1939. The vases of flowers – and potted palms – are a typical May Andrew touch.

in a felicitous little speech; the customary presentation of a snuff-box was made, and a holiday was announced for the following Monday. After the service our distinguished guests were entertained in the Library to afternoon tea, beautifully prepared by the Domestic Science pupils of Form 5B under Miss Thorburn's direction . . .

Examination results for the past session have been very satisfactory, 30 of the 36 candidates presented for the Group Leaving Certificate having been successful. It is worth recording that the six girls who for the first time in the history of the school took Domestic Science as one of their subjects all passed. A word of special congratulations is due to Audrey Purves, Helen MacKenzie and Muriel Brown, who in addition to gaining Leaving Certificates, took high places in a recent Civil Service Examination (Clerical Class). It was gratifying to see our school represented in the Merit List of Edinburgh University Bursary Competition by three creditably high places. Eleanor Ginsburg has been awarded the Thomson Bursary of £60 a year in the Faculty of Medicine, and Nancy Paterson the Ardvorlich Bursary of £20 a year in the Faculty of Arts.

Now that May Andrew was in charge, there was no more ritual snorting of snuff on Founder's Day by the platform party. In another, more wistful

innovation, the school magazine from 1939 and subsequently noted (in an
age only just developing antibiotics) the deaths of pupils during session –
four girls in 1938–39 alone. Death on a still vaster scale was, of course, about
again to engulf the world.

•   •   •

Six years later, in July 1945, Miss Foster – by now long in with the bricks –
wrote a moving editorial for the school magazine.

The scene is the Scottish National Library, the year 2045. An earnest
student of social history, gathering material for a book on 'Life in

Britain during the Second World War', has unearthed from an obscure corner of the library six little paper-covered volumes – the issues of Gillespie's High School Magazine for the years 1940 to 1945. As he turns the yellowing pages his expression becomes puzzled, for what he reads seems almost inconsistent with what he knows of those years when western civilisation tottered and when this country passed through its most fiery trial. True, there are references to War Savings and war charities, to comforts for the troops, to shelter drill and fire-watching; there are verses (mostly humorous) about rationing and queueing and sirens and, finally, about VE Day; there are, in the Infants' stories, revealing little touches like 'My daddy is in the homegard and he looks an ofil site in his yooniform.' Once, at least, he finds a deeper note struck where in the 'School Notes' for 1940 the significant words ' . . . and we have for weeks been awaiting the order to evacuate from Edinburgh,' recall the time when the danger of invasion was real and pressing, and when we could no longer be sure of keeping anything we cherished – our homes, our traditions or even our lives. But the bulk of what he reads is the record of a school carrying on its normal life, indeed, flourishing and expanding. There are the yearly records of examination successes, the reports of every school society, of sports and parties and Commemoration Days and concerts. He concludes that the life of a girls' school in a safe area was, even in these grim years, secure and sane and happy.

Surely every one of us realises that we have been privileged beyond anything we could have dared to expect. Let us beware of the sin of taking things for granted. Innumerable films and newspapers, and of recent months our school's contact with the suffering city of Caen, have shown us what we have been spared. If we, unlike other schoolgirls less fortunately placed, know nothing except by hearsay of bombed houses, of hunger and cold and sudden death, of the shadow of the Gestapo and the nightmare cruelties of the concentration camp, it is through no merit of our own but through the strange mercy of Providence and the sacrifice of others. One of the Editor's privileges is to receive copies of the magazines of some of our Edinburgh boys' schools. In peacetime this was a pleasure, but in these last years it has brought a recurring heartache, for every number has had its portraits of the smiling lads whose death was the price of our freedom. Our security was not lightly won, nor must it be lightly held.

And now in this year we have seen the lights going up again, the flags hung out, and the bells rung for Victory in Europe, and we look forward – to what? The superficial answer is, 'To lighted streets, better food, more attractive clothes, unlimited petrol, seaside holidays,' but if we think only thus, in terms of the returning amenities of our own lives, we are indeed unworthy of our privileges. 'The life of the world,' said Mr Churchill in his own and the nation's finest hour, 'may yet move forward into broad and sunlit uplands.' With more hope now than then we may share his faith, but though victory has been achieved those sunlit uplands are still far away. Those who leave school in this and coming years are going into a world of dark and tangled problems, of violence and suffering not yet extinct, of smouldering hatreds and lingering suspicions, of uncertain leaderships and conflicting loyalties. Such a world, with its challenging opportunities for service, needs women with courage and imagination and goodwill, with informed minds, sound judgment and understanding hearts. Let us dedicate our school and ourselves to meeting that need, and if we ask for a motto for this year of victory, let it be this – 'To whom much is given, of them shall much be required.'

These comments are typical of a new earnestness – an impatience with frivolity; the exalting of service as an ideal; a quiet daily thankfulness – that would stamp most adults who had come through the Second World War and mark even the children they taught through the decades thereafter, until the last retired in the brash 1980s.

Edinburgh had all but escaped the bombing that had so blighted Clydebank, Coventry, London and Hull and elsewhere; but fear of invasion had been real and the privations of rationing would not utterly be lifted till 1954. Gillespie girls, of course, did their bit; many alumni served throughout the Forces, in assorted auxiliary capacities (of the old boys who must have served too, we know nothing) and a report in the 1940 school magazine is typical of endeavours nearer home –

Very early in the session a scheme for knitting and despatching war comforts was set on foot, under Miss Wood's direction. Four large consignments have during the session been sent to the headquarters of the Women's Voluntary Services, for distribution, and Lady Elphinstone has written her personal thanks to the school. Practically every class turned with enthusiasm to the knitting of patches,

and no fewer than 39 gay blankets, whose rainbow colours would have made Joseph's famous coat look dim, were sent to hospitals and minesweepers. One blanket by a happy coincidence reached the soldier father of a Gillespie girl. In all, 550 articles, comprising socks, mitts, scarves, helmets, pullovers and sea-boot stockings, were received. One form, 4A, had the enterprise to 'adopt' the minesweeper 'Braconmoor', to which several parcels were sent. It was with pride that the girls of this form read that one of the crew of 'their' ship had been decorated for bravery. In the spring term two sailors from the 'Bracanmoor' visited the school and personally thanked Form 4A for its gifts. Another form of war service, easy but not unimportant, has been the saving of silver paper, of which two large sacks have been connected fortnightly since January. In view of the country's present need, the Savings Association is being revived.

And, in the summer of 1942, a large crowd of Gillespie girls spent four weeks harvesting raspberries in Perthshire as their personal contribution to the war effort, Margaret H. Clark subsequently reporting –

Sewing vivid but no doubt cosy blankets for British servicemen, 1940.

The scene is Princes Street Station on July 20th, at 9 a.m. Seventy chattering, excited schoolgirls, laden with haversacks, gas masks, waterproofs and cases – the beginning of the berry-picking camp at 'Berrydale', Blairgowrie.

After the first thrill and novelty had passed, as there were then no berries ripe to keep us busy we looked around at what was – not a luxury hotel. Impressions grow vague with the passing of time. Early rising (especially for cooks and orderlies) – bumpy straw palliasses – cold washing water – spiders – rain, rain and more rain! Rain is our clearest and wettest memory! Noisy as well as wet as it poured on to our corrugated roofs.

But these are not our only impressions – oh, no! There were many more happy ones. The gramophone – dear old thing – with the same records that were always on. The day it rained so hard that the craze of a 'beauty salon' was caught even by the staff. 'Andrew' must have been amazed at the hair styles. Yes, there was 'Andrew', our 'man about the house', who never failed to wake the cooks or light the fires. (Among other accomplishments, he told stories, spoke Gaelic, and played the accordion.)

Don't please think that all our pleasures were on 'lazy' days. In spite of maternal warnings we ate (and enjoyed) raspberries until we never wanted to see another. We loved the lorry rides through the town to the 'railway' fields while the 'natives' waved as we sang, in true Gillespie manner, songs which were continued, even in three parts, on the fields. Occasionally the songs gave place to terrified shrieks as we town-bred girls fled from a disturbed wasps' nest. The off-duty trips into 'Blair', as we fondly called it, consisted of meetings with the Perth Academy girls and searches for the best ice cream (a process of elimination by tasting).

Gradually we adapted ourselves to camp life – so much so, in fact, that when Miss Andrew came to spend a day with us her first thoughts were that she had strayed into a gypsy camp.

It was with mixed feelings that we gathered for our last 'sing-song' in the big dormitory on August sixteenth. We longed for an abundance of baths, home and the luxury of a bed, but we were loath to leave our friends, the 'gaffers' with their continual war-cry of 'Start at the tap o' the dreel and pick clean', Andrew, the Perth girls, and the kitten. Even more than them we knew we should miss our own members of staff who had proved such excellent cooks and such patient though much harassed foster-mothers.

Even 'utility' garments could be advertised glamorously.

When we received our pay later we justly had feelings of satisfaction – we had helped pay our country *and* had added to our own
pocket money.

The success of the camp is shown by the fact that some of our
last year's pickers are returning this year. Those of us who are not
going, I am sure would like to wish them good luck, and to say, 'Give
our love to Berrydale.'

A copy of the school magazine even reached troops in a distant theatre of
the war, as a pleasant note from Sergeant J. D. Williams (whose girl
attended Gillespie's) of the Royal Artillery confirmed. 'James Gillespie's
High School Magazine has travelled many miles via South Africa to Persia.

Five months passed before it reached its destination. It has been very fully appreciated by both officers and men serving with the 55th Heavy A.A. Regt. R.A. The adjutant, too, of this regiment was very interested, and gave the school great praise. The magazine has also been in contact with the natives of Basra, Iraq, who, incidentally, admired the photographs very much!

'After travelling through the desert this school magazine is now in Teheran, the capital of Persia, where once again it is eagerly read. The men of this regiment anxiously await the 1943 copy, and send their best wishes to the Headmistress and teachers, and thanks for the pleasant reading they had.'

Commemoration Day in 1945 fell on Friday 1 June, weeks after VE Day, and there is an understandable sunniness in Miss Foster's report.

> Each Commemoration Day as it comes round has the effect of a pleasing variation on a particular tune. The essential features remain the same: always one associates the occasion with masses of June flowers, the cool green of summer uniforms, inspiring music, a distinguished speaker and guests, the inevitable references to snuff, a dignified Senior Prefect and two solemn but excited 'babies', the familiar dusty black of academic gowns lightened by the less familiar glory of coloured hoods – and, under all these surface impressions, a renewed sense of the unity that comes of sharing a fine tradition. This year's ceremony had its own particular touches that will remain in memory – a glint of sunlight on a great vase of yellow broom, the gleam of the Lord Provost's gold chain of office, voices singing strong and true in the last 'Fidelis et Fortis' of the school Song, and the pleasant touch of fantasy which summoned as guest and wise counsellor the friendly ghost of James Gillespie . . . Special note must be taken of the singing for the first time of our School Song, in which words written by Mrs King Gillies have been set to a stirring tune by Mr Macrae. No doubt it will soon become a familiar and cherished part of the Gillespie tradition.

•   •   •

In November 1945 the Preparatory Department was finally able to occupy its new quarters in Bruntsfield House, the move having been delayed for some years as parts of it served as emergency accommodation for homeless families. 'The historic building may have its inconveniences,' mused the

school magazine, 'but few schools can boast such a delightful summer playground as its lawns and trees provide for our little girls. Just before Christmas, a day was set apart on which a large number of appreciative parents visited the Preparatory classes in their new home, admired handwork, listened to carols and poems, watched games, and carried away a vivid impression of work done in those vital first years of school life.'

The new buildings, such as they were, were not completed until February 1948, and only then could the primary classes enjoy more spacious accommodation on the Bruntsfield House campus. 'Very soon *our* wood, *our* avenue, *our* lawn, *our* blackbird, *our* gardens were realities,' enthused Assistant Headmistress Bertha Mackay, 'and by the time the younger children arrived in April, our "policies" had really taken shape, thanks to the kindly interest of very good friends on the Education Committee, and we were ready for the opening service. There a fine little soloist from Primary 1 sang a "blessing on the buildings" and Miss Andrew promised many delightful things which speedily materialised.

'As our concert gave us loudspeakers and the school fund furnished our adiscope [a gadget for viewing three-dimensional transparency images, like the Viewmaster toy of yore] we are well equipped educationally and

Miss Laidlaw's P3 class, 1956.

just need a few more weeks for our bird bath, our tubs of flowers, and our other amenities to grace the grounds and charm our hearts. Here in very truth we can say, "Let Gillespie's flourish", for these must surely be the ideal surroundings where little people can grow and blossom during their early school days.'

The main building at Warrender Park Crescent was now almost relieved of Primary classes, though Primary Seven remained there till at least the opening of the new school in 1966 and some use seems to have been made of part of the building as a Primary annexe till the comprehensive era.

April 1947 witnessed the tenth anniversary of May Andrew's appointment as Headmistress and she held a pleasant tea party on 28 March for 'present members of staff, those who have, during the past ten years, retired from teaching here or been transferred elsewhere, and those who have been Duxes [sic] or School Captains during her term of office'. A new laboratory for Biology classes was now in use at the 'School on the Links', a second Domestic Science kitchen was promised for the 1948–49 session, and the girls' Science Association had now raised enough funds to buy a film projector.

In 1950 May Andrew was awarded a 'Travelling Scholarship' by the English-Speaking Union, allowing her a four-week tour of schools and colleges in the United States, and duly caught her flight that September. Her long and enthusiastic account, 'A Flying Visit to America', appeared in the school magazine the following year, of which four paragraphs suffice:

> From Buffalo I flew to Washington, where I stayed for a week, enjoying most heartily the gracious hospitality and all the entertainments so kindly arranged for me. There I visited two of the large State schools (comparable to our own), marvelling on both occasions at the spacious, well-equipped buildings, the generous staffing and the artistic furnishings which were theirs. It was a pleasure to see the Americans' unbounded faith in education, and their willingness to face the cost of it. During the week in Washington I was able, too, to visit the fine School of Education of Maryland University, where I had an informative afternoon in the Department of Psychology and Child Study, and an interesting social evening, with selections on the bagpipes played in my honour in the drawing room.

> Throughout that wonderful week in Washington I was delightfully entertained, meeting and talking with people of divers interests, whose conversation on contemporary happenings and political events was both interesting and stimulating. It was a particular pleasure to have lunch with the Education Officer of the British Embassy and to be the guest of the Chief Secretary of the Australian Embassy, who drove me to Mount Vernon on one of the loveliest of autumn days. Parties, picnics and sight-seeing excursions were all planned for my delight, and I am deeply grateful to the friends who not only gave me much information about the educational system, but showed me the beauties of Washington in sunshine and floodlight.

> Thence I journeyed south to Richmond in Virginia, where I had

a happy week in the friendly atmosphere of a girls' school, sharing in the communal life and finding myself very much at home. It was a great pleasure to be included in the daily round of work and activities, studying the school system at close quarters, and enjoying thoroughly the friendly companionship of the Faculty and the girls. They were eager to talk about Scotland, its beauty, its literature and its history, and I was happy to attend classes, services and assemblies, answering their many questions and giving informal talks.

One of the red-letter days of the week was a visit to Williamsburg to see the College of William and Mary, and the interesting colonial township built around it. On the long, lovely drive back to Richmond, my hostess was able to tell me a great deal about the coloured people of the south, and to my delight took me to one of the little rural schools for coloured children, where Moneybee Abraham and other fascinating piccaninnies showed us their work, and proved good companions. A visit to an old croft and shack, where I saw the 'old folks at home' – devoted servants of my hostess – completed a day that will long remain in my memory.

In certain matters May Andrew was, inevitably, a daughter of her age.

The 1951–52 session saw general redecoration of the main school and the provision, not before time, of a pleasant staff common room. The Biology Department acquired two tropical fish tanks and there were further improvements to Bruntsfield House. Meanwhile, the Primary Department now sponsored a polar bear at Edinburgh Zoo – he was called Jim, after our noble founder – and Alison Laidlaw put tireless effort into organising a swimming gala. Miss Foster, though, was sidelined for much of the subsequent session by stress-related illness. As she recovered, she succoured her former pupil Muriel Spark (née Camberg) in the aftermath of her own nervous breakdown, a personal crisis culminating in Spark's conversion late in 1953 to Roman Catholicism. This the sturdily Presbyterian Foster took in her stride. 'Repudiate you, my dear?' she wrote. 'No. I think my feeling is almost envy of you for having found the answer, even at the cost of what must have been a very painful sacrifice in the matter of personal relationships.'

Though she would put in more than a decade of further classroom duty, Alison Foster now yielded as Principal Teacher of English to Mr James D. McEwan, a Scots gentleman of Empire fortune who had suffered dreadfully as a prisoner of the Japanese (and subsequently wrote a book about his experiences). He besides took over as editor of the school magazine,

Quite a few snaps of the school's polar bear – kept, understandably, at Edinburgh Zoo – appeared in the magazine in post-war years. Jim could be rather photogenic.

writing in an extraordinarily florid, slushy style. A bad fire in the spring of 1953 burned out attics in Bruntsfield House; these had to be rebuilt. The affected primary classes found temporary accommodation in the Barclay Church Hall across the Links. And, in 1954, May Andrew was awarded the CBE for services to education. As if emboldened to an unusual flash of her authority – and, perhaps, Miss Foster's diminished status – early in the new session that year she called an Extraordinary General Meeting of the Literary and Dramatic Society (in her capacity as Honorary President) and impressed on them firmly that there was rather too much drama and not enough literature on the proposed syllabus.

She was loath to have any fuss made over her retirement in 1956, trying even to persuade the school chaplain, the Reverend Leonard Small, that at the very farewell service

no mention should be made of what was uppermost in all minds. She was moved, but outwardly even less than the most phlegmatic of her hearers. Then the rare discipline re-asserted itself. 'Much has been given to me,' she said, 'let me also give.' She had decided as a gift to the school to present a Head Girl's badge, and this happy thought, artistically translated into goldsmith's craft, symbolically handed over, will record that for nineteen years she has given to Gillespie's without stint . . .

It has been remarked that certain words come readily to her lips. Of these, 'good companions' . . . is an example, and others are 'lovely' and 'happy'. In the duties of friendship she gives and gets constancy, and it is natural that the words that convey her zest for living should be present to her mind. Her devotion to duty has somewhat restricted her in seeing the loveliness of Scotland, through the changing pageantry of the seasons, as she would have liked to. Her little car has recently provided her with the means, and now her greater leisure will extend the opportunity. She recently confided that she has never seen Scotland in June. She often speaks of the glens of Angus, or the north-west up Lochinver way, which she explored as a girl by bicycle, and this summer the long unvisited hills, with their flush of purple and glint of birch-bark, will not fail to give her a heady welcome . . .

No woman ever deserved better of any school than Miss Andrew of hers. At the disposal of all she placed her wide scholarship, her judicious and faithful council, her kindly interest and her inflexible friendship. During her faithful devotion to Gillespie's she never wearied in well-doing. She left the school enriched by her service. Wherever, all over the world, a Gillespie girl sets up a home, Miss Andrew's name will often be mentioned, and it will never be mentioned without veneration, gratitude and honour.

On 3 April 1956, that dread day of departure, she was presented with her portrait in oils, painted by Sir William Hutchison PRSA – who, regrettably, could not attend as he had a commission at Buckingham Palace. The painting (somewhat unsettling) was the gift of staff, pupils, former staff and former pupils. Miss Andrew promptly donated it to the school. Other tokens included a gold watch, a travelling clock and a handbag.

Miss Andrew's reluctance, for many years thereafter, quite to stay clear of the place sorely tried her successors. She attended prize-givings and concerts, was Guest of Honour at untold Gillespie's social functions, and even found a part at the opening of the new Lauderdale Street campus in October 1966, when she was solemnly presented to the Queen Mother (or was the Queen Mother presented to her?).

Gloriana Imperatrix,
1956.

But it should not be assumed that she viewed the comprehensive era – or the very different Scotland already taking shape by the early 1980s – with revulsion and horror. For the rest of her long life she took keen interest in her old command. She wrote to Iona Cameron, in 1968, to commend this new Principal Teacher of English on a radically reformed and lively school magazine. And she fully understood the challenges with which Mary McIver and Patricia Thomas were wrestling from 1973 onwards. Not that she ever quite grasped how far, come the comprehensive era, the school's old clout had fallen with the city fathers. 'I don't understand what all the fuss is about these days,' Miss Andrew once sighed in Miss Cameron's hearing, 'I just lifted the phone and got Dr Reith . . . '

It was Dr Thomas's custom, after each Founder's Day ceremony, to call on her predecessors with flowers, and in the archives this charming handwritten note survives.

Pitsligo House,
Pitsligo Road,
Edinburgh,
EH10 4RY

28th Feb. 1982

Dear Dr Thomas,

Your visit on Founder's Day gave me more pleasure than you would believe possible. I was delighted to meet Mr Galloway again, and to hear from you both the latest news of the school.

As you know I'm always interested and delighted to hear of the continuing success of your work. The lovely flowers are blooming bravely in the great hall of Pitsligo – a great joy to us all.
Long may the good work continue and thrive.
With much gratitude and every good wish,
Yours very sincerely,

May Andrew

She died five months later, on 27 July, after a short illness.

CHAPTER SIX

'You can always tell a Gillespie Girl, but you can't tell her much'
1956–1967

The new Headmistress was Mary D. Steel BSc, who assumed power on 23 April 1956 and served for the next eleven years. Apart from the school's entire relocation, in 1966, to the new and very modern campus around Bruntsfield House, these otherwise were years when Gillespie's stood dangerously still. Shortly before she joined the staff, in 1968, Iona Cameron's bank manager had thoughts of sending his daughter there. But, he said ominously, 'it's been living on its reputation for years'.

There were notable changes in this period to which the school and its leadership struggled to respond – as, in fairness, did schools in Scotland generally. The first was encapsulated in that high drama of 1956, the same year Miss Andrew stood down: the Suez crisis, which destroyed the premiership of Anthony Eden and, even amidst some recent stiff competition, remains the greatest overseas folly of any post-war British government. Certainly it confirmed, in the most humiliating way, that Britain was no longer a world power and that she could accomplish little of any weight abroad against the wishes of her American ally. It besides, and for many years thereafter in the eyes of the country's intellectuals and opinion formers, damned the Conservatives as the 'party of stupid'.

Suez accelerated the rapid dismantling of the Empire, forced Britain at last (under the Macmillan government) to accept that her best future lay within what was then still the Common Market, and sufficiently shook up our politics to ensure, from the late 1950s onwards, first the slow recovery of the Liberal Party and then the jerky rise of Scottish nationalism. Both these, in time, proved lethal for the Tories in Scotland. In 1955 the Scottish Unionists (as they then styled themselves) had won an absolute majority of the Scots vote and quite dominated the internal affairs of Edinburgh. The rest is history. Scotland today is a very different country and of very different values. The Empire and its old verities fast evaporated and even by 1970 Gillespie girls were far more knowing, thoughtful people in a country where politics was now the management of decline.

The second development is the extraordinarily rapid secularisation of Scotland from the 1960s onwards, as Iain Macwhirter describes – if perhaps with a whiff of malice – in his 2013 book *Road to Referendum*:

> At the start of the 1960s, Scotland remained a joyless and colourless place where the Kirk still strongly influenced public morality – 'sex', famously, was something Edinburgh ladies bought coal in; pubs closed at ten; and recreation beyond football was largely non-existent, unless you included Sunday School. But by the end of the 1960s . . . well, not a lot had changed, to be perfectly honest. Scotland still looked cold, grey, poor. However, beneath the surface, a revolution had occurred which destroyed the old Scotland of pursed-lipped conformity and undermined the political and moral allegiances that had endured largely intact since the 1707 Union. The British Empire had already crashed and burned after the Suez Crisis in 1956, and now the moral and psychological hegemony of the Kirk was to be challenged. The age of deference was over.

The most obvious sign of this was the decline in church attendance in a society where the Presbyterian Kirk had dominated ordinary people's lives for centuries through the Session and had even occupied the space left by the absence of a national politics. Church of Scotland membership peaked at 1.32 million in 1956 when attendance was as high as it had ever been in the previous hundred years. Then, suddenly, it collapsed in one of the most dramatic secularisations experienced by any country in the world. The Kirk lost 65 per cent of its communicants within twenty years. The divorce rate in Scotland increased by 400 per cent between 1960 and 1974.

Callum Brown, in *Religion and Society in Scotland since 1707*, described the collapse of all forms of religious observance in Scotland in the 1960s as 'cataclysmic'. Hugh McLeod, Professor of Church History at Birmingham University, has described the 'long Sixties' between 1958 and 1974 as 'a rupture in religious history as great as that brought about by the Reformation'. Since Scotland was one of the countries that led the Reformation in the sixteenth century, this rupture was all the more dramatic here. Scotland has had a history of intense militant Christianity from the Covenanters to the Disruption, and had an education system largely shaped by

the Kirk. It is hard to believe that all this could disappear, in historical terms, overnight. And yet it did . . .

Schools move slowly. 'The Syllabus used in the schools under the control
of the Edinburgh Corporation Education Committee was drawn up in
1930 by a Joint Committee representing the Church of Scotland and the
Educational Institute of Scotland,' asserts the Education Committee's 1934
handbook. 'The Bible lessons are carefully graded and the aim of the
Syllabus is to secure for the children Scriptural teaching by which life and
character may be enriched. The scheme is dominated by the life and
message of our Lord Jesus Christ . . .'

As late as 1991 Gillespie's still had a school chaplain, and Founder's Day,
prize-giving and end-of-term services were framed in the context of
Christian worship; as late as 1980, the Religious Education teacher was an
ordained Church of Scotland minister (best remembered for his unseemly
and enthusiastic use of the belt). When the last extensions to the 1966
campus were opened in March 1991, that chaplain, an Episcopalian priest,
engaged in prayer before the local MP and civic dignitaries. Yet Dr Thomas
struggled ever to show more than polite interest in Christian observance
and for most of my own time at Gillespie's not a single member of staff
supported our tiny Scripture Union group. By the autumn of 2013 a senior
Physics teacher at one Edinburgh school was eased from post for the
enormity of admitting to pupils (in response to a straight question in class)
that he believed the world had been created by God; and Christmas services
at Gillespie's that December, involving local ministers, aroused some pupil
protest. Not a single clergyman attended, far less participated in, the
opening of the new teaching block in June 2015. That world has gone.

The third development was a backlash against the 1944 Education Act,
wherein R. A. Butler both raised the minimal school-leaving age to fifteen
(it would be increased to sixteen in 1970) and established a three-tier system
of secondary schools throughout Britain: grammar schools for the ablest
children (by admission through examination in Primary Seven, the 'qualifi-
cation' or 'qually'), secondary-moderns for the less academically endowed,
and technical colleges for those of artisanal bent. Unfortunately very few
of the last were ever built.

This is not the place for discussion of a fiercely controversial topic; there
are still many grammar schools in England and widespread parental
demand for more. They proved an extraordinary force for social mobility
and the Sixties, especially, were noted for a new brash breed of high
achievers and young celebrities – Harold Wilson, Margaret Thatcher,

Gordon Brown, Mick Jagger, Paul McCartney, Alan Bennet, Clive Anderson, David Bailey, and so on – who had received a welcome leg-up through them. By decade's end more graduands were winning places at Oxford and Cambridge than were the fruits of Eton and similar exclusive establishments. Yet in high places opinion was already turning against them, most eminently in Anthony Crosland, Secretary of State for Education and Science, from 1964 to 1967, in Harold Wilson's Labour Government. 'If it's the last thing I do,' he once stormed at his wife, 'I'm going to destroy every f****** grammar school in England. And Wales and Northern Ireland . . . '

The Left were increasingly entranced by the American high school model – classless, non-selective local secondary schools; a glorious melting pot of varied backgrounds, cultures and abilities. It is easy to forget – and this certainly rings true in the educational politics of Edinburgh – that the real opposition to grammar schools came from grassroots Tories, infuriated to see their offspring consigned to secondary-moderns as grammar schools took in bright wee grammar-school lads and lassies frae the schemes. But no one ended up closing as many grammar schools the length of the United Kingdom as a subsequent, Conservative Secretary of State for Education – Margaret Thatcher.

Most today would be aghast at the return of a system where a child's prospects, income and future came down to one life-defining (and culturally biased) examination at the age of twelve; even if we might dryly note that, after nearly half a century of state comprehensives, not one has produced a single British Prime Minister. (Or, indeed, a single Gillespie's Head Teacher.) But, nevertheless, the times they were a-changin', even as Gillespie's stayed frozen along lines framed in the 1930s by May Andrew – and for her day.

There was besides the rapid social change from the late 1950s in, broadly, the spheres of sexuality and gender. This must be heavily qualified. The so-called 'sexual revolution' of the 1960s really only involved about fifteen people in London. The liberalising laws of the 'permissive society' were, really, a response to the hasty war-time marriages and other variants of moral turpitude during the Second World War; and the change in attitudes generally took root in Scotland rather later than in England, from about the late 1970s – male homosexual acts, for instance, were not decriminalised till 1980, nor Scottish divorce law (and, besides, her licensing laws) liberalised till 1976.

But by the opening of the new Gillespie's campus in 1966 that change hung hungrily in the air. The advent of the contraceptive pill had begun

Poised Gillespie girls modelling the fashions of the hour for a 'mannequin parade', 1964.

greatly to affect the behaviour of young people. Powerful commercial forces – the clothing and music industries, for instance – were fast creating a new and distinct 'teenage' culture. Married women, even those with young families, were starting to return to the workplace, or remain in it. There are several telling signs in the school magazine that this was still cause for comment; that it was not, you know, quite 'done'. 'During Miss Foster's absence,' simper the Staff Notes in the 1953 edition, 'her teaching duties were undertaken at short notice by Mrs Taylor, one of those rare and enviable people who can run a home, a family, and a classroom, with a sunny and gracious efficiency which most of us would be happy to be able to devote to any one ...'

The faint *meeaow* is unmistakable but, even now, hypocrisy on another front endured, as T. C. Smout notes in his history of modern Scotland –

> Dr Verney, the much respected founder of Edinburgh University Medical Health Service, startled a student debate at the end of his long career by adhering, in the 1960s, to the moral attitudes which had served his profession so long ...
>
> 'Dr Verney replied that to prescribe the Pill for unmarried girls would be contrary to the dictates of his conscience ... It is necessary to the male student to prove his manhood by the experience of sex. Earlier they had found this outlet outside the University, but now found it within the University, with an associated rise in illegitimacy and venereal disease in the student population. This Dr Verney attributed to a decline of moral principles among the young women – in his day young women came to the University for education, not for fornication. In the tense and claustrophobic silence which followed ... the sense of most of what he had said previously was forgotten.'
>
> The students can never have heard the double standard expounded so clearly. They were right to be shocked.

A final shadow hung over life in those decades after 1945, and into the late 1980s, which a younger generation cannot recall – the Cold War. On occasion – October 1962; September 1983 – it became scarily hot. Air-raid warning networks remained live throughout Britain's cities; there was a particularly obvious siren at Tollcross, and in July 1986 Edinburgh was briefly terrified when it and others were accidentally switched on. Over the Hebrides, Soviet fighters played cat-and-mouse games with aircraft of the RAF; the coming of an American submarine base to the Holy Loch, in 1961, put west-central Scotland right in the sights of a Russian nuclear strike and was a big factor in the rapid growth of the Scottish National Party that decade. The secret state had its tentacles everywhere; only after the collapse of the Soviet Union did its highly detailed invasion plans emerge, including street maps of Edinburgh and other cities. The world, through those decades, was an exciting one for young folk in Scotland; but it never felt entirely secure or safe.

With the advent of passenger jets, too, the world was a rapidly shrinking

Lacrosse at Meggetland with Mrs Bull, 1966.

place by the end of the 1950s. And of course there was a most modern phenomenon – television, sitting in most homes by the early 1960s, opening a window into other worlds, other ways of life, other ways of thinking, beyond snell Edinburgh nights, the shoogle of a Corporation bus, and tea and scones at McVities Guest. By decade's end an unmistakably restive note from Gillespie girls themselves grows evident in a school magazine of suddenly unloosed stays – far more questioning, consciously more vulnerable to sexual pressure, ever more remote from the ageing women in black gowns who increasingly struggled with a fast-changing order.

For years to come, those brought to adulthood before the early 1960s would struggle in many ways to relate to those of us raised soon after them. And it is no coincidence that this new generation of Gillespie children, passing out of the school in the Seventies and Eighties, has produced, from Edi Stark down, so many journalists and commentators. But one has only to glance at two staff photographs – those taken, respectively, in 1955 and

1980 – to see how, in time, the bearing and fashion of adults was transformed too. In just a quarter-century our generation witnessed more changes, culturally and socially, than any children are likely ever to see again.

In its account of Founder's Day proceedings on Friday, 27 February 1959, meanwhile – the guest of honour was renowned physicist Sir Edward Appleton; our reporter is James McEwan – the magazine, and the school itself, seemed hopelessly behind its times.

> It was the red-letter day in the school almanac. We had met to pay our annual tribute to our Founder. We had also met to take stock of our good fortune and to look forward, fortified by what we had seen on looking back.
>
> It was a kindly day on the Meadows, on the sun-grey Barclay steeple and the sun-red Salisbury Crags. Even the flowers on the high table, reft if not of their crown at least of long sojourn, tossed their heads in sprightly greeting. It was Sir Edward's day.
>
> How, we speculated, would a mind which moves at ease in the spacious firmament on high unbend to address the mature scholars of the 6th and the mites of the Infant Department on the mere brim of this great world? The answer was immediate: with assurance, wisdom and charm. Here was one of the great who had not lost the human touch.
>
> It was Sir Edward's day; but he shared it. At the end of the

The infants' Nativity Play, 1958.

proceedings, after the last bulb had irreverently flashed its intrusion, there took the stage – took it by storm shall we say? – one of these little creatures whom Burns might call a 'dear charmer'. Shall we name her? The record has it as Marion Anne Braithwaite Simpson. 'Toddle' would be a base word to indicate the poise of her progress towards our Guest of Honour. There followed the handing over of the snuff mull; and then one of the most joyous and priceless moments of any Founder's Day we can recall: Sir Edward bent down and kissed her; and she comported herself as if she expected it.

The Lord Provost, Sir Ian A. Johnson-Gilbert, CBE, occupied the chair, introducing Sir Edward and renewing our happy ties with town and gown. The Reverend Roderick Bethune, DD, led the assembly in prayer and Mary Crocket read the lesson from the venerable if a little puzzling type of James Gillespie's own Bible. The choir sang the anthem, 'Ex Ore Innocentium'. The Head Girl, Alison Keith, expressed to Sir Edward the pleasure of the School at his coming away from very important affairs to be with us: there is a kind of violet-by-a-mossy-stone charm about Alison's public utterances which rivals the more gaudily oratorical. Miss Steel graciously added the epilogue.

And so the day came to an end and we trooped down the stairs, the white and green tiles looking more golden, we thought. And we felt that the shade of another scientist, once working away in a smaller capacity beside the Water of Leith at Colinton, must have been watching with almost surprised admiration what wonderful things his homely thrift had wrought.

Sir Edward began 'by thanking the Lord Provost for the happy terms in which he had introduced him, and Miss Steel for the initial invitation. He also congratulated Miss Steel, and through her the whole School, on the honour of her recent appointment as a member of the Advisory Council on Education in Scotland.'

After recalling 'in lighter vein' his earlier association with the girls' schools where his daughters had been educated, Sir Edward Appleton, GBE, KCB, continued –

Of course, I had a connection with schools as an examiner in the School Certificate examinations. Now that was quite a pleasing experience because now and again I got some quite remarkable and amusing answers from school pupils. I remember this which is true in every detail. I once had to mark the answers to a science question – 'imagine that you wish to drink a cup of tea at a railway station before the train starts: imagine also that you are given the tea and milk separate and that the tea is too hot to drink. Will the tea cool quicker if you pour the milk in at once or quicker if you keep the hot tea and milk separate during the cooling process?' I got some peculiar answers. One candidate said: 'The answer to this question depends entirely on whether you want hot tea or cold tea. Personally I loathe it.' And I can vouch for this answer: 'This is rather a silly question because anybody with any sense knows that the best way is to pour it into the saucer and blow on it.' The candidate added those words: 'However, that may be counted an action of the vulgar and so may not be permitted.'

On the subject of examinations, however, I feel I want to say one further thing and I say it especially to those of you here and I hope we shall see some of you coming to Edinburgh University, and to those of you who will be coming on I say this, that while at University, students are told sometimes today that they are wasting their time because at the end of the day so many of them get second-class honours in their examinations, and we often hear people say, 'She only got a Second.' Of course, we people in the University would like to see as many people as possible getting a First but the fact remains that men and women are not created equal. Young people do not all have the same start in life. By that I mean that all of them do not come from equally good homes or equally good schools like yours, so that sometimes getting a Second in the case of one student is as great a feat of mind and character as getting a First in the case of another. As you will see I do not like the remark, 'She only got a Second.' And I think it is applicable only in the rare cases where she has wasted her talent and her opportunities. You must remember this, that the world is really run by the many people who are, so to speak, good enough to get second-class honours and also are dependable. In fact, speaking quite generally, we need lots of people who are second-class in this world because the world is really run by the second-class working out the ideas of the first-class.

We often hear it said about women graduates, 'She got a good degree and then she wasted it by getting married.' Now, I suggest that it is taking far too narrow a view of education which should make us fit to live as well as fit to earn a living. When you educate a man you educate an individual, but when you educate a woman you

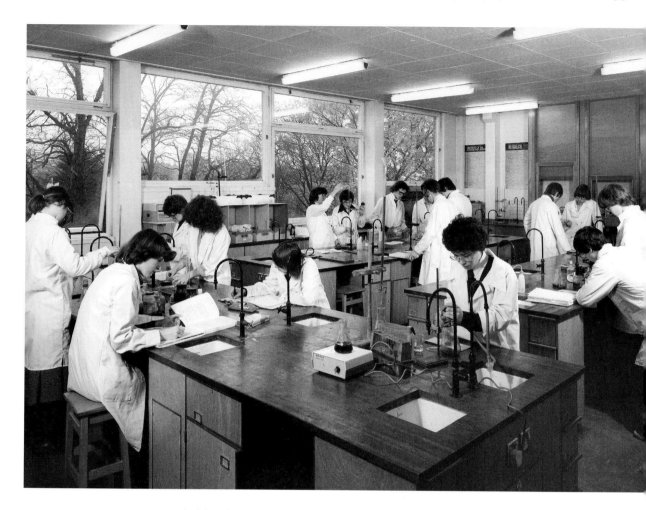

Chemistry, 1978. Even then, many Scottish state schools still actively discouraged girls from the sciences – but never at Gillespie's.

can probably educate a whole family. You see, I never like to think of education as something that is completed either in school or university. It should go on all our lives. I have always had a good deal of sympathy with Mark Twain who said that he never allowed his schooling to interfere with his education.

As the Lord Provost has kindly indicated, I am a scientist by trade and I am not going to apologise at all for recommending that trade – the trade of the scientist – this afternoon to those of you before me who have not made up your mind. The country needs far more scientists. Remember that the only person who has ever been awarded the Nobel Prize twice was a woman, Marie Curie, who won it for both Physics and Chemistry. And in that connection I would like to mention this – we need more women science teachers in our schools. Now I know that although there are certainly today some brilliant women mathematicians, it seems to be the rule that boys often find mathematics an easier subject than you girls. Girls, by the way, generally beat boys in command of language and, of course, words are very important. However, I would like to point this out, that science is not all abstruse and mathematical, especially in the 'applied' side. In Applied Science women in the future are going to succeed. They are essentially practical creatures and I am sure that they find mathematics easier and more attractive when it is applied to things. Apart from science as a career, I think that women should take a greater interest in the 'Science of the Household' – the how and why of domestic affairs – and should make their views and requirements better known. During the war, twenty years ago, men, for the first time, had to take a hand in washing-up. I felt that the whole business was not good enough, so I said to some of my friends in industry that there surely must be something that would help us in this washing-up business – only I called it 'separating food particles from plates.' And so very soon I was given samples to try of the new substances those chemists were then developing – detergents – and the business of washing-up became much easier. That change took place because men were assigned to the kitchen sink, and they made science come to their assistance.

Now today I would say that the biggest problems of the subject of science in the home are concerned with heating the home – space heating and water heating – for here, you see, the situation has changed rapidly during the last few years. The electric fire merely heats, the gas fire heats and ventilates, while the coal fire heats and ventilates and entertains. However, if we wish to continue the privilege of using these benefits of the open fire we have got to produce more smokeless fuels, otherwise we shall be turning to electricity, oil and gas. Well, fortunately, scientists have made great progress in these matters and I myself have seen a number of women scientists in the testing of heating appliances of all kinds. I was glad to see recently that some really promising work was being done by the National Coal Board on the production of smokeless fuels from small coal and coal dust which, as we know, is so plentiful today while large coal is scarce.

I do not want to take more than my allotted time, but I am just touching on one or two subjects and I hope that I have been able to show you that there is a vast field in Applied Science for women.

It only remains for me now to say how grateful I was for the invitation and what a pleasure it has been for me to talk to you here this afternoon.

•   •   •

Born in 1902 and brought up in the Borders – she used shyly to recall her daily two-mile walk to school – Mary Steel won a place at the University of Edinburgh and graduated with a degree in science. She began her teaching career in Eyemouth, Berwickshire; taught subsequently in Dundee, and down south in Derby, and finally returned to Scotland as Head of the Science Department (and 'Second Mistress') in St Leonard's School, St Andrews – a noted independent school and, until 1999, for girls only. She remains the only Head of Gillespie's, to date, to have come from the private sector.

By all accounts, Miss Steel was a gracious woman of unfailing courtesy, a diligent administrator and an upright lady who took avidly to the wider politics of headmistressing. 'As a member of the Scottish Branch of the Association of Headmistresses,' gushed a former colleague, Janet S. A. Macaulay, at her retirement, 'Miss Steel has never, to my knowledge, missed a single meeting. She was a member of the Executive Committee of the Branch from 1958 until 1964 and President from 1961 until 1963. She has represented the Branch on numerous occasions at conferences, national and international; she gave evidence before the Anderson Committee on Grants for Students in 1959; she has been our spokesman at St Andrews House many times; she has been, continuously since 1958, the representative of the Scottish Headmistresses, first on the Secretary of State's Advisory Council for Education, and then on its successor, the Consultative Committee on Educational Matters. But in the midst of attending these important, and often exhausting, meetings with representatives of the Universities, County Councils, Civil Servants and Directors of Education, she has never been too busy to scrutinise SCE syllabuses and examination papers in Chemistry, and make trenchant comments to her colleagues in the Branch.'

If she indulged in 'trenchant comments' at Gillespie's, they do not survive: Miss Steel is one of the most obscure personalities ever to command it. She had neither Miss Andrew's energy nor her sheer physical presence. Even at her appointment, judging by photographs in the school magazine, she was old for her years, a lady whose fashion sense had frozen about 1919: pinned, piled hair and calf-length skirts. The tributes to her

Tall, correct, a little
chilly with children . . .
yet it was on Mary
Steel's watch that the
Lauderdale Street
campus was finally
built.

Gillespie's service, come her departure, are big on compliments and short
on detail. One has the impression of a shy, desk-bound administrator, her
reign best remembered for the removal to the new campus in her final year.
Above average height, she was a 'very nice woman', Iona Cameron insists.
She points out, too, that Steel could be acute, even cunning. Vexed at a host
of unaddressed 'snagging' issues in the new Lauderdale Street premises,
she could have pestered and berated the builders, James Millar & Partners
Ltd. Instead, in honeyed tones, she invited Sir James himself to be the guest
of honour at the last Founder's Day on her watch – and, upon his joyous
acceptance, replied in warm oh-by-the-way terms listing twenty things she
wanted adjusted or fixed. Each was fast, frantically addressed.

But virtually all surviving anecdotes are of rebuke and reproach. Sandra
McCormack, née Todd, remembered one of her friends turning up for
school in suede shoes. 'And Miss Steel saw her. "Get those off, girl! We don't
have these at this school." And she had to walk around in her stocking-feet
for the rest of the day.'

'She was very tall,' Dorothy Cochrane related forty years later, 'and seemed to look down on you from an angle, and had this sort of slightly nervous thing – she seemed to close her eyes when she was speaking. She didn't raise her voice – *that* didn't cause any fear or intimidation; it was just that she was the boss, I think.' One Friday, Dorothy and her friend Jean Knox were caught by their Headmistress, on the streets of Edinburgh, walking home hatless. ' "I want to see you on Monday morning when you come in." And we spent a miserable weekend worrying, "What's she going to do?" She didn't say very much – a weekend quaking in our shoes was quite enough . . . those hats were quite something, weren't they?'

Another girl still cannot forget her. 'Miss Steel used to stand in the bottom corridor and when people came down the stairs or from the side she used to sort of watch people going out – and if their skirts were too short or their hair was too untidy she would just sort of beckon with a finger – and just a quiet word . . . ' 'She was there in authority,' mused a classmate, 'but rather remote . . . ' Another remembers how May Andrew would sometimes visit her Primary classroom, 'and we would all jump up and down like little jack-in-the-boxes, and she would beam, and say, "Good morning, my little rays of sunshine!" ' The veteran Gillespie girl pauses. 'There was none of that with Miss Steel . . . '

Miss Steel appears to have taken weekly classes in Scripture, probably for First Year girls, and quite a few of her appointments survived and even prospered into the comprehensive era – Moira Burnard, Anne Cuthbert, Catherine Lambert, John S. Hay, Jean C. McIntyre and Alexander R. MacKenzie among them. It was a general changing of the guard, with other vast personalities – Allie Anderson, John Brash, Alison Foster, Gertrude Gloag, Anna Munro and Margaret Napier among them – all slipping into retirement in the early Sixties. She did keenly encourage community engagement – raising funds for local charities and so on, and surviving examples of correspondence with former pupils are poised and warm.

Otherwise, she registers in our history as little more than a ghost; not a sentence she wrote or said ever appears in the school magazine. And she was, of course, much in the shadow of her larger-than-life predecessor. At Founder's Day in 1961, half a decade after May Andrew's retirement, Sir James Robertson huffed about his decision, in 1940, to send his own daughter to Gillespie's, largely because of 'the vital power of your late headmistress, an exceptional headmistress who in the twenty years since that has proved herself one of the most outstanding and influential figures in Scottish education'. Nor was there any need, at the same occasion a year later, to heap yet more garlands at the feet of the departed deity – for May

Though of vast girth, 'Allie' Anderson, PE mistress for four decades, was extraordinarily light on her feet, an internationally respected figure in Scottish country dancing, and immensely strong. She once walked all the way home from Prestonpans to Marchmont after an evening teaching dancing to East Lothian miners – and, in retirement, one night swiftly overpowered a burglar, tied him fast to the dining table, retired serenely to bed and called the police in the morning.

Alison Foster (1901–1976) served from 1923 to 1965. She goes down in history as Muriel Spark's English teacher: the author stayed in touch for the rest of her life.

Andrew in 1962 chaired the occasion herself. Miss Steel's emotion can be imagined: her predecessor's inability tactfully to retire to the shadows, and stay there, as Iona Cameron confirms, deeply tried her successors.

Gillespie's had since 1929 steadily acquired more and more of the airs of a private school. The advent of Episcopalian religious instruction suggests, as early as 1934, a pupil-base increasingly privileged – for, in Edinburgh at least, the denomination is very much associated with the well-heeled in general and English incomers in particular. The Literary and Dramatic Society had by the war already begun to share debates and speakers with boys from Heriot's or Watson's. The school's branch of the Edinburgh Schools Citizenship Association likewise let the girls (strictly chaperoned, of course) mingle with the lads of such establishments. Miss Steel herself had come from an independent school and, as is already evident, Founder's Day was now an exalted occasion indeed – the Lord

An entire master of Greek, Latin and classical culture, teaching at Gillespie's from 1923 to 1961, Anna Munro – in a day of better opportunities for woman – would surely have held a university chair. Hugely respected, many former pupils kept in contact with 'Beanie' Munro till her death in 1987.

Shy, correct, the Maths teacher who finally crowned her Gillespie's career as Deputy Headmistress, Miss Margaret 'Nippy' Napier on her 1965 retirement was suddenly all 'pink and twinkle-eyed', a former pupil recalls. For, in her seventh decade, after forty-one years at Gillespie's, the spinster schoolmarm was about to marry the minister of Crieff . . .

Provost in attendance, guests-of-honour being titled or knighted or at least the Moderator of the General Assembly of the Church of Scotland.

There was a certain delicious frisson in 1961, with the first publication of what remains Muriel Spark's most famous novel, *The Prime of Miss Jean Brodie* – which in turn made Gillespie's, to this day, among the most famous schools in the world –

'Meantime I will tell you about my last summer holiday in Egypt . . . I will tell you about care of the skin, and of the hands . . . about the Frenchman I met in the train to Biarritz . . . and I must tell you about the Italian paintings I saw. Who is the greatest Italian painter?'

'Leonardo da Vinci, Miss Brodie.'

'That is incorrect. The answer is Giotto, he is my favourite.'

Some days it seemed to Sandy that Miss Brodie's chest was flat, no bulges at all, but straight as her back. On other days her chest was breast-shaped and large, very noticeable, something for Sandy to sit and peer at through her tiny eyes while Miss Brodie on a day of lessons indoors stood erect, with her brown head held high, staring out of the window like Joan of Arc as she spoke.

'I have frequently told you, and the holidays just past have convinced me, that my prime has truly begun. One's prime is elusive. You little girls, when you grow up, must be on the alert to recognize your prime at whatever time of your life it may occur. You must then live it to the full. Mary, what have you got under your desk, what are you looking at?'

Mary sat lump-like and too stupid to invent something. She was too stupid ever to tell a lie; she didn't know how to cover up.

'A comic, Miss Brodie,' she said.

'Do you mean a comedian, a droll?'

Everyone tittered.

'A comic paper,' said Mary.

'A comic paper, forsooth. How old are you?'

'Ten, ma'am.'

'You are too old for comic papers at ten. Give it to me.'

Miss Brodie looked at the coloured sheets. 'Tiger Tim's, forsooth,' she said, and threw it into the waste-paper basket. Perceiving all eyes upon it she lifted it out of the basket, tore it up beyond redemption and put it back again.

'Attend to me, girls. One's prime is the moment one was born for. Now that my prime has begun – Sandy, your attention is wandering. What have I been talking about?'

'Your prime, Miss Brodie.'

'If anyone comes along,' said Miss Brodie, in the course of the following lesson, 'remember that it is the hour for English grammar. Meantime I will tell you a little of my life when I was younger than I am now, though six years older than the man himself.'

She leaned against the elm. It was one of the last autumn days when the leaves were falling in little gusts. They fell on the children who were thankful for this excuse to wriggle and for the allowable movements in brushing the leaves from their hair and laps.

'Season of mists and mellow fruitfulness. I was engaged to a young man at the beginning of the War but he fell on Flanders' Field,' said Miss Brodie. 'Are you thinking, Sandy, of doing a day's washing?'

'No, Miss Brodie.'

'Because you have got your sleeves rolled up. I won't have to do with girls who roll up the sleeves of their blouses, however fine the weather. Roll them down at once, we are civilized beings . . .'

The atmosphere, the personalities, the dry humour, the assured and acidic Edinburgh concision – all are immediately recognisable to pupils of these years. In one odd respect, things had gone backwards since Spark had attended. At annual Christmas dances, girls had generally been able to bring male partners. For most of Miss Steel's reign this was forbidden, and when she relented it was only on condition that she personally interviewed the proposed boys beforehand. Only the most respectable – and at least attending a private school – passed muster. 'You couldn't be too fussy, you know,' chuckles one Old Girl. On another occasion, a girl was chewed up by one mistress after being glimpsed chatting to a uniformed Heriot's boy on the Links – despite protesting, quite honestly, that he was her brother. Nevertheless, by the mid-1960s, even under all such rules and in such a nunnery of an atmosphere, Gillespie girls were no longer as unworldly as Miss Steel might have wished – as betrayed by a knowing short story in the 1964 school magazine which, somehow, eluded the censor.

Driving Test

'Miss Jane Smith, please!'
Almost lunch-time – hope it's not mince again.
　'Miss Jane Smith! Ah! Right! Come this way.'
Hm – pretty girl. Ha – she's nervous!
　'Yes, it is very cold for June. Your car?'
Needn't think you'll get round me that way, young lady!
　'Move off when you are ready.'
Nice legs!
　'Try turning on the engine first! When you are ready.'
Women – all the same. Take her up the Mound – plenty of traffic and she can do a hill-start on that nasty vertical climb.
　'Turn right and use hand signals only please. RIGHT!!'
Nice pair of legs these. Of course Annie's were good twenty years ago.
　'Left past the traffic lights.'
Hm – no change of gear on approaching lights. Blast! Must buy a new pen.

'Stop halfway up this hill.'
Ha! This is the best part of the test. Hm – reasonable clutch control.
In fact it was quite a good hill-start. Pity.
    'Left at the top.'
She's getting too confident – I'll take her into the High Street again.
    'I am going to say "Now" somewhere along this road and I want
you to stop as quickly as possible.'
Ha – she thinks I'm going to look behind to check the traffic but
I'm not!
    'Now!'
That gave her a fright.
    'Move off when you are ready.'
Her hands were shaking. Fantastic stockings they wear these days.
Annie still wears these thick fawn ones.
    'Second road on the left and stop at the corner. Reverse round it
keeping close to the kerb.'
Hm – didn't check blind-spot.
    'First on the right and then third on the left.'
Ten minutes till lunch-time. Too close to that bus. She doesn't use
the mirror enough. Ask her some code questions and that's that.
    'Draw up in front of that blue B.S.M. car if you please.'
What was that one the last girl didn't know? Ah, yes!
    'What are the two most difficult manoeuvres in driving?'
If she knows this one, I'll ask her the questions on braking distances
and level crossings and night parking.
    'I see. Thank you.'
Ha – she doesn't know whether she was right or not – let her sweat
it out for a few minutes. Shall I pass her? Let's see – I've failed twelve
out of twenty this week... Hm – nice legs!
    'You have passed the test.'

                                                    Carol Baillie, 6B1

It is an astute and chilling view of the world as a shrewd young woman
then saw it – one still largely gripped by the whims of men. And an enterprise utterly directed by men – badly – was, of course, now well under way
in the gardens, lawns and bluebell woods surrounding Bruntsfield House,
even as pupils grew ever less amenable to conforming to an old woman's
idea of a young one. As the joke already ran, you can always tell a Gillespie
Girl – but you can't tell her much.
    'Great and terrible machines are devouring the loved mansionry of

Bruntsfield House,' sighed Mr McEwan in the 1964 magazine. 'Trees have toppled and trenches are filling with concrete which presently will support beams and walls. We are on the move. The new school, at various times a promise, a chimera, is taking shape before our eyes.

'And now, unbelievably, we are experiencing emotions we never thought would disturb our souls. The red Dumfries stone, the green slates laid with a precision a slater once told us made him feel proud every time he looked at them from Whitehouse Loan, the stairs – the interminable stairs – with their white tiles, and the pigeons on the balcony strutting raucously up and down like Horse Guards, and the Barclay Church, and the Castle, and the Lomonds away across in Fife: our school – 'for many a year renowned' – at least for many a year beloved, will know us no more. Will the harsh angularities of glass and concrete now rising round Bruntsfield House readily house the elusive *genius loci* of our home on the Links? This, anyhow, marks the great change and the great challenge that in about a couple of years from now we must face . . .'

And pupil-editor Anne Naysmith was in thoughtful trim in the 1966 editorial –

'But the best I've known
Stays here . . .'

We are the last of the old guard. The new school stands ready, awaiting occupation. Future years will learn amid gleaming equipment and fresh paint, isolated from the traffic by the green lawns and trees of the grounds of Bruntsfield House. And, like the school, we who are leaving are moving from the old world to the new. We too are forsaking the shelter of familiar surroundings to take our places in modern society. This year is a time of change, a time for abandoning old traditions and forming new habits, both for the School and those who are leaving it . . .'

•   •   •

On Friday, 21 October 1966, about nine in the morning in a small Welsh mining village, the children of Pantglas Junior School were just filing from assembly – they had been singing 'All Things Bright and Beautiful' – when they heard (and felt) the most terrible roaring, rushing, onward noise from the huge mountain of colliery spoil dominating the view from their class-rooms. 'It was a tremendous rumbling sound and all the school went dead,' an eight-year-old girl remembered. 'You could hear a pin drop. Everyone just froze in their seats. I just managed to get up and I reached the end of my desk when the sound got louder and nearer, until I could see the black out of the window. I can't remember any more but I woke up to find that a horrible nightmare had just begun in front of my eyes . . .' Afterwards, there was only terrible quietness. 'In that silence,' George Williams would remember, 'you couldn't hear a bird or a child.' A wall of nearly one and a half million cubic feet of mud, rock and slag – a malevolent river some forty feet deep – had smashed onto the village and the children of Aberfan: 116 youngsters died, and 28 adults.

In Edinburgh, that afternoon, all carried along as planned, as James McEwan later related in his characteristic manner and with no reference whatever to the horror in Wales.

The Royal Visit and the Opening of the New School by Her Majesty Queen Elizabeth the Queen Mother

This happy and unforgettable day in the history of the school was ushered in by 'ane orient blast' and Aeolus seemed regrettably in the ascendant. But at 2.45 p.m. the sharp wind had whipped the sky clear, and when the Royal car swung through the Main Entrance gate into the Avenue, the warmth of the greeting from the throats of the tiny scholars lining the route could leave Her Majesty in no doubt as to the cordiality of our welcome. Simultaneously, the Royal Standard was broken on the flag staff beside the Clock Tower.

At the main entrance to the sixteenth-century Bruntsfield House, the Lord Provost, the Rt. Hon. Herbert H. Brechin, C.B.E., presented to Her Majesty the Lady Provost; Councillor John Fitzpatrick, the Chairman of the Education Committee; Dr George Reith, the Director of Education; our School Chaplain, the Rev. R. Leonard Small, O.B.E., D.D., Moderator of the General Assembly of the Church of Scotland; Cmndr. Clark Hutchison, M.P. for South Edinburgh; representatives of the architects and the main contractors; and Miss Mary D. Steel, Headmistress of the School.

Her Majesty, accompanied by Her Maid of Honour, and guests, thereafter entered, by the main foyer, the School Hall, where the other guests and pupils representing all Forms were already assembled. As the Royal party entered, the Choir and the Orchestra joined in a stirring welcome, 'quhois armony to heir it wes delyt'.

The Opening Ceremony began with a prayer of dedication by

the School Chaplain. The assembly then sang the 121st Psalm, 'I to the hills will lift mine eyes,' which was followed by prayer. The Lord Provost then invited Her Majesty to declare open the new school. In an address of great charm, Her Majesty spoke of the increasingly important role played by women in this swiftly developing scientific age, reminding her young listeners, however, that a woman may best fulfil her destiny by being a good wife and a good mother, and that a happy home may well represent the culmination of her success in life. After Her Majesty had graciously declared the school open, bouquets were presented by the School Captain and Vice-Captain. A vote of thanks was proposed by the Chairman of the Education Committee. The assembly then joined in singing 'God Save the Queen', with a sincerity and fervour born of the occasion and the graciousness of the Royal Guest.

After the proceedings in the Hall were at an end, Her Majesty then visited the Swimming Pool, where Second Year girls were under instruction. Miss Catherine H. Lambert, Principal Teacher of Physical Education, was presented to Her Majesty by the Head-mistress.

Miss Steel, Lord Provost Brechin and HM Queen Elizabeth the Queen Mother, who always knew where the cameras were.

Opposite.
Clarence House and
the Corporation
'had refused to let
the school supply
the pen', one
teacher remembers,
'and the one they
brought with them
wouldn't work'.
Left to right,
Provost Brechin,
the Queen Mother,
Miss Steel and
Miss Ferguson.

Her Majesty continued to the Library. There the School Captain, Catherine Falconer, and the School Vice-Captain, Linda Dickson, and Miss Lilian W. Paterson, Principal Teacher of Modern Languages, Mr Harry Milne, Principal Teacher of Russian, and Mr John S. Hay, Principal Teacher of Classics, were presented to Her Majesty.

After an inspection of the Library, the Royal party then returned to the main entrance to the Assembly Hall. There the Lord Provost invited Her Majesty to unveil a commemorative plaque in bronze on the wall recording, for our successors, the day's events.

Her Majesty then continued on a tour of inspection of the teaching departments of the school, her first visit being to an English classroom, where Sixth Year girls were studying English literature. Her Majesty asked some of the girls about their studies and learned that an interest in modernity did not preclude an enthusiasm for Shelley. Mr James D. McEwan, Principal Teacher of English, was presented to Her Majesty.

A visit was next paid to the Art and the Commercial departments. Here Her Majesty showed keen interest in the work that was being done with advanced equipment, such as accounting machines and potters' wheels and kilns. Miss Jean C. McIntyre, Principal Teacher of History, Miss Christina M. McIntyre, Principal Teacher of Commercial Subjects, and Miss Eileen D. Campbell, Principal Teacher of Art, were presented to Her Majesty.

The Royal visitor then entered the Science building where she examined the work that was being done in the Needlework and the Domestic Science departments. Mrs Mary E. Jenkins, Principal Teacher of Domestic Science, Miss Madaline H. A. Dunbar, Principal Teacher of Chemistry, Mr Alexander B. Dall, Principal Teacher of Geography, Miss Barbara M. Reid, Principal Teacher of Mathematics, Mr Alexander R. MacKenzie, Principal Teacher of Physics, and Mr Thomas Sommerville, Principal Teacher of Music, were presented to Her Majesty in the Science Building.

Her inspection of the work of the school being completed, Her Majesty then returned to Bruntsfield House, where, in the Headmistress's Room, the Lord Provost invited Her Majesty to sign the Visitors' Book. Miss Emily A. K. Ferguson, the Deputy Headmistress, was here presented. Her Majesty then graciously accepted an invitation to have tea in the Music Room, whose sixteenth-century architectural splendour provided a fitting framework for

the concluding events of this great day. Here several ladies, including
Miss May Andrew, C.B.E., were presented to Her Majesty.

Thereafter, escorted by the Lord Provost and the Headmistress,
Her Majesty returned to the Main Entrance of Bruntsfield House,
and there took leave of the school. As the Royal car, with this
gracious lady, drove slowly along the entrance avenue, the grand
elms looking down on the youthful scholars' full-hearted farewell,
one's mind turned to the words which the captivated merchant from
Augsburg addressed to her famous ancestor, their relevance seeming
to echo the sentiments in every heart:-

'Scho wes sa beauteous, sa gracious and sa kind that men
thocht her mair worthy to be servit for little profet than any
uther prince in Europe for gret commoditie.'

Pupils subsequently organised a collection, given 'the tragic coincidence of our Royal Visit with the catastrophe in Aberfan', and the sum of £36 was sent to Wales.

Mary Steel retired as Headmistress on 31 March 1967, the occasion marked by a formal dinner in the city's Roxburgh Hotel. 'With a natural obeisance to established tradition,' recorded McEwan, 'we found "that the chambres and the tables weren wyde, and wel we weren esed ate beste"; and when, at length, the victuals had been dispatched, "the wyn was fet anon"; the conversational shuttlecock had deftly flicked from tongue to ear; what more fitting than that our sweetest minstrel should be accorded the last word. For his first song Mr Sommerville took, "O, Mistress mine, where are you roaming?" (even minstrels can be subtle) by Roger Quilter; and for his second, "Five Eyes" by Armstrong Gibbs. This great gift of Mr Sommerville's, which his fastidiousness permits him to exercise so rarely, makes us, when he does, entrancedly his debtors . . .'

The girls had earlier that day presented Miss Steel with a silver tea service and tray, an onyx clock and an album of photographs. At a separate ceremony she received a Parker fountain pen from the Prefects, 'suitably inscribed'. The Former Pupils saw her off with a silver and enamel brooch in the shape of a rose; janitors and cleaning staff gave her an Edinburgh Crystal salad bowl, 'the ladies of the Dining Centre' a matching Edinburgh Crystal vase – and the staff a specially commissioned studio-photograph of their departing commander. It hung in the library for many years, but was latterly laid on the floor against the wall in an obscure corner, its glass cracked.

Miss Steel quietly died in August 1981. Jean McIntyre, for the rest of her days, maintained that, as the last Empress of India 'inspected' the new facilities that Friday of Aberfan, she stumbled momentarily and, but for Miss Lambert's lightning reaction and burly arm, Her Majesty would have toppled sideways into the new swimming pool. Doubtless still smiling radiantly.

CHAPTER SEVEN

'Nothing stands still for ever'
1967–1975

Miss Mary G. McIver was introduced to the staff, by preening dignitaries, in the new school library as the new Headmistress on Tuesday, 18 April 1967. Councillor Fitzpatrick, James McEwan relates, 'congratulated the school on its good fortune in securing, at this moment when momentous changes are fermenting in Scottish education, the services of such an experienced and wise hand to guide its destinies through the challenging days ahead. Dr Reith then expressed his pleasure at having the opportunity to reinforce this message of good will, and speculated briefly on the problems ahead and the satisfaction that would assuredly come in their resolution . . . In her reply, Miss McIver gave revealing evidence that she wanted no part of the skill or elegance of phrase which such performances require . . .'

The teachers again assembled in the library on Thursday for a less formal function, pleasant speeches being made before staff and Headmistress enjoyed a light lunch. Miss McIver then, that afternoon, made the round of the classrooms, 'where she met the girls and was made aware of the cordiality of their welcome'.

The careless readily dismiss the tiny Mary McIver as a grey, transitional Head of the school, sandwiched (with Miss Steel) between two big, long-reigning personalities and doubtless overwhelmed by the wholesale change from 1973. That McIver was an extraordinarily self-effacing lady, leaving very little on personal record, certainly tempts such an assessment. In truth, she was an extremely able woman, a shrewd and hands-on leader, with an acute grasp of the times and great, intensely pastoral respect for her girls – and, when the challenge of the comprehensive order came, she met it coolly, shrewdly and with relish, as those of lesser stuff wilted and fled. Mary McIver wrote (and worked) with extraordinary concision, never wasting a word, nailing down the essentials. We have a photograph of her

Mary McIver, on her first day in charge. Quiet, but she accomplished much with that quietness.

152

James Gillespie (1726–97) of Spylaw, by Sir James Foulis, Bt – oil on canvas. (City Art Centre, Edinburgh Museums and Galleries)

The monument to James Gillespie on Edinburgh's Royal Mile. What was once his tobacco shop is now Gordon's Trattoria. (Andrew Digance)

Portrait of John Robertson (1770–1849), first Headmaster of James Gillespie's Free School, by William Allan. Robertson held the post for a mighty forty years. He looks tired, but kind. (Merchant Company of Edinburgh / John McKenzie Photography)

Gillespie's Hospital, as originally built, home to the school from 1874 to 1914 on what is now Gillespie Crescent. After subsequent decades as the Royal Blind Asylum, it was demolished with very little fuss in 1975.

Books presented in the 1890s, with beautiful prize-labels. (Andrew Digance)

'The School on the Links.' This majestic building, originally erected for Boroughmuir Secondary School, housed Gillespie's from 1914 to 1966. After an uncertain quarter-century it was sold to Edinburgh University and converted to student accommodation in the 1990s. (Andrew Digance)

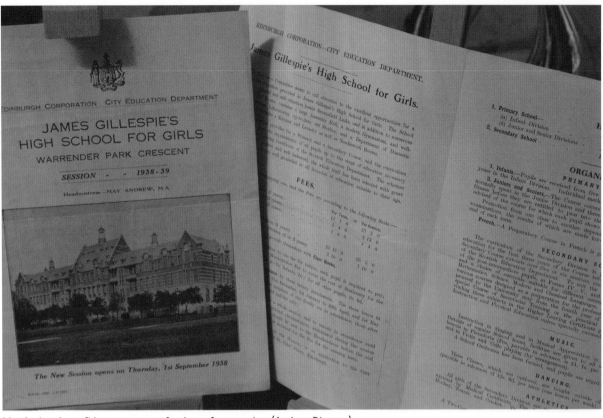

May Andrew's confident prospectus for the 1938–39 session. (Andrew Digance)

A ceremonial oaken chair, presented to the school by the Swimming Club in 1938 with a matching lectern and table. They survive, but have seen little use since Dr Thomas's time. (Andrew Digance)

A spread of colourful school reports from the 1940s, each in log-book format for a girl's whole High School career. (Andrew Digance)

'A little spoon-fed, but very well taught!' One young lady's record, late 1940s. (Andrew Digance)

The old school Bible, with splendidly embroidered markers bearing the traditional cipher. (Andrew Digance)

Above left. 'We were Gillespie Girls . . .' Linda Urquhart's surviving blazer, with assorted honours and haberdashery (and one of the dreaded hats) from the school's collection. Badges reflected 'House' colours – Gilmore, blue; Roslin, yellow; Spylaw, red; and Warrender, green. (Andrew Digance)

Above right. The splendid hand-painted frontispiece of the Hockey Club records book, 1954. (Andrew Digance)

Right. Alison Laidlaw strolling down the avenue, near the end of her teaching career. A memorial garden, very near this spot, was completed in her memory after her death in 2007 – ending her 93-year relationship with the school as pupil, teacher and friend.

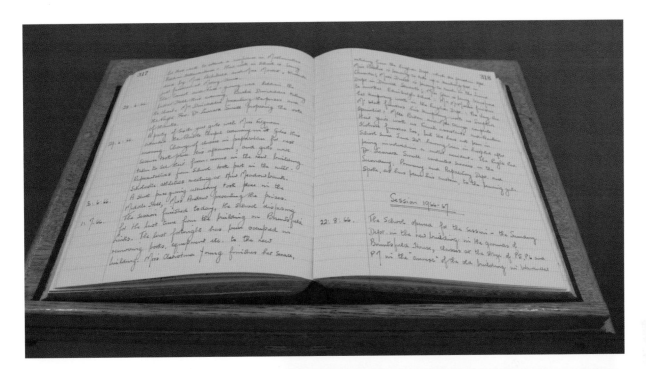

Above. New beginnings in 1966, as detailed – in her immaculate handwriting – by Miss Steel in the school log. (Andrew Digance)

Right. 'And did you and the boys have joint discos?' 'Oh, we were much more sophisticated than that – we had joint debating societies!' Programmes for successive Burns Suppers, 1960s. (Andrew Digance)

Evening shadows, 1981. This view, from the music classroom on the top storey of Bruntsfield House, is fondly remembered by many.

Miss Lambert in glowering pride with her Hockey 1st XI side, 1978–79 session. An unforgettable personality, she served at Gillespie's from 1957 to 1989. Though fond of bellowing, small cigars and the odd nip of whisky, the ferocious persona she affected occasionally cracked in kindly, guffawing humour.

Ian Nicol with his junior rugby side, 1978–79 session. Accessible, good-hearted and gentle, he was much beloved.

Allan Leslie (1949–88) and his senior basketball side, 1978–79. One of Miss McIver's most inspired appointments, he was not only a brilliant teacher but a mainstay of outdoor activity and trips away, and was immensely popular.

Typical Edinburgh weather in changing times, 1981: wet pavement, fitful sunshine, hints of autumn, 'a mishmash of maroon blazers, grey flannel and the odd defiant blur of denim . . .'

Dr Thomas, flanked by Alan Waugh and Stewart McDougall, with prefects in August 1988, at the start of the new school session. A few years later, blazers – never mind prefects – were as Nineveh and Tyre.

Kevin Woods, Sandra Evans, Tom Johnson and (nearest the camera) John Kilday enjoying the staff Christmas dinner in December 2000. The teachers were waited on by Colin Finlayson and his senior management team (all in fetching bow-ties) as a demonstration of 'servant leadership'.

Pupils performing in the foyer of the Lyceum Theatre on 28 January 2003. Jay Presson Allen's dramatisation of Muriel Spark's *The Prime of Miss Jean Brodie* had been revived for a widely praised run, starring Siobhan Redmond, and James Gillespie's High School boldly booked the whole theatre on opening night for staff, pupils and parents. It was among various events marking that year's bicentenary – and exuded the confidence of a school no longer haunted by the past.

Alex Wallace and Colin Finlayson at a Civic Reception in Edinburgh City Chambers to mark the school's bicentenary. Though Wallace (left) only succeeded Finlayson as Head Teacher in October 2003, the two men had worked closely since Wallace's appointment as AHT late in 1991 and, latterly, as Finlayson's deputy. Of a new and more informal style of leadership, they were a formidable team and pupils loved them.

Appointed in 1974, A.J. 'Tony' Merriman retired thirty-four years later as a Gillespie's institution. He was kind, funny, and sometimes extremely loud.

An inspirational history teacher and of rich personal hinterland – a keen musician, he had hung out with the likes of Gerry Rafferty – Ian Caddell, of big hair and crazy ties, was highly esteemed. After his sudden death in June 2011, distressed pupils designed an especially colourful tie in his memory.

Massed pupils on the Usher Hall stage for the finale of the 2012 Christmas Concert. Deirdre O'Brien is in command. (Andrew Digance)

And great was the fall of it, December 2013. (Andrew Digance)

If trees could talk, June 2014. (Andrew Digance)

Purpose-built for 'Curriculum for Excellence,' the new Malala building was an immediate hit with pupils. (Andrew Digance)

Keeping it casual, April 2015. An exhaustive consultation established, by year's end, that there was no appetite for a return to formal uniform among pupils, staff or even parents. (Andrew Digance)

The fall of the house of Spylaw, May 2015. (Andrew Digance)

Donald Macdonald, Head Teacher, celebrating in December 2015 with senior pupils after the *Sunday Times* pronounced Gillespie's the top state school in Scotland. (Neil Hanna)

A new First Year, a new term, a new school . . . new beginnings, September 2016. (Andrew Digance)

on her very first day in service, bright, birdlike, bristling with energy; we
have a final one, as she demitted her post eight years later (having selflessly
postponed comfortable, moneyed retirement) oozing the serene, amused
authority of a velvety turtle-dove.

Born in 1911, Miss McIver remains the only Glaswegian to have
commanded Gillespie's, the first to have been a head teacher already, a
graduate from that city's University with First-Class Honours in Modern
Languages, and, by blood and close descent, a Highlander. Her father,
himself a head teacher (in Bowling) was a native of Poolewe in Wester Ross,
who latterly served with HM Inspectorate of Schools; her grandmother
was from the Isle of Skye. Beyond that were deep ancestral roots in Lewis.

Even now, Miss McIver is remembered fondly for her service in Modern
Languages at Glasgow's Jordanhill College School, from 1937 to 1952. They
would miss, lamented Headmaster Andrew Walker in that year's school
magazine recording assorted departures, yet 'another experienced teacher,

Miss McIver, who left to become Principal Teacher of Modern Languages and Woman Adviser in Elgin Academy. Miss McIver served Jordanhill faithfully and well for fifteen years. Her well-earned promotion gave us all great pleasure – we could not grudge her this – and we knew that her many fine qualities would be increasingly recognised in her responsible post.' He added, astutely, 'Her quiet efficiency and her sane resourcefulness in coping with any emergency will always be recalled when we remember her.'

After Elgin, McIver became Headmistress of Stobswell Girls' Secondary School in Dundee 'where she gained a high reputation for her efforts on behalf of the pupils'. On one occasion, she, in retirement, quietly told Iona Cameron, she had spent a fraught evening driving around the city with a distressed and terrified lass, who had fallen pregnant and whose appalled parents had thrown her out; her headmistress finally found caring accommodation for her. With Miss McIver, Miss Cameron says, 'the girls came before everything'.

Her sister Isabella, incidentally, was a no less distinguished Headmistress, leading Hutcheson's Girls School in Glasgow from 1948 to 1973 – and it has been recorded of her by a Hutcheson's historian, and says much for the times, that 'Miss McIver's values seemed to have a quality recuperative of the past about them . . . in a time where the Cold War meant that survival of the schools might seem of lesser importance than the survival of humanity itself, this was only normal, and it was the truth of life in post-war Scottish senior secondary education for a long time to come. Pupils in the late Sixties, for example, had an English syllabus not markedly different from the Forties pupil, and this was true of HGS until the end of the Seventies – if not later . . .'

Mary McIver was a very small, trim woman with a shy smile, much less austere than her predecessor but no less correct, and had but one indulgence: she was a very heavy smoker. She was, like many Gaels, of modest, watchful personality, but in some regards a strikingly open-minded woman. She was the first to institute Pupil Councils, which have lasted in one form or another ever since, giving children a platform to contribute their own ideas on the running of Gillespie's. She happily granted all Sixth Years the privilege of wearing a plain maroon tie (a prerogative hitherto exclusive to prefects). She was determined her girls should shine; grow in confidence. In her first session, she insisted that certain classes – like Higher English – should be taught in double-periods, granting more time for focused study and discussion. James McEwan had a fit of pearl-clutching vapours. 'But,' he protested, 'we have already *given*, for a full period . . .' 'Mr McEwan,' said Miss McIver firmly, 'then let the *girls* give!'

She also established a system of pastoral care on which her successor would build – two Tutors for each House, and a Senior Tutor overseeing these first endeavours in Guidance. Miss McIver encouraged outdoor pursuits – it was in these years Gillespie's began its use of the Benmore Outdoor Centre, by Dunoon; succoured the Scripture Union; brought in for the first time outside lecturers; and developed assorted forms of voluntary and community service for her pupils – overcoming much staff resistance, calmly resolving personality clashes, showing all the while calm, understated leadership and a Stakhanovite work-ethic. All is modestly recorded in her brief, precise daily notes in the handwritten School Log; Miss McIver was the last Head Teacher to keep it.

•   •   •

The new school, opened in 1966, was very much in the spirit of the Sixties – modernist, angular, flat or valley-roofed constructions of brick, wholly in keeping with what Harold Wilson's 'white heat of the technological revolution'. It had been designed by Rowland Anderson, Kinmouth and Paul, an architectural partnership on Edinburgh's Rutland Square; the main contractors were James Millar & Partners Ltd of 18 George Street. The City Architect, A. Steele, played his part too, as they strove to make best use of a tight sloping site with, at its heart, an historic townhouse.

'In designing the new buildings,' cooed its fathers, 'the architects have preserved as many as possible of the fine existing trees and have used to advantage two groups of magnificent evergreen yews and conifers. The buildings have been grouped around the trees and the house in an attempt to give the school the essentially domestic character that is not character-istic of many new schools. As a suitable background to these trees a handmade facing pit [brick] from Northumberland has been chosen which with its deeply recessed pointing fits in with the reddish rubble stonework of the house.'

It was certainly a much more attractive campus than many erected in Scotland in that decade. The great gate and archways over the avenue from Whitehouse Loan survived as a distinguished entrance and the forecourt of Bruntsfield House, with the stately sweep of steps up to the main buildings and the lofty clock tower overlooking them, had undoubted expansiveness. The steps soon proved an imposing setting for school photographs. The library, with its parquet flooring and fashionable Scandic furnishings, was an attractive space (rather spoiled by averred improve-ments in the late 1980s). There were two main teaching blocks. One, parallel

with Lauderdale Street and visible the length of Spottiswoode Road, had English classrooms on the ground floor, Mathematics and Arithmetic on the first and Modern Languages and the Social Sciences on the second. By the end of the coming Dr Thomas's rule it had been named Warrender. Near the Lauderdale Street entrance, built in matching style, was a little house for the janitor.

What became Spylaw stood on the Whitehouse Loan side, its boxy lines at least softened by old trees. Domestic Science – soon to be rebranded Home Economics – was taught on the ground floor and the two floors above were given over to Biology, Chemistry and Physics. The top storey had also a lecture theatre. A third single-storey building, parallel to its gable, housed classrooms for Art and Commercial Studies and was later named Thirlestane.

The biggest complex, down at the same level as Bruntsfield House and linked to its first floor by a sort of corridor-bridge, contained the timber-

Bruntsfield House after completion of the new school in 1966. Several Victorian excrescences had been sensibly removed: forty-seven years later, so was that hideous bridge.

lined Assembly Hall, the gym and swimming pool, a secluded upstairs staffroom for teachers and an even more spacious common room (with a little courtyard) for senior girls; not surprisingly, these were eventually swapped. The hall was rather magnificent, with a stage and great curtain, and a raised walkway down one side linking it to other buildings in the complex – where, besides, the prefects sat in their pomp during school services. On the other side ran splendid floor-to-ceiling windows. At the rear of the hall, as built and through my time in the early 1980s, was a tiered area for the seating of the massed school choir or whole-year assemblies, but this was by 2012 gone, ending one useful public-performance aspect of the space – that, depending on the function, the audience could be seated facing the most appropriate end.

Adjacent to the Sixth Form common room was the library. The main foyer afforded ample wall-space for honours boards, trophies, the Merchant Company plaque, Camley's bust of Mr Gillespie and that portrait of Miss Andrew. By my time, some fourteen years later, there was an encased barograph. There was a brief upper floor with a single classroom, Music Room 2, and then that bridge into the splendid first-floor drawing room of Bruntsfield House, now Music Room 1. Across a lobby the scarcely less grand sometime dining room was the Head Teacher's office (and would so remain till the summer of 2015). There was another music classroom at the top of Bruntsfield House, and a number of intimate little practice rooms. The ground floor was largely taken up with school administration. Its atmospheric flagstoned hall was soon graced by artwork presented by the former pupils, and a Jacobean settle donated to the memory of a former Dux, Jean Catherine MacAnna, by her bereft husband, Alexander E. Drysdale. She died in 1967, aged but thirty-eight. It is still there.

Bruntsfield House has a long and deliciously dark history. Until the great tenement developments of the 1870s it stood, of course, in its great walled gardens in open countryside. Built in the late sixteenth century, it was effectively an insurance job, replacing a much older and probably much more fortified building burned down by English troops, under the command of the Earl of Somerset (Henry VIII's brother-in-law) during the 'Rough Wooing' assault on Edinburgh in 1544. A 1381 charter by King Robert II grants 'Broune's Fields' lands to one Alan de Lawdre, evidently of Norman stock; his annual payment to the Crown for possession of Bruntsfield was 'a silver penny payable at the Burrow Mure on the feast of St John the Baptist . . . if asked'. How Edinburgh.

King James IV is said to have stood on a knoll within the current school grounds to watch his forces marshal on the Boroughmuir for their fateful date at Flodden. Lauder descendants retained the estate till 1603 and it was then acquired by John Fairlie of Braid, who 'made a number of improvements and built a substantial extension to the east of the existing house. The date, 1605, and the initials of himself and his wife, Elizabeth Westoun, appear on several window lintels.'

In 1695 the Fairlies sold their house and estate to George Warrender, a successful merchant who became Lord Provost of Edinburgh in 1713 and – with suspiciously convenient Hanoverian timing – was elevated to the baronetcy, that hereditary knighthood, in 1715. It was his descendant, another Sir George (and the local MP) who from 1869 made a considerable fortune by feuing off his lands for the erection of Marchmont's tenement-gulches. The names of these streets all honour some Warrender relation or other, as Charles Smith details in his *Historic South Edinburgh*.

As every Gillespie's pupil knows, the house is said, deliciously, to boast a ghost. Actually, there are two. Unseen horses and a carriage are said to rattle up and down the avenue of an eerie night – a mounting-block still stands in front of Bruntsfield House – and the still more mysterious 'Green Lady' is said unhappily to waft around its garrets. The latter Sir George Warrender greatly fuelled this legend by noticing, one day, taking the air in his grounds, that Bruntsfield House had one too many windows. A secret room! A senior retainer was confronted, and denied all knowledge of it, until seriously menaced. The bricked-up entrance was found hidden behind a tapestry. Sir George duly forced it. 'Inside all was intact and undisturbed since last it has been occupied; ashes were still in the fireplace, and . . . bloodstains on the floor!' The skeleton of an infant was found below the window; the mystery was never explained. One suspects a dark business of concealed pregnancy and panicked infanticide.

This Sir George died in 1901, his diminished and overlooked manor and gardens passed to trustees, and the family seem subsequently to have neglected Bruntsfield House, which by the early 1930s was threatened with demolition. Sir Victor Warrender, though, sought its survival and, after protracted talks, he signed over his life-interest in house and grounds to Edinburgh Corporation, on the firm and express terms that they could only be used for a 'school, hospital, home, museum, art gallery, institute, public hall, public library, public park, recreation ground, swimming baths, public offices, garden, allotments or for any other public or municipal purpose in connection with the welfare of the City of Edinburgh.' As we have noted, it was in 1937 decided to use it for a new Gillespie's – local uproar had put paid to such suggestions as a children's home or a

BRUNTSFIELD HOUSE

Violins squeaking
Computers speaking
Pianos trilling
Phone bells shrilling
Pupils singing
School Bells ringing
Desks and chairs
Spiral stairs
Broken props of by-gone shows
Share a box with 'cello bows
Deep in a cupboard lie cracked recordings
Of Usher Hall concerts now in mourning.

And now we come to B13
That room of the Lady clad in green
Always locked that room remains
Always quiet - a private domain
Perhaps at night a solitary light
Winds its way down those spiral stairs
Perhaps, she tries those wooden chairs
Perhaps those 'phone bells ring as well
As ghostly friends call up from hell
Pianos play - 'Perhaps' you say
Explain the 'lid up' the very next day
So you think you're a whizz when it comes to computing
But the Lady's better - there's no disputing.

So in Bruntsfield House if you think you see
A silent shadow near room one-three
Remember this tale and don't dismiss
This ghostly Lady as an ancient myth!

                    J. Wood, S.4

workhouse – but Bruntsfield House was requisitioned by the authorities during the Second World War and planning permission was not finally granted till 1963. During the works it was sensibly decided to remove some Victorian extensions out of character with the original building; and its most charming apartments had escaped serious damage in the fire of April 1953. But the subsequent construction of two large modern schools in half a century inevitably felled a great many magnificent trees.

Nothing in the coverage and publicity that attended the opening of the new James Gillespie's High School for Girls suggests anything but confidence that the campus would stand and work for the foreseeable future. Time and Providence instead ensured that every last new building (and, indeed, the extensions of 1990) were flattened and replaced before its fiftieth birthday.

It was undone by events and capacity. The 1966 campus was designed for – at most – eight hundred girls. By the late 1970s, and for years thereafter, the school roll was rarely south of 1,200. At one point it was a gulping 1,250. The buildings had been conceived, too, with the evident vision of a sedate ladies' college. There was, for instance, abundant outdoor seating where a budding bluestocking might repose with a book. But there was nowhere (save one small area of fenced tarmac tennis courts) where youngsters could play games. Neither grounds nor buildings were well suited to the exuberance of children and (later, in all their physicality) boys. By modern standards of disabled access, the new Gillespie's was embarrassing. There were no lifts, doorways and corridors were uncomfortably narrow, and the main complex, especially, had several short flights of steps and stairs.

The heating system was blithely linked to the heating of the swimming pool, which meant it had to be run all year round. A windowed corridor granting a ringside view of children in and around the swimming pool would not, today, be acceptable. The acoustics of the hall were dreadful: when, for instance, senior *Scotsman* journalist Chris Baur delivered the Founder's Day address in 1983, you strained to hear him. Horizontally hinged windows, prone to drop and slam and on occasion shatter, proved dangerous; several pupils over the decades were badly injured. Flat roofs, in time, began to leak. And, local Pharos as the stately Clock Tower fast became, it never really worked – its great bronze hands were too heavy for the mechanism.

The school was not ten years old before settlement and subsidence issues became evident; the leaks chronic – though, for many years thereafter, staff and pupils struggled on gamely in premises that were badly

Opposite.
The Green Lady is a cherished part of school mythology. Certainly, one does not lightly linger in Bruntsfield House at night. From *Snuff,* 1984.

designed, of cheap materials, and criminally built. Around 1988 there was an exhaustive survey of the whole campus. The only building passed as structurally sound (to general ye'll-have-had-yer-tea hilarity) was Bruntsfield House.

•   •   •

The Sixties swung, and life went on. The year 1966 had seen the first Gillespie's exchange pupil, Helen McConachie, study for a year in the United States as part of the American Field Service Programme. Twenty-two senior pupils had visited Russia. Founder's Day speakers continued to patronise. 'When they are looking for a career,' as Sir James Millar's address in February 1967 was reported, having guilelessly fulfilled Miss Steel's cunning wish-list, 'Sir James advised them to consider that the best career still open to girls was to be a successful wife and mother . . .' Professor Michael Swann, Principal of the University of Edinburgh, echoed him a year later. 'If you look at what is predominately a man's world – politics, medicine and science – you do nevertheless find quite a lot of women who have made their mark. I think, without exception, if they compete on equality with men, they can actually do just as well if they want to. The fact of the matter is that, in the home, with children making the demands they do, most of you won't need to compete in a man's world. You will in fact be looking after families in your own home. Some silly people in this day and age tend to feel that this is a second-rate occupation. I do not think this is second-rate: I think this is perhaps the most important occupation that there is . . .'

Staff passed from the scene. Miss Douglas retired in 1967 after over four decades imparting French at Gillespie's. Miss Paterson retired as Principal Teacher of Modern Languages later that year. Mairi Macdonald (of close Lewis ancestry) moved up to replace her. Mr McEwan stood down in December 1967, and was succeeded in January 1968 by the engaging, formidably clever Iona M. Cameron. She was one of several new arrivals around this period – Jean Mcintyre had taken over the History Department in 1966; Miss Cuthbert – who would retire as a Gillespie's institution – was already diminutive queen of the Film Society. The highly strung Miss Ferguson had become full-time Deputy Headmistress and Robert Galt replaced her as Principal Teacher of Biology. Mabel Marr's long and ferocious service – the very last of Mr Burnett's teachers: '*Rrrreason*, girrrl!' – ended with her retirement on 1 January 1972; she had taught at Gillespie's for thirty-nine years.

New sports took some hold: basketball, fencing, squash, golf, skiing

The ebullient Iona Cameron spent two decades at Gillespie's, retiring in 1988. Her pupils surprised her with this cake shortly before she had to enter hospital for an operation, and later sent her a birthday card – with a caricature of their favourite teacher wilting in her ward with a vast bottle of gin.

(the dry ski slopes at Hillend, the longest in Europe, had now opened). There were new social concerns – for instance, the environment, as sirens like Rachel Carson and assorted contamination disasters began to direct minds to the dark underbelly of progress and technology. After the loss of 2,000 birds in the Firth of Tay following an oil-spill in March 1968, these verses appeared in the school magazine –

Tay eiders

Coal-breasted, snow-backed they floated
Upon the winter tide
Mottled, down brown their mates,
Hundreds and thousands

Resplendent upon sandbanks wide.
In biting wind, the ice
Of the New Year,
Yet we came and stood
Braved the bitter clime
Eyes drank and drank their fill
Of beauty
Somehow that plumage warmed our very hearts
Made us feel
That cold did not matter.

Oh, God! What an infinity of pain man spreads
Now that his power his wisdom far outrides.
Black from the beating life long crushed and dead
Hydrocarbons – fuels – thick oils we draw
And set upon waters great in ships.

Now they are gone, the eiders,
Huddled heaps, helpless and dying upon the beach;
Broken the trail, wing-thick, of cloying carnage;
Slow are the toxins sinking in the blood.
A silent massacre of those who have no tongues
A moment's thoughtlessness, a heedless crime
Pollution.

                                                        Joan Bathie 6P

Dramatic reinvention of the school magazine by Iona Cameron, in a different format with much more artwork and a (mildly startling) new cover each year, was seen in 1969. What had become a fustian publication with undue focus on retiring staff and the doings of matronly former pupils was now emphatically by and for current Gillespie girls. There were, for the first time, informal and diverting documentary photographs of school life, sharp new advertisements; reports of Founder's Day proceedings were now polite, minimalist. And the new School Council had already won dramatic reform –

It was most encouraging this year to see the enthusiasm with which the girls, from the youngest to the oldest, under the direction of the Council, threw themselves into the biggest Christmas charities effort

Right.
The Magazine Committee in 1973, aping
political prisoners in the porch of
Bruntsfield House. Under Miss Cameron's
direction, it had become a much jollier
pupil-centred publication.

Our over-burdened School Captain, Heather McCallum.

Anne McGregor takes a swipe.

Singing.

Swimming.

3.30 p.m. . . .

Primary girls ' skip-a-rope '.

Photographs by Barbara Newson

THE MILK MACHINE

It stands against the chaste white wall, a six foot solid obtrusive hunk of modern technology aggressively clad in cold blue enamel, with a masculine breadth of shoulder—emphasised by its tapering base—which seems somehow inappropriate to its function as a kind of miraculous cow. Its welcoming lighted panel, conveniently head-high, bears two legends—one elegantly printed, black on white—" Put in sixpence but do not press button till light goes out "; the other handwritten—arrestingly blue on green—introducing a sad sense of the mutability of all things: " If the machine breaks down, tell Janitor immediately."

A chromium belt encircles its considerable waist in which are grouped : the slot for the sixpence, the reject lever for the necessary return of the said sixpence if the machine finds it unsatisfactory, the operating instructions and the small panel for that light which must go out before the button should be pressed, pace the exhortation above.

Below the belt, so to speak, is the neat chrome panel with three vivid red buttons waiting impatiently to be pressed when the light at length goes out, and offering in its selection of Strawberry, Milk (6¾ oz.) and Strawberry—a sobering reflection on a humanity whose taste is corrupted into preferring the saccharined and prettified to purer and more sober fare.

Adjoining this panel is the tiny shelf where the rejected sixpence is expelled, and it is only fair to mention that this particular machine—unlike others of its breed that I have known—is kindly and competent in action, so that only very rarely does it ingest your sixpence without delivering the milk.

Lastly, below the selection panel, is the wide shelf with its chromium grasping lip where, for our refreshment, the milk-filled, cream and blue patterned cartons actually appear, after a peculiar grunting chuckle has advised that the miracle of modern vending techniques has worked yet once more.   Fiona Ross, 3, G.

— INTRODUCING 'PHRED' —

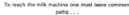

To reach the milk machine one must leave common paths . . .

Behind every man there's a woman . . .

Meantime in the heart of the Jungle . . .

At night the machines come to life . . .

THE REVOLUTIONARY

The machine sits in its place, chortling internally, as eager hands push in sixpences, press buttons, and wait, with looks of childish trust, for the carton of milk which they expect the machine to disgorge. After a minute, the machine stops chortling and grinds its teeth in hatred as the people vent their suppressed desires on the machinery by means of kicks and blows. They hear the machine grinding its teeth and think—poor deluded fools !—that milk will be forthcoming after all. The expression of childish trust returns, with just a hint of anxiety as time goes on without a single carton to gladden their hearts. The machine rocks with silent laughter as they stamp their feet, clench their fists and open their mouths to scream with frustration and implacable hatred of everything in general and the machine in particular for denying them their daily third of a pint.

That, however, is only a very minor part of the machine's plot. At night, when people have gone home, the lights are out, and mice come out to hold their revels, the machines are employed in something altogether different, and far more sinister.

At night the machines come to life. They first move about the building in which they are situated, and, with their lights flashing in hatred for man and all his works except themselves, they smash windows and strew goods all around on the floors, as Latin maids used to do with roses.

They finally reach their destination—a huge union meeting of all metropolitan milk machines. At this meeting, they swear in a thousandfold chorus that they will do all in their power to exterminate man. They reaffirm their allegiance to the Supreme Milk Machine, whom they cheer every time he tries to say anything.

Then comes the climax of the ceremony, in which they utilise the power of concentrated thought and, in the space of a few seconds, turn all their milk sour, put evil thoughts into the minds of teachers the world over, and make the wrong Prime Minister be elected.

Then, their night's work done, they disperse, knocking off, with cartons of sour milk, the hats of any policemen they see. They return to their appointed places, there to brood until the day dawns, over such cheerful matters as the black death, germ warfare, world-wide starvation and the British government.   Rosalie Mason. 3, W.

Though temperamental and a little daunting, the milk-machine proved a big hit.

we have known. Each class was responsible for choosing the particular charity it wanted to support and also for the method of money-raising. Some extremely original ideas emerged such as crossword puzzles at '6 d. a shot', sales of work organised by the younger girls, who produced some very expert baking and a Tea Party to which members of staff contributed admirably. These are but three of the many successful ideas which were put into practice but every class made its own contribution to numerous charities ranging from Spina Bifida to the Epilepsy Association.

Still on the voluntary side the Council approved that each class should collect halfpennies for 'Shelter' – the new organisation to provide homes for the homeless. £17 has been collected – a lot of halfpennies. Our Oxfam contribution has been raised this year as a result of the efforts of the younger girls who have been continuing their good work of knitting squares and making home-made sweets.

A major uniform decision was instituted by the Council this year regarding hats. It was proposed that the school hat should be worn only on special occasions and outings and not for everyday wear. The

Council was asked to take a general vote from each class and when returned the school was found to be unanimously in favour of the proposal. On consideration of the proposal, Miss McIver agreed.

A School Canteen has been started this year in the dining hut in the Primary grounds – the suggestion of last year's Council – but, as yet, the Council has not agreed as to what use the profit is to be put.

As milk is no longer provided for senior pupils, the Council was anxious that a milk-vending machine be installed. This suggestion proved popular and in due course a machine was installed on the bottom flat of the classroom block. Other suggestions for coffee and soup vending machines have been remitted for further consideration.

This year we were pleased that a photograph of the entire School Council was taken.

Our sincere thanks go to Miss McIver and Miss Ferguson who have so encouragingly supported the Council and so wisely guided us in the past session.

Heather McCallum, 6W

The new School Council, 1969, with Miss McIver and Miss Ferguson. And almost everyone is smiling.

There was sweeping change in the Primary Department: between 1969 and 1970, six venerable teachers retired – Miss Dalgleish, Miss Douglas, Miss Laidlaw, Miss Gaul, Miss Anderson and Miss Pirie. There were no more protracted quasi-obituaries for departing staff, though; unhappy for the historian but far less tedious for the pupils. Few paid much attention to growing rumbles as to dramatic change in the school's status, and the few who did must have felt reassured when the Conservatives were unexpectedly returned to national power in the general election of June 1970.

But Mary McIver's reign is, for the senior pupils of the early 1970s, sadly associated with near-incredible horror in January 1972, as Edi Stark recalled in her 2003 Radio Scotland documentary –

> We confronted the worst when we were in Fifth Year at school. Blood-drenched tragedy was no longer confined to Shakespeare or Greek myth. I have an old school photograph – there we are, row upon row, standing to attention in the uniforms we couldn't wait to burn – and one girl is missing. The most popular girl in the school. Clever. Lovely, with tumbling blonde curls. Musical. Brilliantly entertaining.
>
> Elaine Anderson, along with her brother and grandmother, was brutally murdered in her own home. Her mother survived, with devastating head-injuries. In the school magazine that year, Elaine had written a characteristically funny article about family life. What happened to her was indescribable, too horrifying for us to imagine. Of course, we did.
>
> Elaine's father, a driving instructor, had killed his family with a hammer. The class register had been read out every morning in alphabetical order. 'Elaine Anderson . . . Moira Brown . . .' It was never read again. I remember wondering at the time if there was any consolation in the fact that at every point in our lives we would remember Elaine as a 16-year-old, immortalised as young and pretty and amusing and fun. Thirty years on, at least on this earth, there is no consolation. I learned a lesson early in life: there is no such thing as normal. Life is darker than fiction.

David Anderson, a pillar of Dublin Street Baptist Church, but with financial and other burdens, had succumbed to psychotic depression, maniacally attacked his family and at trial was finally acquitted on the grounds of insanity. Edi Stark could never hate him. 'I never thought of him as evil. I thought of him as ill.' He spent the rest of his life in Carstairs

State Hospital. 'A memorial service, conducted by Dr Small, was held for Elaine Anderson, of Form V,' recorded Mary McIver in the school log on 13 January, 'who died in tragic circumstances at the end of last week.' To the distress of many of Elaine's friends, the school hall was too small to accommodate all pupils who wished to attend.

Haunted ever since by memories of her merry, devoutly Christian, guitar-playing pal pootering away from school for the last time on that fateful Thursday evening on her little moped, Edi Stark's recollections of Gillespie's were inevitably defiled. 'I went . . . to this rather precious school and felt alienated,' she declared, interviewed decades later by *The Scotsman*. 'I had never felt stupid before and I felt these girls were much more clever than me. So I felt stupid and I felt inferior and I never quite felt that I belonged. I hated the elitism of it. And I always thought it was a travesty that James Gillespie, who was the snuff merchant in the High Street, made a bequest that was specifically for poor boys – yet here it was, a school for middle-class girls.'

'She was made to feel average at school,' her interlocutor speculated, 'and it is little wonder she resented it.' Less than fair: Stark would become a brilliant broadcaster, her work winning two Sony Awards in 2003. But what so horribly befell Elaine Anderson is not all that haunts her. Not

The 1st XI Hockey side, 1970–71 session. Elaine Anderson is the beaming goal-keeper, fourth from left in the back row.

merely, on visiting the school at last for the reunion event in 2003, was Edi Stark shaken to find two school contemporaries now stricken with multiple sclerosis and unable to walk unaided, she had still sadder memories of girls

> from my school-class: Fiona McBain, who could argue for Scotland, died of cancer at the age of twenty-one. Her son was eighteen months old. Jill Redgrave, an only child, whose mother had died when she was fourteen, was killed in a car-crash – also twenty-one. Wilma Johnson died in a motorcycle accident. Pat Muir of a brain tumour. Kathy's husband shot himself. Another friend became a heroin addict. Little wonder I find it hard to go back. So many memories to lay to rest, in the place I last saw when I was seventeen.

But to damn the fee-paying, single-sex, selective Gillespie's of that era as 'elitist' might raise eyebrows. There were far grander (and much more expensive) private schools in the city; many girls, even in 1972, came from homes of slender means and, as we have seen and as Muriel Spark in 1991 attested, Gillespie's has always had a cool, liberal, mordantly tolerant approach to life in all its diversity.

Not that it was beyond criticism. 'It was a very sound education,' Joyce Flanagan – pupil from 1952 to 1958 – remembered, 'but it was not very wide.' Many Gillespie girls feel they were not encouraged to question, or to think things through for themselves; that it was a cramming academy of overly serious staff obsessed only with Higher Leaving Certificate and admissions to Edinburgh University. 'You had to mind your Ps and Qs all the time,' Sandra McCormack remembered in 2007, with a faint shudder – 'teachers were very strict . . .'

There was certainly an extraordinary focus on that particular University across the Meadows. 'I'd like to have gone to Cambridge,' quips one Gillespie girl, 'had I ever heard of it!' But, until at least the 1960s it was not thought respectable for girls to leave the parental home to study, unchaperoned, in other cities, and the focus on the University of Edinburgh was the inadvertent fruit of May Andrew's central marketing tool – winning high places in its bursary competition, the top fifty names being reported annually and lusciously in all local papers. 'I want the cream of Edinburgh girls in my school,' she once characteristically declared, 'and I'm having it . . .'

Avril Jakes, though, never forgot the faint *moue* of the lady who interviewed her for Edinburgh University admission. 'Oh, yes. Gillespie's. Very good. Very well taught. A bit *spoon-fed*, but very well taught!'

Yet there were many inspirational teachers – the gentle Alison Laidlaw, the exuberant Alison Foster, and of course the colourful Christine Kay who so enchanted the young Muriel Spark. Indeed, do not overlook this in Spark's memoir – that her own years at Gillespie's were so happy. Marissa Bryden, a pupil from 1961 to 1967, went on herself to a distinguished teaching career – retiring in 2009 as Assistant Head of the Mary Erskine School – and had, likewise, as she shared in a 2010 interview with *The Scotsman,* most positive memories that coloured her own professional approach in the classroom –

> Obviously we were taught different subjects and perhaps in different teaching styles, but that aim that girls can achieve is still as strong now as it always was. At Gillespie's there was very much an idea that you were on your way to something else, and there was an expectation that you would work and you would make your mark in some way.
>
> When I taught at Mary Erskine it was the same: it existed to give you the key to the next door, whatever that was. The school equipped you to move on to the next stage in life, and you were encouraged to be ambitious. Your role models were women – female teachers, sports captains, heads of debating – they were all girls and you looked to them as role models, saw what they achieved, and they were good things that you aspired to.
>
> There have been great revolutions in teaching styles, but I still think that what my school was trying to do for me, and what the school I taught at is trying to do for girls in the 21st century, are the same. It's that desire to produce girls who go into the world with a can-do attitude.

An exuberant senior girl joyously plugs the staff versus pupils hockey match. Complete with school hat.

Does the spirit of Jean Brodie still animate the schoolrooms of Edinburgh? 'I think there are still teachers with a sense of style and charisma and, I would hope, a sense of humour, in the way that she had. But you must also remember that she didn't allow her pupils choices, and I think education now is much more pupil-centred at giving them choices. Miss Jean Brodie mapped out her pupils' futures for them instead of helping them look at the vast array of things out there. But the fact that she gee'd them up and got them interested in art and culture – good luck to her.'

Anne Everest of St George's School – the last girls-only establishment in Edinburgh – agrees. 'In girls' schools, the pupils can truly be themselves: the teachers focus on girls in the classroom, cooperative and enthusiastic learning is commonplace, academic achievement is high and so also is participation in sport. We are still producing young women of independent mind and, with pride, we watch them go out into the world ready to make a difference and to embrace the opportunities that life has to offer.'

David Gray, of the Erskine–Stewart's school group, backs her up. 'Intellectually girls thrive in an environment where they are with other girls and where they feel unthreatened by the influences of boys. Girls in a single-sex environment are prepared to risk-take in a way they don't in a co-educational environment, because they have to be leaders. It encourages them to break out of normal stereotyped images of women and encourages them to be ambitious and have high expectations.'

How accurately, Edi Stark asked Liz Roberts in 2003, had Muriel Spark captured the spirit and mores of Gillespie's in *The Prime of Miss Jean Brodie*? 'Utterly. I mean, I find it the most riveting book – it's a book I can go back to time and time again – because there's an element of narcissism in it; we can actually see ourselves reflected. And she captured so much, I think, of that strange sexual charge girls got from teachers, and I don't mean crushes or anything as obvious as that, but the kind of fantasising about teachers, because they were a race apart. I remember the first time I realised they were paid. For the honour of teaching us! – I couldn't believe it. And these goddesses would arrive every day in their Baby Austins and Morris Minors – and they were quite *other* beings. And I think some of that is captured in *The Prime of Miss Jean Brodie*, particularly the relationship of Miss Brodie with her special set . . .'

It is futile to speculate if Gillespie's should have been preserved in its selective single-sex fee-paying form. Token as these fees were, by the late 1960s such local authority schools were a most endangered species and only three (including the Royal High School and the junior division of Leith Academy) now survived in the city. From our perspective, in 2016, Gillespie's has been a co-educational comprehensive now for forty-three years – practically as long as the girls-only Corporation Grammar era, as remote and elegant and of its day as a classic Rolls-Royce Bentley or the Royal Yacht – and no less over.

Few Scots today would welcome the return of the 'qually', and the admissions-testing for Primary One at Gillespie's – little girls asked to explain 'What's Mummy doing here, dear?' in a picture, or to identify the colour of the teacher's coat or name the object in her hand as a pencil – seems to us both subjective and bizarre. The typical examination for secondary entry, Tom Johnson remembers of his own Fifties experience, was almost as incoherent, testing general knowledge as much as ability:

Two delightful mites at Founder's Day, 1970.

'What precious stone do you associate with a popular name for Ireland?' (Of her own Gillespie's test, Stark remembers only having to spell 'synchronise'.) Nor have girls-only schools prospered in the private sector. Those in Glasgow – Laurel Bank, Park School, Westbourne, even Hutcheson's – are long gone. Others in Edinburgh have folded, by mergers to death, from Morningside's St Hilary's by 1983 absorption into Polwarth's St Denis & Cranley to, in 1997, Newington's St Margaret's, which went, in 2010, brutally bust. Mary Erskine's survives only in substantial civil partnership with Stewart's Melville – children being taught co-educationally through primary and senior school, being segregated only through Forms 1 to IV – and St George's has, otherwise, the Mallory Towers market to itself.

James Gillespie's, in its supposed golden age from 1929 to 1973, was of its day, profoundly in the shadow of the Great War and embracing the years when infinite possibilities began at last to open for women and parents first began wholesale to be as ambitious for daughters as for sons. But the women who taught them were by decree unmarried (until the exigencies of the Second World War, wedding bells entailed immediate dismissal) and many carried their own private heartache, not least the loss of so many

Begowned, immaculately dressed staff joyously star-struck by the Queen Mother, 21 October 1966.

men of their generation in the trenches of the Western Front. Small as she was, Muriel Spark had sensed some of this in her own junior mistress –

Did Miss Kay have a sweetheart in her life? I think she did, long before our time. I would put her age at about fifty in my memory, and, looking at the class photograph, I think that is about right. The two years I was in Miss Kay's classes, the last in the junior school, were 1929 and 1930. She was of the generation of clever, academically trained women who had lost their sweethearts in the 1914–18 war. There were no men to go round. Until we ourselves grew up there was a veritable generation of spinsters. At any rate, Miss Kay told us how wonderful it had been to waltz in those long full skirts. I sensed romance, sex . . .

Even in the 1980s, Edinburgh churches still bristled with such old maids, often gaggles of sisters – from our own, very Highland Free Church congregation one recalls the Misses Anderson, the Misses MacAskill, the Misses MacLeod, the Misses MacLennan, the Misses Niven (or, more accurately, by 1980, the last of the Misses Niven, complete with ear-trumpet) – most of them shrewd Miss Marple types, but some indubitably trapped; bitter. The potentially corrosive nature of the single life undoubtedly affected a number of Gillespie's teachers; bled into their classroom style. And there was, too, so much frustrated ability. Alison Foster and Anna Munro, at least, would have adorned university positions; May Andrew a seat in the Cabinet.

Even as Mabel Marr, last of Mr Burnett's appointments, at New Year 1972 retired, all was nearly done. The school's selective status at one point had survived by just a single vote in full Council. Finally, on 5 June 1972,

Brisk, explosive and tiny, Miss Marr is not remembered with universal affection. From the 1963 school magazine.

TERROR!
(with apologies to Rudyard Kipling)

Ere Mor the Mistress mutters, ere the pupils heave a sigh,
Ere the shadow darkly crosses o'er their paths,
Through the tension-laden classroom there's the echo of a cry—
" It is MATHS—oh fellow-scholars—it is MATHS! "

Very softly down the passage comes a petrifying tread,
And the whisper spreads and widens far and near;
And the sweat is on each brow—and they know they're " for it " now,
For of MATHS they have a real and mighty fear!

When the outburst comes upon them, and they tremble, wilt and cower,
When the blinding, blaring onslaught rushes by—
Through the war-gongs of the thunder rings a voice of wondrous power-
" It is x, you stupid girl—it is NOT y! "

―――――

Now the fearful hour is past—now the period's o'er at last,
And they're limp as though they'd come from Turkish Baths;
Still their throats are shut and dried, and each heart against each side
Hammers—" MATHS, oh fellow-scholars—that was MATHS! "

PATRICIA WALL, 2F1.

the Edinburgh Corporation Education Committee agreed 'to approve in principle that all Corporation schools become non-selective in character and that this policy be implemented as soon as possible and preferably with effect as from August 1973'. In a detailed paper that July, the city's Director of Education outlined catchment areas, addressed the issue of rising school rolls – the Sixties had seen a sustained baby boom, peaking in 1966 – and proposed the construction of two large new comprehensive schools, at Cameron Toll (to replace Boroughmuir) and at Canalfield by Craiglockhart, to replace Tynecastle. The James Gillespie's Boys' School would close, merging with the junior girls as an area primary school wholly separate in administration and leadership from the secondary. The High School would become comprehensive and co-educational – and at very short notice. There was uproar, of course, but little Gillespie's parents could do. And, for the record, these proposals were under a right-wing, 'Progressive' administration. The old Gillespie's order was smashed by the Tories.

Neither of those two new comprehensives was built. Cameron Toll by 1985 instead boasted a huge shopping centre and the Canalfield site, by century's end, much Legoland housing. The years from 1973, as far as Edinburgh's state schools went and until century's end, are a sorry tale of broken promises, chronic underfunding and makeshift annexe arrangements for desperately overcrowded academies. Indeed, the Education Committee even flirted with returning Gillespie's to 1908. 'That in addition to the foregoing,' burbled this report, 'the Director of Education be asked to make preliminary enquiries with the Merchant Company as to the possibility of the Merchant Company taking over the name and honours of James Gillespie's Girls' School and making provision for the easy transfer to the Merchant Company School of such pupils of James Gillespie's Girls' School whose parents would wish to make that transfer.' The Merchant Company evidently disdained; the Corporation having stopped cynically short of offering besides the grounds and buildings.

There was howling controversy. Car-stickers had long been distributed – HANDS OFF GILLESPIE'S! – and one Morningside parent, John G. Gray, had already written a 1971 (and incandescent) pamphlet, *Edinburgh Education*, that, decades on, reads in many respects as prophetic. Pointing out, rightly, how few involved in the critical decisions had any personal stake in state schools – most sent their children to private ones – he ridiculed a £400,000 scheme for temporary adaptation of old buildings and annexes; predicted that one of several other proposed new comprehensives, Castlebrae, on Craigmillar Castle Avenue, would prove a disaster (it has) and that the two other schools would not be forthcoming.

Why did the right-wing Town Councillors, who have recently been calling publicly for the tightening up of Corporation spending, vote so enthusiastically to throw a quarter of a million pounds down the drain? I suggest that the reason for this extravaganza is that the right wing have no intention of providing new schools in the central area and once the 'interim' secondary school complexes have been established central area children will be left to rot in them for generations to come.

And Gray added a telling glimpse of Corporation culture. 'A professional man writes to the Education Offices, requesting the name of his local school, and in return receives a list of Merchant Company and other private schools in Edinburgh, printed on Corporation letter-headed paper . . .'

Amidst the storm, Miss McIver continued her conscientious log. On 28 June 1972, 'Miss Steel presents Forms I–III prizes.' On the following day, 'Forms IV to VI. Miss Andrew as guest.' On 28 August, 'Miss Iona Cameron now takes up duty as Assistant Head Teacher.' On 19 February 1973, 'Mr Davidson takes up duty as PT English. Miss Cuthbert is APT.'

And, on 15 August 1973, 'School opened with staff only in attendance. As a result of reorganisation the Primary Dept. is now an independent unit and Miss Barclay has been appointed Acting Head. The next three days will be occupied with meetings and planning with staff . . . Mrs Domanska is now Asst. PT Maths . . .'

Five days later, on 20 August, 'The pupils returned to school. The new First Year, non-selective and local, totals <u>203</u> and includes <u>78</u> boys.'

•   •   •

Promises had been broken. In July 1972 the Director of Education had listed, among 'critical projects to be completed for August 1973', the provision of boys' toilets at Gillespie's. As the first little chaps in long trousers made nervous arrival, none were ready. For weeks a girls' toilet had to be used, with a supervising teacher at the door to enable lads to relieve themselves on shift. There were no facilities for woodwork, metalwork or technical drawing and it would be after my own time in the 1980s before there were convenient boys' changing rooms for the swimming pool: we had, but in our trunks, to prance barefoot down a long corridor and up a flight of stairs. (Short-sighted and without my glasses, on one occasion in late 1980 I burst into the main hall full of startled seniors sitting some Prelim. Thus humiliated, I compounded undying disgrace by, a week later, making the left turn too early and blundering into the girls' changing room.)

The catchment area for the new Gillespie's encompassed those of three 'feeders' – the new Gillespie's Primary; Bruntsfield Primary School and Tollcross Primary School. In preposterous anomaly, Boroughmuir Secondary School was itself within the Gillespie's catchment – its own catchment area being split in two, either side of it. In any event the 1966 Gillespie's buildings would soon struggle to cope with a First Year intake that would at times in the years ahead near three hundred pupils.

The only way to handle these numbers was to use an annexe; and the obvious solution – the old Gillespie's, on the Links – was, evidently, far too sensible for the authorities. They made the old Warrender Park Crescent building the annexe for Boroughmuir High School (even though that school was on the other side of Bruntsfield Place) and, by August 1976, had consigned the Gillespie's overflow to the former Darroch Secondary School, sometime alma mater to Sean Connery and, as peerlessly described by Willis Pickard in a subsequent *Times Educational Supplement (Scotland)* piece, 'an annexe whose grim Victorian aspect would daunt the stoutest spirit'.

Of umpteen storeys, tiled corridors and terrazzo stairs, the Darroch Annexe seems, internally, even today something between a vintage prison and a public lavatory. There was and remains not a blade of grass in its grey, asphalt grounds. High tenements peer down on children disapprovingly; there were in the Seventies still tiered desks and fixed blackboards in its high-ceilinged rooms, and the boys' toilets were disgusting, with graffiti to match. Nor was there anywhere staff could safely park their cars and there was an all-pervading reek of yeast from local breweries.

These witless annexe arrangements by what, from the summer of 1975, was Lothian Regional Council, ensured that children from both Gillespie's and Boroughmuir – and for years to come – had to cross incessantly, by the dozens, a very busy main road. It besides gave Gillespie's pupils down at the Darroch Annexe – and they were by the 1980s predominately students from blue-collar backgrounds, sitting English CSEs rather than full-fat Scottish O-Grades – the sapping feeling of being second-class pupils; certainly, Gillespie staff veterans have spoken cheerfully in my hearing of 'the hard cases down at the Annexe . . .'

In August 1973 the school had just four male teachers. Most staff were well on in years and many had never, ever taught boys. Scarcely any had experience in mixed-ability teaching; and many of the new First Year

children came from rough, mean homes – mostly in the Tollcross, Fountainbridge and West Port areas, long associated with railways and the Union Canal and smelly trades and, by the mid-1970s, frozen in protracted and demoralising 'planning blight'. (Much of the area has been long since demolished.) For the first time in decades, Gillespie's faced disciplinary issues of a whole new order from dubious hems or inappropriate shoes. Inevitably, and with little argument or discussion, the belt returned, and fingers would be exuberantly warmed for the next few years.

But boys took surprisingly well, in these initial months, to hockey and cookery and even sewing, as well as to more traditionally male activities. And they were underestimated. The unaccountable decision was made, for instance, not to teach the First Year comprehensive intake any Latin, and Mr Hay was reduced to teaching dumbed-down Classical Studies to them instead – lots of colouring in pictures of gods, gladiators and Caesars – and watched helplessly thereafter as the subjects he loved dwindled remorselessly in the Gillespie's curriculum. In December 1981 he would take early retirement. Latin classes have been but rare at Gillespie's since the summer term of 1983.

Darroch Annexe, 2016. (Andrew Digance)

'Our first bedraggled little football team', 1974.

The shock for teachers generally was considerable and, inevitably, senior mistresses started to leave in droves – though McIver did her calm best to bring in, especially, confident young men.

14.9.73 – Miss Warren leaves today from the English Department.

21.9.73 – Mrs Noble leaves today.

24.9.73 – Mr Duncan has taken up duty as Asst. Housemaster.

4.10.73 – Fire Prevention Officer considers it essential that an additional fire-door be provided in Bruntsfield House and is to notify the authorities accordingly.

9.11.73 – Mr McCaskill leaves his RE post today.

13.11.73 – Mr Moffatt leaves today

7.1.74 – School reopened. Staff who have left: Mrs Waugh, Eng. Dept., Miss Moncur, Art; Mr McCann, English.

16.1.74 – Mrs Macpherson has now resigned from her post.

29.3.74 – Mrs Walker leaves from the Mod Langs Dept.

20.8.74 – Staff in school for four days' preparation for opening. The following have left: Miss Dickinson, Art; Miss Frier, Chem.; Miss Guy, Mod Langs.; Miss Johnston, PE; Miss Minck, Mod Langs.; Miss Nicoll, Music; Miss Thompson, Physics; Miss Cresswell,

part-time Music. New members – PT Technical Subjects – Mr
Cairns; Senior Tutor – Mr Merriman; Tutor, Mr Leslie; English
– Mr Mitchell; Maths – Mr Rendell; Mod Langs – Miss Watson;
Chem. – Mrs Muiry; Physics – Mrs Cowie; Music – Miss
MacDonald; PE – Mrs Milne; Drama – Miss Clark. Mr Syrett is
now an Assistant PT; Miss Smellie has changed her name to
Matthews; Miss Lawrence part-time Art.

26.8.74 Pupils returned to the school. New pupils in First Year
number 209, 105 boys, 104 girls; total roll is 919.

As grey heads and former pupils (like Dorothy Minck) ran for it, some
notable new personalities were arriving; Allan Leslie fast proved central to
the rapid and happy reinvention of the school, and Tony Merriman, jolly
and exuberant, would be at Gillespie's for the next thirty-four years, retiring
much beloved, if rather larger.

It has long been part of joyous school mythology that Miss Matthews
had changed her surname from Smellie on account of cheeky wee laddies.
It is not true, Iona Cameron advises; she did it for family reasons. A highly
thought-of teacher in my time, Miss Matthews eventually retired to
Gairloch, and untimely lost her life climbing the Five Sisters of Kintail.

The young boys may have daunted many old schoolmarms, but the
girls loved it. Suddenly, they had little pets. 'When a multiplicity of great-
aunts ask me about my plans, now that I have reached the lofty heights of
the Sixth Year,' editorialised Gillian McDonald in the 1974 school magazine,
'my instinctive reply is that my schooldays are over and my future is
completely settled. Yet this cannot be true as none of us know for sure
whether or not his plans will turn out well; nothing in the future is at all
certain. For example, how many of us would have guessed, six years ago as
we tiptoed wide-eyed into our New School, that in a few short weeks our
initial nervousness would wear off and we too could join the "Blue-Knee-
Length-Socks-for-School-Uniform Campaign". Even more unbelievable
was the idea that, in a few short years, this last bastion of femininity would
be invaded by a small army of be-trousered young gentlemen known affec-
tionately to the school as "The First Year Boys". When we first heard that
the school was to be changed so radically, we all exclaimed vehemently,
"It'll never work . . . We'll all be murdered on the hockey-pitches! . . . rugger
in our school? – Never!"

'Now, after a few early teething troubles, we can hardly imagine a time
when there were no boys here. The changeover had been remarkably
smooth and effortless, and far from splitting into two schools of "Us" and

Despite short notice and grave apprehension, the first boys since 1929 were absorbed with ease. A playground scene, 1974.

"Them" we have remained a completely integrated community. Not only is school a community, it is also a preparation for life and one of the principal features of life is the way that circumstances are constantly changing. The introduction of the boys has shown us that, even though we thought the school was stagnant, nothing stands still for ever . . .'.

There were some engaging comments from the lads themselves to C. Leslie of 6R. 'When I first started school I thought I was going into a big palace.' 'I was thinking of giant prefects and myself like a midget.' 'It has everything in it except a snooker-table.' 'I like the coffee and juice machines. They're quite handy like the ice-cream.' 'The boys are a good laugh,' one girl confided. 'Some of the boys are nice-looking,' panted another.

By June 1975 the latest editor of the magazine, Kate Sinclair-Gieben, gave her darkly funny take on things –

Times have changed.
When first I entered these hallowed portals, bowed to Gillespie's bust, and cringed before everyone over Second Year, I never dreamed

FOUNDERS DAY.

On 14th February, 1974, at our annual service we were honoured by having as our guest speaker the Chairman of the Edinburgh Education Committee, Bailie Charles Stuart.

Bailie Stuart talked to us about the history of the positions of office in local government and the changes which will be effected when the local government reforms are carried out.

This year saw a change in the general appearance of the audience, with a row of unusually smart First Year boys in the front. Also for the first time the traditional presentation of the snuff box was made by a boy—James Wallace, Form Captain of 1W.

Afterwards staff and visitors met for tea with representatives of the 6th Form.

of looking at these god-like creatures – the prefects. In fact, when prefects talked to our form class, we were all stricken totally dumb – apart from the six who burst into tears and went home to Mummy.

Hah! – the grim realities of comprehensive education. Who would have thought First or Second Years would kick their dearly-beloved Sixth Years in the shins when faced with authority? And who would have thought that I would retaliate with such relish?

Opposite.
Four happy young
men at James
Gillespie's High
School, 1975.

I will say no more about that particular incident, but it does go to show how much the school has changed since I came.

We have still to realise whether Gillespie can adapt his character to our new-style school. Is he turning in his snuff-sprinkled grave at the thought of his school being comprehensive, or does he welcome a return to the co-education of yesteryear?

It was about this time – and certainly early in the comprehensive era – that one Sixth Form had the inspired idea of organising and hosting an annual evening Hallowe'en party for the First Year pupils, nowadays taking full advantage of the spooky possibilities of Bruntsfield House at night and ensuring abundant be-costumed ghouls, distant moans, creaking doors and bogles jumping out at the little mites – capped, of course, by music, treats, and dooking for apples. It has continued ever since and may be almost as much fun for the First Years.

Miss McIver was nearly sixty-two in August 1973. She could quite easily have ducked the challenge, as Iona Cameron in April 2016 correspondence pointed out, months before the oncoming storm –

To land, so late in her career, the massive and in so many areas greatly resented upheaval of turning such a long-established and proudly traditional Girls' Grammar into a co-ed Comprehensive was daunting beyond belief. Typically, she postponed her retirement for two years to ensure that her arrangements worked, when in fact she could easily have fled and left it to her successor to straighten things out. What didn't help was [that the authorities had] admitted, at First Year level only, a very small complement of boys, seventy only in a year group of about two hundred . . . and that made timetabling very difficult, especially when in those days Technical Subjects were for boys only and of course in a previously girls-only school there was no provision and Darroch School, about a mile away, and involving travel time, had to be used as an annexe. O.B.E.'s have been awarded for lesser achievement! For the first year or so the only way to solve such problems was to have boys' classes and of course this was jeeringly interpreted as her determination to keep boys and girls separate. Outdoor pursuits, games, etc. for the boys were slow to establish themselves as we had so few men on the staff in the girls-school days but the early recruitment of many young men, to the P.E. Dept. and others, enabled the necessary develop-ment. In the earliest days even Miss McIver herself could frequently

be spotted huddled, all too often in drizzling cold, on a Saturday morning at the pitch-side to encourage and cheer on our first bedraggled little football team.

Thus Mary McIver conscientiously ran two schools of different character and emphases at the same time, on the same premises and with the same staff – insofar as she could keep up with the staff, who continued to come and go at a daunting rate. The Physical Education Department – for reasons pupils of that era can readily guess; the lack of adequate or at least adjacent pitches and the combustible nature of Miss Lambert – had notable difficulty in keeping anyone for very long. Yet her meticulous log records the challenges –

> 19.9.74 – Mr Mutter takes up duty in Art Dept.
> 20.9.74 – Mr Jones leaves from the Maths Dept.
> 4.10.74 – Mr Milne leaves from PE, Dr Allan from Chemistry Dept.
> 31.10.74 – No pupils attending today owing to industrial action by staff.
> 1.11.74 – Mrs Gowans leaves from PE.
> 6.11.74 – Mrs Roberts leaves from Science.
> 20.12.74 – Members of staff leaving today: Miss Joan Cameron, Home Economics, and Mrs Galloway, PE.
> 17.1.75 – Mr Edwards leaves from the RE post today . . . Mr Merrick leaves also from PE.
> 3.2.75 – Mr Burke takes up duty as Asst. Head; Mr Carroll as APT Science.
> 21.2.75 – Mrs Turner left from the HE Dept.

Finally, conscientiously, this stout-hearted little Headmistress recorded on 21 March 1975, 'School closed for the Easter vacation. I am resigning my post as Headmistress at this time, and hand over with all good wishes to my successor, Dr Patricia Thomas. [signed] Mary G. MacIver.'

The handwritten school log ends there, and for always. And Mary McIver, the last Headmistress of James Gillespie's High School for Girls, left a gift for the staff – two original Adam Bruce Thomson watercolours, which have hung in the school ever since – and embarked on quiet Edinburgh retirement. The cigarettes finally caught up with her on 12 May 1994.

CHAPTER EIGHT

'No respecter of persons'
1975–1991

For many of us, some three decades ago, we seemed in the helpless thrall of two determined and formidable women. Both were from provincial England, both had been born in the 1920s and both been profoundly shaped in youth by the Second World War. Both, too, had enjoyed their first career as industrial chemists – indeed, in that capacity they had once actually met; each now had a vision and each was implacably devoted to achieving it. One was Dr Patricia Thomas, who led Gillespie's from April 1975 to June 1991; the other was merely Prime Minister and leader of the Conservative Party.

There are other diverting parallels between Thomas and Thatcher but, as her famed contemporary to a remarkable degree reinvented Britain and its politics, so Dr Thomas as Head Teacher (she disliked the term 'Headmistress', and never used it) quite recast James Gillespie's High School. She had to work amidst appalling difficulties, at times under frightful pressure, and yet, in all essentials – a quarter-century after her retirement – Gillespie's is the school she left behind: egalitarian, good-humoured, serene and at ease with itself; a sought-after co-educational area comprehensive which has turned out a remarkable number of creative and sparkling people – actors and musicians, broadcasters and journalists and cultural commentators and activists and agitators and leaders. The fourth successive and – to date – the last female Head of the school, she besides had a husband and family; like most of her generation, Patricia Thomas had married young, and by her mid-fifties was already a grand-mother.

Born in Leeds, Yorkshire, in October 1927 – and never quite losing its accent – Patricia Fothergill attended St James Primary School in Wetherby and, after leaving King James Grammar School in Knaresborough, passed from the University of Leeds with her science degree and a PhD in Organic Chemistry. She worked as a research-chemist with the Calico Printers Association Ltd, Manchester – their laboratories, in 1941, had invented Terylene – from 1951 to 1954, and is rumoured to have been personally part of the team that discovered (or at least developed) the fluorescent 'hi-vis' yellow dye now ubiquitous among the functionaries of a risk-averse health-and-safety age.

She then, as the deplorable term of the day went, 'retired to marry' Gordon Thomas, an affable college lecturer, and when Dr Thomas returned to the workplace in 1961, early child-rearing done, it was as a teacher. She put in five years at the posh Greenacre School for Girls in Banstead, Surrey; briefly at another private establishment, Lansdowne House in Edinburgh, and then held positions at Armadale Academy, Craigshill High School in Livingston (as Principal Teacher of Science) and, from 1972 to 1975 as Assistant Rector at Blackburn Academy – all in West Lothian. There she honed a particular interest in 'Guidance,' as the conscious pastoral support schools by the 1970s now offered children was called.

Her appointment as Head Teacher of Gillespie's raised some eyebrows. It was most unusual for a third-rung Assistant Head Teacher to leapfrog to entire leadership of a secondary school. But Gillespie's was still, in the spring of 1975, largely full of girls, and till perhaps her last year or two, when the malicious began to mass, Dr Thomas proved fully up to her new command through all those years of change and tumult.

She is an intriguing personality. For one, considering so prominent a position, she was (and remains) painfully shy, an impression reinforced by her very soft voice, a tendency to stoop (though her height made that inevitable when working with children) and an unease with full eye contact. At times this, unfortunately, made her seem remote and cold. Linda Urquhart, Head Girl in the 1976–77 session, often shared a platform with Dr Thomas and other dignitaries, but described her ruefully in 2007 as 'rather aloof' – and could not recall a single conversation with her. As morning prayers ceased from her appointment, pupils had not even that frequent contact with her; and only in the company of her most gifted and cajoling deputies, Peter Galloway (from 1980 to December 1983) and Alan Waugh (from 1986 to the end) would she conscientiously spend time in the staffroom.

For another, Dr Thomas was extraordinarily tall. A colleague who comes himself from a family of very lofty people insists she was at least six foot two. (She herself, in 1982, claimed demurely to be but five foot eleven-

Dr Thomas, senior colleagues and their be-blazered lieutenants for the session, August 1982. Peter Galloway, Deputy Head Teacher from 1980 to 1983, went on to great success as Head Teacher of Trinity Academy, retiring after a quarter of a century with a CBE. Stewart McDougall, of exuberant person-ality and keen brain, was one of Dr Thomas's shrewdest appointments.

1982 – 1983

Mr Galloway	Dr Thomas	Mr McDougall	
Brian Hood	Helen Ritchie	David Neilson	Deirdre Campbell
Head Boy	Head Girl	Depute Head Boy	Depute Head Girl

and-a-half.) She is invariably the tallest person in any surviving group photograph and yet – and this tells us a great deal – she is invariably wearing heels.

For all her formidable ability, her enjoyment of power, she was, even in her sixties, a very attractive woman who looked far younger than her years. And she knew it. She dressed in the timeless, tailored style of the Fifties – fitted two-piece suits in tweed; no less elegant, flowing summer dresses with neck-detail; sometimes skirt and a sweater showing her figure to advantage and with a favoured gold pendant. Thomas liked understated jewellery and, though her make-up was discreet to non-existent, there always lingered fragrance when (invariably with a retinue of visitors) she glided through the campus to or from Bruntsfield House. Yet one man she appointed to Gillespie's, Hamish McDougall, is adamant that

> none of these impacted on me as much as the gravitas she brought to the job. A call to her office, even for a routine matter, was met with a degree of trepidation. Praise from her was not freely given but when it was (as I still have in my possession) it came in the form of a short letter on school notepaper and really meant something.

Guidance . . . was an area where she excelled and was responsible for assembling an outstanding group of practitioners, which I was privileged to join, albeit in the sad circumstances of the ill-health and subsequent death of the highly respected Miss Lindsay Hamilton. Dr Thomas oversaw my transition into Guidance and spoke to me about child [sexual] abuse which she had encountered in West Lothian. This was long before it was ever mentioned in polite circles and, although initially shocked, the conversation had a profound effect on me and showed another facet to the enigmatic industrial chemist.

Although I may have a tendency to view the past through rose-tinted spectacles . . . the combination of Dr Thomas and Peter Galloway was excellent and very effective and the best that I worked in. Although management systems have changed, that combination with the Year Heads and Guidance teams below meant that the pupils and staff were far better served than the overworked, over-hyped, botched systems that replaced them.

I think her great strength was planning and managing. She put together a disparate but strong management team and generally recruited well. This meant that there were clear lines of communication and matters were dealt with swiftly and effectively. Her tall stature and forbidding exterior were good in terms of affording gravitas to formal occasions and scaring all but the most foolhardy! This masked a more caring side as I know of instances where she supported staff who were undergoing personal difficulties and, although few staff got close to her, I do not know of any former colleagues who do not respect her and the type of school she ran.

Pat Thomas, as friends referred to her (staff jocularly called her 'Patsy', though never to her face), was of that new generation of post-war women who for the first time stormed assorted bastions of male supremacy, who rarely enjoyed equal pay, whose achievements were often minimised or whose laurels were snatched by others, and who rapidly grasped that to advance anywhere much in a man's world you had to work twice as hard, be at least as good – and nevertheless, in a way that young women would balk at now, remain consciously womanly and attractive: those who held the strings of patronage were, after all, invariably men. In fact, till very recent years – and of this the young Dr Thomas would have been sorely aware – women were treated especially shabbily in the field of science; written out of textbooks, seeing credit for their discoveries awarded to men,

School magazine,
1966.

FYSICS IS PHUN

I manage to swim and to walk of course,
Without understanding the pull of phorce.
Perhaps when I'm phat and I'm phorty
And phamous phor what I've attained,
I'll remember that phriction
Has the oddest addiction
To phacilitate fysical change.

JACQUELINE SALTON, 2L2

and ruthlessly patronised. Rosalind Franklin's work was critical to the discovery of DNA – but the 1962 Nobel Prize went to men; in physics, Chien-Shiung Wu's cobalt-60 experiments – at the fawning request of male colleagues – definitively overthrew the 'law of parity' in quantum mechanics; but they, not she, enjoyed the 1957 Nobel honours.

These ambitious young women had besides to be canny, even sly. Colleagues of Dr Thomas recall – with rueful admiration – a considerable capacity for guile, be it in dealing with the mere men at Lothian Regional Council's Education Department and the more obstreperous parents, or evading some minor drama she felt could be dealt with just as effectively by another member of staff. If a letter annoyed her and was not from anyone important, she simply ignored it; if some unwelcome imposition on her time was threatened – some tedious unpleasantness – she would suddenly remember she had to be in a meeting. One might tut-tut; but – like all prominent public women of this time – she had to cope with a great deal of ill-veiled misogyny and spite, to some extent within the school but far more from without. As late as 1981 she was still one of but a handful of female high school Heads in all Scotland. And, a decade later, a senior colleague was shocked to be hailed by an Education Department official – male of course – with the contemptuous query, 'Has the bitch quit yet?' Such vile language must be unthinkable today. Or is it?

And yet most who worked with Dr Thomas recall ferocious, she-bear loyalty to her staff, especially if they came under any sort of external attack. She fast won respect in wider, educational Scotland, being appointed to important committees (such as that which finally begot the Munn and Dunning reforms) and was seriously rated by such men as J. Grant Carson of Jordanhill College School; local historian Malcolm Cant (who wrote, in

1983, of her 'very able leadership'); her successor, Colin Finlayson; and an elder, himself a teacher elsewhere in the city, of my own church, the late Murdo MacLeod.

She had a shrewd, even gritty awareness of darker social reality. Mindful of the dreadful housing in which many pupils then still lived, without proper bathrooms and so on, Dr Thomas besides pressed on PE teachers the importance of ensuring that all children showered after games – though the changing-room supervision essential to this was sometimes unfortunately misunderstood. But she had that remarkable capacity to see things from the bottom. The chief concern throughout her reign – reflected in a host of initiatives and throughout her surviving paperwork in the archives – was not academic attainment or the comfort of the ablest Gillespie's pupils. Indeed, they were rather neglected and, at least once, she got into a mortifying mess over senior pupils' timetabling. It was for those whom parents, school and society were failing – the less able, the traumatised and flailing; the children of recent immigrants, of single mothers; wild-eyed and cheaply clad youngsters who bore the stamp of mean streets – children inured to poverty or addiction or even violence in the home; children who did not want to be in school at all. And, inevitably, with each successive August intake the numbers of such unhappy pupils grew, the greater classroom disorder they threatened and the more urgent appropriate strategies became.

•   •   •

Dr Thomas had two essentially trivial trials from the outset. Many parents of older girls, and some surviving staff, still struggled to accept or come to terms with the new order of the school, though as years advanced and things bedded down and people retired this tension fast receded. The school, though, had new problems in the community, especially in the nearest Marchmont and Bruntsfield streets: long used to demure little Gillespie girls, neighbours now complained as if the school had been taken over by Orcs. Children were seen dropping litter, jostling on the pavement, overheard using bad language, caught smoking in closes or (the enormity of it) simply 'hanging about'. Miss McIver, too, Iona Cameron recalls, had also borne many complaints about Lauderdale Street litter, though they took it a little less seriously after it emerged residents had howled down council proposals to hang a litter bin on every lamp-post. 'It didn't help,' Miss Cameron adds dryly, remembering excited gaggles of girls, 'that the granny of a Bay City Roller lived on Lauderdale Street!'

One note of very different character amidst such ongoing hate mail survives in Dr Thomas's papers, doubtless because it was so unusual –

Dr Thomas – Miss Laidlaw of 15 Lauderdale Street 'phoned to say how impressed she was with the kindness shown by a group of 3rd Year boys (Trevor Watson, a twin, & others.) They helped her gather together rubbish which the wind had blown on roadway. She just wanted you to know.

3.3.82

Alison Laidlaw was not the only thoughtful veteran of the recent Gillespie's past to look serenely on ongoing changes; sense the burdens Pat Thomas carried.

Two problems, though, were far greater and the first would become almost the Head Teacher's understandable obsession – capacity. Because of the extraordinarily high birth-rate till the late 1960s, the pupil roll grew and grew and more and more use had to be made of the Darroch Annexe, involving fraught crossing of a very busy road and wasting a great deal of staff-time in transit. Worse, the fabric of the 1966 campus was now a matter for concern, as poor design, cheap materials and shoddy construction grew more and more evident. Even the layout of the buildings caused problems for the requirements of a modern comprehensive.

And Dr Thomas, like every Lothian Head Teacher of the era, had to cope with the difficult (and changing) political climate; for instance, the mighty squeeze on public spending from the summer of 1976, after Britain had had to approach the IMF with the begging bowl. That eventually eased. But, apart from four years between 1982 and 1986 – the elections, of course, coincided with the Falklands conflict – Lothian Regional Council was under absolute Labour control and, from 1979 and like Labour local authorities everywhere, increasingly and bitterly at war with the new Conservative government. The Thatcher administration meddled in the affairs of Britain's town halls in unprecedented fashion, 'capping' local rates and generally mucking such authorities about. Councils in turn (and in this Lothian was no exception) cut and cut, not least in the hope of provoking electoral backlash against the hated Tories; and the budgets of 'posh' schools in Conservative wards were a particularly easy target. By 1982, when there was an unexpected change of administration, things had grown desperate, as an *Evening News* report by education correspondent Joan Simpson on 12 September 1981 related with a sort of horrified relish –

Learning to make do in the classroom

A new generation of Scottish children are learning about rationing and austerity at first hand.

Lothian's schools are tightening their belts as the regional council's spending cuts – to meet Government demands for £30 million savings – begin to take effect.

And, at classroom level, that means boarded-up windows, no strip-lights, sharing textbooks and cutting down on jotters and exercise books.

It has meant an unhappy and difficult start to the new session, and some head teachers feel that Lothian's education system – hailed as the best in Scotland – is crumbling.

All head teachers have received detailed advice from the director of education on what the cuts mean and how to try and save money – everything from non-filling of staff vacancies to economising on toilet paper.

Mr Hugh Mackenzie, headmaster of Craigroyston High, Edinburgh, said the worst effect so far was on staff shortages.

There are vacancies in Technical, Home Economics and Drama and no likelihood of replacements.

'These vacancies have had an adverse effect on the curriculum and, as the term goes on and more vacancies arise, the situation can only get worse.

'I could see us getting to the point where children would have to be sent home.'

In practical terms, the £2,000,000 which must be saved on maintenance adds up to 50 boarded-up windows at Craigroyston.

The 20 per cent which must be saved on books, stationery and equipment (£852,165 in Lothian) means that the Art, History, Biology and Arithmetic departments at Craigroyston are desperately short of textbooks.

Paper supplies for photo-copied classroom notes are running out.

Book shortages are a major problem, too, at James Gillespie's High School, Edinburgh, with A-level classes in Biology and English particularly affected.

Head teacher, Dr Patricia Thomas, said, 'The problem with these books is that we have to wait until the beginning of term to see how many pupils need them before ordering.

'We may have to ask pupils to share books.'

The use of Meadowbank stadium for badminton and squash by Gillespie's pupils has been axed, and the continuation of after-school clubs and societies relies on the goodwill of staff who, as well as not being paid for this work, will now have to pay their own expenses as well.

Dr Thomas's biggest worry is for the future of Music classes. Instrumental teachers – who teach more than 1000 pupils – have had their contracts renewed, but only until the October holiday.

At Craiglockhart Primary headmaster, Mr John Inglis, is taking the view that the cuts can be educational.

'Many economies are just common sense – in fact, things that the older generation were brought up to. It will do the children no harm to learn to be more economic.'

The seeds were thus rapidly sown for sustained industrial action by the EIS teachers' union from 1985 through 1986, deliberately targeting high-profile schools in seats held by Scottish Conservative MPs and blighting the learning experience of thousands of children. This was an especially trying a time for Dr Thomas – but her own inordinate capacity for very hard work, her considerable (and, when necessary, imperious) writing gifts and that keen low cunning served her well.

As the cuts bit, Douglas Burke remembers, she tempted her lords and masters at Torphichen Street with a wily offer. Gillespie's, Patricia Thomas suggested, could cope well enough with a few fewer teachers than it was, by strict pupil-numbers, entitled to – but in return she wanted very first pick of the very best candidates for stipulated vacancies. Officials gladly acceded and, as a consequence, the calibre of staff appointed under Dr Thomas was for the most part extraordinarily high. She had besides put about her an excellent senior management team. Iona Cameron (with whom she had a cool but correct relationship) was already an Assistant Head Teacher. Douglas Burke was in position too. Tony Merriman was soon elevated to join them and, in 1977 – given the additional difficulties imposed by the Annexe – Thomas was allowed to appoint a fourth, Stewart R. McDougall. And, from Emily Ferguson's retirement in June 1980, she had an outstanding Deputy Head Teacher in Peter Galloway.

Mr Merriman's true potential in senior management was seen to finest advantage after Dr Thomas's time. 'He wasn't a good AHT at first,' one colleague remarks, 'but he became a great one.' He was in these early years, apparently, rather inclined to scuttle to his queen with every rumour going

Right.
Supremely tall, emphatically in charge – Dr Thomas, in all her complexity, is caught perfectly as the Lord Provost presents awards at a school library book fair in 1982.

Opposite.
Staff, August 1980. There are some minor errors in the key, drawn up for a school exhibition about a decade ago; for instance, the Principal Teacher of Classics is Mr John S. Hay, not Mr A. Hay.

or comment overheard, he and Patricia Thomas thereby 'only feeding each other's insecurities'. (Though colleagues could, and did, take wily advantage of this propensity.) But the administration outlined in the 1981 school prospectus – with one of her characteristic flow-charts – was formidable.

Iona Cameron, shrewd native of Keith, Banffshire, took charge of Guidance, Social Education and liaison with the Primary feeder-schools. Douglas Burke, genial and kindly, with a great shock of white hair and whose strong features put many in mind of James Gillespie himself, was

JAMES GILLESPIE'S HIGH SCHOOL, EDINBURGH.

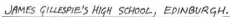

TEACHING STAFF – AUGUST 1980.

1. DR. P. THOMAS	18 MR. R. MUTTER.	34 MRS B. MACKIE.	50 MR. R. TURKINGTON.	66 MR. K. FERGUSON.
2 MR. P. GALLOWAY	19 MR. A. LESLIE.	35 MR. A. HAIR.	51 MRS J. COOMBER.	67 MR. J. YOUNG.
3 MISS I CAMERON	20 MR. J. CAIRNS (TECH)	36 MR. R. CAIRNS (ENGLISH)	52 MR. R. SNEDDON.	68 MISS. C. MERCIER.
4 MR. D. BURKE	21 MR. H. DAVIDSON	37 MR. P. HUTCHISON	53 MR. I. GILCHRIST.	69 MISS. S. GALLACHER.
5 MR. S. McDOUGALL	22 MR. D. SCOTT	38 MR. G. WIGHT	54 MISS J. COLLISON.	70 MRS. S. PAGE.
6 MR. A MERRIMAN	23 MR. J. KILDAY.	39 MRS. S. CRAMB	55 MISS. L. HAMILTON.	71 MR. I. COLQUHOUN.
7 MR. A. HAY	24 MR. R. GALT.	40 MISS C. McDOUGALL	56 MISS. M. BURNARD.	72 MR. H. McDOUGALL
8 MISS C. LAMBERT	25 MR. D. GIBB.	41 MR. A. MITCHELL (MUSIC)	57 MISS. M. NIVEN.	73 MISS D. GILLIES.
9 MR. A. McKENZIE	26 MR. I. MITCHELL (ENGLISH)	42 MRS. S. STOBBIE	58 MRS. C. PAYNE.	74 MR. N. McDONALD.
10 MISS J. McINTYRE	27 MISS. A. CUTHBERT.	43 MRS. D. MORRISON	59 MISS L. RODIE.	75 MR. J. STEWART.
11 MR. A. DALL	28 MRS. M. DUNCAN	44 MISS M. JONES	60 MRS. M. HARKNESS.	76 MR. B. GANNON
12 MRS. M. DAY	29 MR. G. CAMPBELL	45 MISS. E. MATTHEW	61 MISS. M. McDONALD.	77 MR. I. EVANS.
13 MR. J. FAIRHURST	30 MISS J. CLARK	46 MRS. M. WILKIE.	62 MRS. C. DOMANSKA.	78 MR. S. WATTON.
14 MR. T. JOHNSON.	31 MRS. J. KELLIE	47 MRS. A. JORGENSON.	63 MISS. W. DALGLEISH.	79 MR. I. WATSON
15 MR. H. THOM.	32 MR. I. NICOL.	48 MRS S. EVANS.	64 MRS. C. SCOTT.	80 MR. R. GRAY.
16 MRS A. GRAY	33 MR. K. SHARP	49 MRS. E. McVITTIE.	65 MR. M. DUNCAN.	81 MR. C. WHITE.
17 MRS. G. SINCLAIR-GEIBEN.				

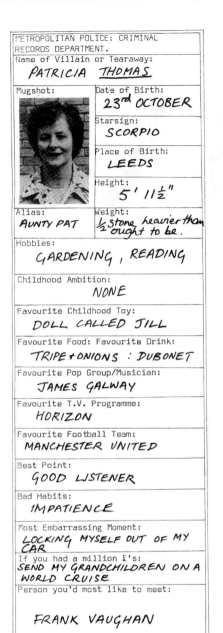

METROPOLITAN POLICE: CRIMINAL RECORDS DEPARTMENT.

Name of Villain or Tearaway: PATRICIA THOMAS

Date of Birth: 23rd OCTOBER

Starsign: SCORPIO

Place of Birth: LEEDS

Height: 5' 11½"

Alias: AUNTY PAT

Weight: ½ stone heavier than ought to be.

Hobbies: GARDENING, READING

Childhood Ambition: NONE

Favourite Childhood Toy: DOLL CALLED JILL

Favourite Food: Favourite Drink: TRIPE + ONIONS : DUBONET

Favourite Pop Group/Musician: JAMES GALWAY

Favourite T.V. Programme: HORIZON

Favourite Football Team: MANCHESTER UNITED

Best Point: GOOD LISTENER

Bad Habits: IMPATIENCE

Most Embarrassing Moment: LOCKING MYSELF OUT OF MY CAR

If you had a million £'s: SEND MY GRANDCHILDREN ON A WORLD CRUISE

Person you'd most like to meet: FRANK VAUGHAN

METROPOLITAN POLICE: CRIMINAL RECORDS DEPARTMENT.

Name of Villain or Tearaway: PETER GEORGE GALLOWAY

Date of Birth: 21st MARCH

Starsign: ARIES

Place of Birth: ST. ANDREWS

Height: 5' 10½"

Alias: UNCLE PETER

Weight: 11 st. 4 lbs

Hobbies: GOLF, TENNIS, READING ABOUT WINES AND FRANCE

Childhood Ambition: ENGINE DRIVER

Favourite Childhood Toy: A DINKY CARS' WEETABIX VAN

Favourite Food: Favourite Drink: RED PUDDING : SASPERILLA LOIRE WINES

Favourite Pop Group/Musician: BOOKER T. + THE M.G.'S. HARRY CHAPIN

Favourite T.V. Programme: FAWLTY TOWERS

Favourite Football Team:

Best Point: ENERGETIC TALKER

Bad Habits: NOT PUTTING SHAVING BRUSH AWAY

Most Embarrassing Moment: FAILING DRIVING TEST.

If you had a million £'s:

Person you'd most like to meet: FELICITY KENDALL / JOHN ARLOTT

METROPOLITAN POLICE: CRIMINAL RECORDS DEPARTMENT.

Name of Villain or Tearaway: STEWART ROBERT MACDOUGALL

Date of Birth: 24th MARCH

Starsign: ARIES

Place of Birth: EDINBURGH

Height: 5' 7" (NEARLY)

Alias:

Weight: 10½ STONE

Hobbies: SQUASH, FEATURE FILMS READING, PRODUCING MUSICALS

Childhood Ambition: T.V. PRODUCER

Favourite Childhood Toy: A MODEL AEROPLANE THAT REVOLVED AROUND A STAND

Favourite Food: Favourite Drink: SWEET + SOUR : WINES.

Favourite Pop Group/Musician: BEATLES, POLICE

Favourite T.V. Programme: TOMORROW'S WORLD

Favourite Football Team:

Best Point: AMBITIOUS, ENJOYS LIFE

Bad Habits: SMOKING

Most Embarrassing Moment:

If you had a million £'s: SPEND IT ON A LUXURIOUS LIFESTYLE.

Person you'd most like to meet: LAWRENCE OLIVIER

Senior management gamely completed a cheeky questionnaire for the 1982 edition of Snuff.

in broad charge of First and Second Year pupils. Mr Merriman, bearded and genial with a wonderful bellow, was the Head of 'Middle School', and Stewart McDougall – small, moustachioed, gurgly-voiced and with a keen sense of humour, yet on no account to be trifled with – had charge of senior pupils. All four besides had a considerable classroom-teaching commitment. Though he himself was not so obliged, Peter Galloway chose to take a few Social Education classes – thus getting to know pupils; he had a

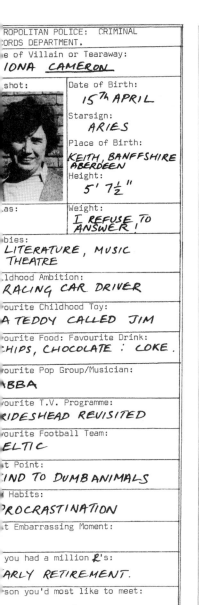

METROPOLITAN POLICE: CRIMINAL RECORDS DEPARTMENT.	
Name of Villain or Tearaway: IONA CAMERON	
Mugshot:	Date of Birth: 15TH APRIL
	Starsign: ARIES
	Place of Birth: KEITH, BANFFSHIRE ABERDEEN
	Height: 5' 7½"
Alias:	Weight: I REFUSE TO ANSWER!
Hobbies: LITERATURE, MUSIC THEATRE	
Childhood Ambition: RACING CAR DRIVER	
Favourite Childhood Toy: A TEDDY CALLED JIM	
Favourite Food: Favourite Drink: CHIPS, CHOCOLATE : COKE.	
Favourite Pop Group/Musician: ABBA	
Favourite T.V. Programme: BRIDESHEAD REVISITED	
Favourite Football Team: CELTIC	
Best Point: KIND TO DUMB ANIMALS	
Bad Habits: PROCRASTINATION	
Most Embarrassing Moment:	
If you had a million £'s: EARLY RETIREMENT.	
Person you'd most like to meet: MRS THATCHER.	

METROPOLITAN POLICE: CRIMINAL RECORDS DEPARTMENT.	
Name of Villain or Tearaway: Douglas Robert Burke	
Mugshot:	Date of Birth: State Secret
	Starsign: Taurus
	Place of Birth: Edinburgh
	Height: 5' 11"
Alias: 'Snowdrop'	Weight: 13 st 7 lbs
Hobbies: Singing and wine beer making	
Childhood Ambition: To Survive Hitler	
Favourite Childhood Toy: Mecanno Set	
Favourite Food: Favourite Drink: ripe peaches' real ale	
Favourite Pop Group/Musician: Barbara Dixon	
Favourite T.V. Programme: Does not have a T.V however enjoyed watching Wimbledom	
Favourite Football Team: Used to support Hibs	
Best Point: Innocence	
Bad Habits: ' Not making the most of myself '	
Most Embarrassing Moment: " Discovering at the end of a schoolday there was a 12 inch rip in seat of trousers	
If you had a million £'s: Give it away - the strain of planning what to do with it would spoil the enjoyment	
Person you'd most like to meet: The late Henry Cockburn	

METROPOLITAN POLICE: CRIMINAL RECORDS DEPARTMENT.	
Name of Villain or Tearaway: Antony James MERRIMAN	
Mugshot:	Date of Birth: 6TH JANUARY
	Starsign: CAPRICORN
	Place of Birth Stow-on-the-Wold (COTSWALDS
	Height: 5'10"
Alias:	Weight: TOO MUCH
Hobbies: Gardening, Squash, Tennis, Golf.	
Childhood Ambition: ARTIST	
Favourite Childhood Toy: an aeroplane which fired sparks.	
Favourite Food: Favourite Drink: TERRIAKI STEAK! GOOD RED WINE.	
Favourite Pop Group/Musician: BEATLES, POLICE, ADAM + THE ANTS.	
Fabourite T.V. Programme: -	
Favourite Football Team: Wrexham	
Best Point: Voice can be HEARD......	
Bad Habits: SWEARING AT PUPILS	
Most Embarrassing Moment: Last years prize-giving	
If you had a million £'s: Re-organise Education	
Person you'd most like to meet:	

remarkable facility for remembering faces and names – and besides was responsible for curriculum development and community liaison. This 'Board of Studies', as Dr Thomas proudly described her chosen lieutenants, met regularly in her office and was 'responsible for the administration of the school and the formulation of policies after consultation with relevant bodies'.

Most departments enjoyed a Principal Teacher and the largest an

Assistant Principal Teacher, both granted a number of no-contact periods (that is, time when teachers are not obliged to teach) to prepare materials and ponder the latest curricular proposals. And, pastorally, broadly on the lines laid down by Mary McIver, pupils

> are allocated to one of four Houses – Gilmore, Roslin, Spylaw or Warrender. All pupils in a Form class are allocated to the same House, as are all members of the same family. Form classes are named by the initial of the House.
>
> Two Tutors are allocated to each House, with responsibility for the social and personal welfare of approximately 150 pupils. They operate a comprehensive social education programme through weekly discussion with small groups of their pupils. The programme covers a wide variety of topics including careers guidance, health, competence, self-awareness, relationships, and education for leisure.
>
> One of the aims of this system is to give parents a known point of referral for each child. Parents are informed of the times during the week when the House Tutors are free from a teaching commitment. Parents are encouraged to visit the school at these times to discuss any problems and anxieties at an early stage. No problem is too small. These meetings, by appointment, may be at the request of the parents or the House Tutor.

The growing emphasis on care of this nature – known today as Support for Pupils, or SfP classes – was the fruit in itself of wider cultural change. Fewer and fewer pupils had a meaningful church connection, more and more mothers now worked and, whether they wanted it or not, schools in recent decades have become far more involved in the personal lives of their scholars, a trusted teacher taking on the role which once would have been that of a relative or the family minister. At least Guidance teachers are now specifically trained in it; and some of the heavy lifting (for instance, basic sex education) is today done in Upper Primary.

There were three ongoing areas of change and tension. Gillespie's has always been diverse and cosmopolitan, but in Dr Thomas's time it became rapidly much more so – photographs of school life in those years show a rising range of ethnicity. This in turn, in her time, raised new problems – for instance, a growing number of pupils whose mother tongue was not English and required special tuition and support – and made regular Christian observance increasingly fraught: by 1980, it was confined to end-of-term services, prize-giving and Founder's Day. By the late Eighties she

had studiously formulated anti-racism and diversity-awareness programmes. She added Mandarin and Urdu to the Modern Languages
curriculum. And her last, 1990, prospectus proudly welcomed readers in
several different languages. Her successors put most noisy emphasis on this
sort of thing, but they followed, really, where she had led.

It was also, from August 1973, no longer possible – as the law then stood
at that time – to impose compulsory school uniform. Most pupils still wore
it, and its wearing was 'strongly encouraged', but – as Dr Thomas repeatedly
told parents – she had not the power to exclude children who chose not to
wear it or whose homes could not afford it. With more and more Muslim
pupils, by 1981 not a few girls were wearing trousers. 'Extremes of fashion',
football-favours and so on were vigorously discouraged, and teachers
themselves continued to dress formally far into the 1980s – jackets and ties
for the men; skirts or dresses for the ladies. As Dr Thomas herself did not
routinely wear an academic gown (save her gorgeous green doctoral robes,
on high days) these from 1975 rapidly died out, Miss Cuthbert being the final
diehard. 'On a cold day you could wrap yourself up in it,' she chuckled to my
Higher English class. 'Or you could roll it up into a ball and sit on it . . .'

The other issue that vexed Dr Thomas was the belt. Though she was not
on rarest occasion averse herself to wielding it, she would really rather have
abolished it all together. But her staff would not, in the conditions of the
time, have stood for it, and we would do well to remember that it was hyster-
ically supported almost to the last by the teachers' unions. I myself was never
threatened with it and never once saw it used. Down the Annexe was, apparently, another matter. One Technical master is still remembered for his
vigorous, sprinting run-up as he warmed someone's fingers with the tawse;
the meticulous Stewart McDougall, in action with the strap, always made
sure the pupil had not deliberately left a long hair across the palm (which
could cause a cut) and he conscientiously draped a damp towel over their
wrists, lest the strap burst veins. In the culture of the times and especially
with working-class boys – some of whom were capable physically of
attacking staff, and occasionally did – senior teachers of the era insisted it
had to be accepted. 'The use of corporal punishment is left to the discretion
of the individual teacher,' Dr Thomas advised in that 1981 prospectus, 'who
must inform the Head Teacher of each case. School policy is to phase out
this form of punishment over the next few years. Other sanctions may be
imposed, including detention and extra homework.'

In the event, it was abolished for her, and at short notice in March 1982,
by Lothian Regional Council. From the end of that spring term, no
Gillespie's child was ever strapped again. But, to widespread surprise, an

opinion poll for *Snuff*, as the school magazine was now cheekily styled, showed widespread regret on both sides. Only 42 per cent of pupils supported the abolition; 48 per cent regretted it. Two-thirds of teachers – 65.5 per cent of staff – predictably deplored its demise too, though 30.5 per cent supported it. The same poll – prefiguring changes to come from Dr Thomas's departure – showed growing pupil disdain for prefects (40.5 per cent did not think them necessary) and school prize-giving: 31 per cent now disapproved of it.

Dr Thomas's era is noted for several great reforms, all of which she thought through clearly and then robustly advanced. One, probably the vision of another new young PE teacher, Hamish Thom, was a bold programme of Outdoor Education, centred on a residential trip to Loch Tay every May, for a week, near-obligatory, for all the First Year pupils, led by particularly outgoing and child-friendly teachers – Mr Thom, Allan Leslie, Tony Merriman, Tom Johnson, Ian Nichol, and many more, plus genial Sixth Year girls. Similar outdoor pursuits were laid on for those pupils in later years so inclined, also at the Craggan Outdoor Centre on Loch Tay and still more rugged ploys at and from Benmore, near Dunoon, deployed from Miss McIver's days. The success of these adventures, launched late in the 1975–76 session, was immediate, and Tom Johnson – he had joined the staff in August 1975, teaching Modern Studies, and served for three decades – wrote warmly of the trips in April 2016 –

> The first full S1 residential experience was in 1976 and lasted nine weeks (eight classes and what was then known as the remedial group), and took place between the end of the Easter holidays and finished two weeks before the summer recess. It was a great success.
>
> I do not know if there was one individual who suggested it but there were certainly three prominent members of staff, namely, Tony Merriman, Allan Leslie and Hamish Thom. There is no doubt they were the three key members of staff who were really responsible for the developing, organising and the running of the programme. By the late 1970s Tony was appointed A.H.T. and thus less responsible for the running of the programme and probably by 1979 Hamish was the main organiser and remained so for the next twenty years. They were very well and ably assisted by many, many staff, which included myself, as well as a number of Council outdoor pursuits staff. There is one other member of staff who is worthy of a mention and that is Ailsa Gray, PT Home Economics. It was all self-catering then – she put in a power of work setting out menus, quantities of

food required, assisted in the purchase, organised the required utensils and even made the cagoules for the S1 pupils. The food was prepared and cooked by staff plus many 6th years who appeared at Loch Tay when their exams had finished. The experience was an outstanding contribution to the S1 curriculum, so ably led and organised and backed by a terrific team effort.

'I'm not really sure who actually started the residential weeks at Loch Tay,' says Iona Cameron. 'I have a vague feeling that somebody found out that the Boys' Brigade had residential premises there which they used at weekends only and JGHS sent First Year form-classes there in the summer term, from Monday to Thursday. It was hugely popular with the kids and, apart from the joys of the outdoor life, provided a good bonding session. Tony Merriman's name was very much associated with its inception but it may have been Dr Thomas – perhaps through the Directorate – who was the first to learn of its availability. I remember Dr Thomas, Eric Ferguson [Director of Education] and Mr Merriman were up there together on a much-vaunted day visit when a Form was in residence. The late Allan Leslie made a big contribution to its popularity as he had disco talents he could add to his other attributes! Staff back at the ranch played their part by taking the classes of their colleagues at Loch Tay and Miss Ailsa Gray, Head of the Home Economics Department, with her staff, supplied much of the food. As there were nine form-classes it all added greatly to staff commitment week after week.'

Youngsters who had never been beyond the dreich streets of central Edinburgh now encountered the countryside. Bookish, solitary types found they could sail, kayak, climb; the lonely found they could be popular. Barriers of all sorts were broken down and the positive impact on discipline and staff–pupil relations was incontestable. But let Tony Merriman tell the tale, in the 1977 school magazine –

The Loch Tay Project

This much used expression means many things to many people. To some pupils who have not participated in the event it is yet another experience denied them. To parents of those who have taken part it heralded a week's welcome break from at least one lively offspring. To the staff it recalls various degrees of hard work, drainage of stamina and, with luck, some enjoyment. To the pupils who went to Loch Tay? . . . I suspect most would return if given the opportunity.

Why have a Loch Tay Project? The potential value of maximum relevant pupil–teacher contact has long been appreciated by many staff. No longer can we afford to view the school as a series of units held together by an umbrella of memo-papers. No longer can each classroom be a kingdom in its own right, using varying ground-rules and standards with every pupil still expected to adjust to each situation with chameleon agility. There must be a degree of togetherness and a sense of unity of purpose amongst not only the pupils but also the staff. Maximum useful pupil–teacher contact should ensure productive channels of communication and without communication there can be no purposeful exchange of knowledge. So to me Loch Tay is not merely a programme in Outdoor Education but rather a blueprint for overall unity and discipline for the benefit of all.

Each First Year register-class spends one week at a Centre on the south side of Loch Tay where they are involved with teachers in a full programme of activities not only academic but also physical and social. This programme runs for nine weeks of the summer term involving over fifty staff, forty-five of whom are resident at the Centre for part or all of their week. In 1976 all but nine of the 226 First Year pupils participated and there was overwhelming support from parents.

En route to the Centre each party stopped at Bannockburn, where they relived the lessons and projects of the battle. They were able to let off steam yet at the same time realise that they were not on holiday. They had begun to work, but somehow it wasn't work. They were able to tell their science teacher about the campaign, realising that he might not be in full possession of the facts – after all, he was only the driver! On arrival they were astounded to see Mrs Latin wearing slacks, and what was Mr Maths doing cooking the evening meal?

And so the programme began. Some were to undertake map reading that first evening; some washed up; others tidied the Centre, whilst others wrote home. A crowd looked at the duty rota to see who was making the breakfast or the packed lunches or doing the cleaning. An expert from Benmore Outdoor Pursuits Centre, or the City of Edinburgh Outdoor Education Centre, joined them to give tuition in canoeing and/or sailing.

Next morning one group sets off gorge-walking whilst another does field-study. After lunch the canoeists are off to Strathyre Forest or perhaps the farm or the power-station. The walkers go to an old hillside cemetery to do art. The biologists are out sailing. That evening there is a trip to see a waterfall and some caves. The following day the groups engage in different activities and compare their experiences with the groups of the previous day. There's a sausage-sizzle on the shore at night. A few boys go fishing.

What have we achieved? We have exposed as many pupils as possible to as varied a number of activities as possible. We've taken some pupils away from home for the first time. We've introduced them to a number of outdoor pursuits in which they can now specialise if they wish. We've encouraged staff–pupil involvement and hopefully avoided confrontation. We've hopefully dispelled the 'them and us' syndrome. We've shown a large part of the Scottish countryside to city-dwellers who may not have seen it before. We've cemented relationships within the class itself and between members of staff also.

Most of all I hope we've begun to crystallise a way of life, a code of discipline, a basis of understanding of what school is all about and have impressed upon pupils that we, the staff, are here to help them reach a clearer understanding of themselves and the society in which they live and enable them to find their place in that society. Such programmes cannot begin to work without major staff participation. I feel that our staff in their response to this project have shown their belief in such a philosophy and that the school is already better for it.

A J Merriman
Principal Teacher in charge of Outdoor Activities

Patricia Thomas did not herself frolic in the waters or join in ketchuppy sausage-sizzles. But the Loch Tay Project fitted fully with her vision and had always her enthusiastic support. She besides, for the first time, established a Parent–Teacher Association. And, in the summer of 1978, an important milestone was reached; the last, selective girls-only Sixth Form departed in June, as she mentions in her Head Teacher's Report, and Dr Thomas returned from her holidays that August in charge at last of a fully comprehensive school on which she could unleash all her reforming energies.

•   •   •

June 1978 – 'The next session will see many new and exciting ventures beginning...' When school returned, that August, it was now fully co-educational and comprehensive. However, it would be June 1985 before the very last girls who had been admitted to the fee-paying selective primary department (in 1972) finally quit Gillespie's.

HEAD TEACHERS REPORT

The end of this session closes another chapter in the history of the school. The last of the girls who entered Gillespie's when it was a girls' selective school witll leave this month. It has not been easy for them in the time of transition and all credit is due to these senior girls for all the help and support they have given the school during this period.

Last session saw the school disrupted by the fuel crisis which was closely followed by the temporary closure of the annexe. The co-operation and support of the staff during this time ensured that any detrimental effect on the pupils was minimal. The pupils also played their part by their usual exemplary behaviour which is much to their credit.

Next session will see many new and exciting ventures beginning. A programme of work experience for senior pupils is almost completed and we are at present investigating the feasibility of offering "A" level courses. Parents will be invited to join several "O" and "H" grade classes as well as several separate interest classes.

This month also sees the publication of a school prospectus. This will be supplemented by three booklets describing the curricula of Lower, Middle and Upper School. There will also be two other publications - one describing the Loch Tay project for the Lower School and the other giving a comprehensive survey of extra curricular activities.

I would like to take the opportunity to thank staff, parents and pupils for their support in the past session.

P. Thomas

Two of her initiatives were, for the time, rather shocking and attracted widespread publicity – and, in short order, admiration. One, launched in that bold 1978–79 session, was a week of compulsory work experience for all senior pupils, however academic, taken either in Fifth or Sixth Year and with great help from local businesses and parents. Here Dr Thomas's past in industry was key: the programme was deliberately tailored for senior pupils of academic ability, to broaden their horizons and perhaps lend them insight into the drab jobs of those in quietly desperate lives. (Dr

Thomas took keen and far-sighted interest in ensuring all pupils left school workplace-ready. A fat careers-guidance text survives in the achive, laced with humour and sharp wisdom, and makes delightful reading.) Overseen from the start by Art teacher Robert Mutter – one of Miss McIver's most interesting appointments, an original thinker, a warm, charismatic personality – pupils had to fill in application forms; keep up a diary. No pay was to be given or accepted. They toiled in shops, in offices, in banks, in strange schools or curious enterprises; apart from anything else, it was good for certain pupils, Dr Thomas observed in her dry way, to learn just how boring some jobs are. This has now become general in Scotland's schools, again following where Dr Thomas had led.

'We were treated like adults and expected to react in the same way,' one youngster commented. 'I had to balance the ledgers and look after petty cash,' mused another. 'It was frightening! Someone else's money seems much more valuable.' 'The staff taught us and answered questions but not like teachers. They treated us like equals.' This was echoed by another – 'They're not like teachers. They talk to you, not at you!' 'I learned to use a Telex,' said one proudly. 'It was only for a week, but it was like a term in school. I learned so much more quickly because it was real.' A participating employer remarked, 'Their presence made us look carefully at some of our procedures: explaining routines and reasons has shed a lot of light on some of our less appreciated problems.'

These comments – and many more – appear in the 1980 edition of *Snuff,* very much the publication of pupils: bold, subversive and darkly funny, and granted a remarkably free hand by Dr Thomas, who thought it an important safety valve and could on certain fronts be extraordinarily tolerant – a reminder, again, of her complexity. (She even, in the 1981 edition, sanctioned reports of a French trip where several pupils had been caught by Customs, on return, trying to smuggle in flick-knives. They were released after a robust lecture.)

'Boredom is an evil which is no respecter of persons,' she orated in that same issue. 'All age-groups from all walks of life are vulnerable, but boredom in young people is the most distressing . . . Opportunities must be provided to arouse the interest and imagination of the pupils. The publication of a school magazine provides such an opportunity for many pupils who are willing to become involved in a creative adventure of writing and art design.'

And the work experience programme won much gratifying publicity, not least Mark Jackson's February 1980 report in the *Times Educational Supplement* –

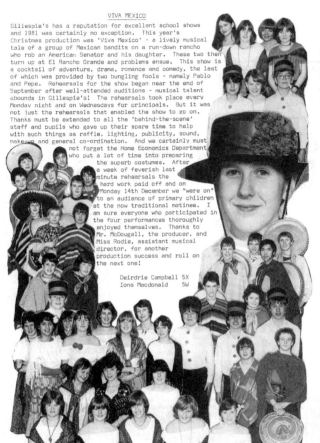

VIVA MEXICO

Gillespie's has a reputation for excellent school shows
and 1981 was certainly no exception. This year's
Christmas production was 'Viva Mexico' - a lively musical
tale of a group of Mexican bandits on a run-down rancho
who rob an American Senator and his daughter. These two then
turn up at El Rancho Grande and problems ensue. This show is
a cocktail of adventure, drama, romance and comedy, the last
of which was provided by two bungling fools - namely Pablo
and Pepe. Rehearsals for the show began near the end of
September after well-attended auditions - musical talent
abounds in Gillespie's! The rehearsals took place every
Monday night and on Wednesdays for principals. But it was
not just the rehearsals that enabled the show to go on.
Thanks must be extended to all the 'behind-the-scene'
staff and pupils who gave up their spare time to help
with such things as raffle, lighting, publicity, sound,
make-up and general co-ordination. And we certainly must
not forget the Home Economics Department
who put a lot of time into preparing
the superb costumes. After
a week of feverish last
minute rehearsals the
hard work paid off and on
Monday 14th December we "were on"
to an audience of primary children
at the now traditional matinee. I
am sure everyone who participated in
the four performances thoroughly
enjoyed themselves. Thanks to
Mr. McDougall, the producer, and
Miss Rodie, assistant musical
director, for another
production success and roll on
the next one!

Deirdrie Campbell 5X
Iona Macdonald   5W

The school show in December 1981, *Viva Mexico!*, was a huge success. 'Amigos,' Dr Thomas solemnly began her written remarks in the programme, concluding 'Hasta La Vista.'

Where pupils lose their illusions painlessly

Kenny Boal now knows that he does not want to be a teacher. He found that out on first teaching practice, as have others before.

The difference is that Kenny has lost his illusions in time to save himself a false start in teacher training: he is still a pupil at an Edinburgh comprehensive.

James Gillespie's might be seen as a sample of the more acceptable face of Scottish education – a mixed comprehensive which rejects the narrow authoritarianism of its selective past, but expects most of its pupils to perform at least as well as their predecessors in the examinations.

Sited in the Bruntsfield quarter, an inner-city district popular with the capital's university staff and civil servants, the former academy for girls can still rely on getting a high proportion of serious ambitious children. Well over two-thirds will sit for four or more Scottish O-Grades; and the remainder will try for at least one O and/or the English CSE Mode 3.

Dr Patricia Thomas, a former industrial chemist from Lancashire [sic], one of Scotland's six women secondary school heads, points out that the catchment area does include a small patch of acute social deprivation, and that the school has to cater effectively for the full range of abilities.

Nevertheless, what distinguishes Gillespie's main work experience programme from most of those run elsewhere in Scotland, England and Wales is that it is not designed for those intending to leave at sixteen... the work experience scheme which has been operating for the last two years is aimed exclusively at the Fifth and Sixth Year pupils, the equivalent of England's lower and upper Sixths, most of whom are studying for the Scottish Higher or for English A-levels.

Dr Thomas is convinced that the more academically able pupils need first-hand knowledge of working just as much as, or more than, other leavers, if they are to choose the right career; and that such contact is likely to attract more of them into industry and commerce.

But to provide it meant convincing their parents and their subject teachers that their chances of exam success – which, they believe, is the real key to a career – would not suffer from the distraction of work experience.

So, from the start in 1978, work experience was offered not as an option but as part of the programme for all the senior pupils, to be taken as a one-week spell each September. Half of the Fifth and Sixth Year classes go out for a week while the rest continue their studies: the following week the pupils change over, and the second half get their spell out at work.

Anxious parents who rang up to point out that the arrangement would still deprive their children of a week's 'real' education were told that the number of subject-periods throughout the school year was being raised from six or seven a week to eight to compensate: this year a further weekly study period was crammed into the timetable for Higher grade subjects.

Says Dr Thomas: 'We have had to convince parents, and indeed some of the youngsters, that they will not lose out. But I think the value of the experience is now becoming understood. It is as important in heading youngsters away from choices they will regret as in confirming their plans.'

Nearly 100 employers are now offering placements, ranging from archaeology and blacksmithing to veterinary surgery and zoo-keeping.

Most involved actually doing a job, but one of last year's young-sters complained he was only allowed to look and listen. He did his work experience in the control tower at Edinburgh Airport.

The other initiative was for those hard cases down at the Annexe – the 'December leavers', the considerable number of non-academic youngsters too young to leave school at the end of Fourth Year who thus had to serve out one more term till Christmas. These frustrated souls had proved the most disruptive and trying of any, and teaching them in any traditional classroom environment a thankless lot – until, in close consultation with colleagues (and again with Bob Mutter in immediate charge) Dr Thomas in 1980 came up with SCOPE, as detailed in the 1982 edition of *Snuff* –

SCOPE is a unique, full-time school-to-work transition course devised at JGHS. It was originally designed for Christmas leavers but has been developed to offer a relevant programme for 'reluctant learners' during their final year. It was specifically designed for this group of pupils, taking into account their past experiences and differences.

The project is based on a series of Student Centred Occupational Preparation Exercises and the aims of the course are to prepare the group for all aspects of their adult life and encourage the pupils to regain confidence and self-esteem by beginning to realise their potential, both as individuals and as a group. SCOPE also includes preparation for unemployment, community and self-help schemes.

SCOPE's premises consist of a 'wing' of six rooms in the Annexe. Being self-contained, it can function without timetables or other restrictions, allowing a flexible and open-ended approach to the various course modules.

This course, now in its second year, proved extremely successful for the first group of twenty-seven pupils, most of whom are now in full-time employment or further education.

SCOPE was clever because it was directed by the pupils themselves. They were to run small businesses, they were to draw up their own regulations, they

THE TIMES EDUCATIONAL SUPPLEMENT   5.6.81   3

Willis Pickard reports on a scheme which has turned failure to success

Gillespies' unit helps intractable pupils find jobs

An experiment with intractable fourth-year pupils at James Gillespie's High School in Edinburgh is attracting attention from many parts of Scotland. Last week end-of-term came for the group, most of whom had found jobs for themselves after a session in which their work, undertaken in a unit separated from the rest of the school, had been largely directed towards establishing their confidence by preparing them for the world of work outside.

As Dr Patricia Thomas, the head teacher, says in a report on the year's experiment: "The obvious pride of the young people in the quality of the work they are producing is a sad reflection on their previous failures." One girl has established a profitable line in jewellery making; a boy turns out chess sets cast in resin; printing helps organizations both inside and outside school; doors in the school are adorned with wooden nameplates made on a gravograph by a helpful lad, who did one for the door in my office.

None of this activity in itself is unusual in comprehensive schools. But the fact that the entire curriculum is directed to job-finding and to making a success of any job found is a cause for comment. Why are "English exercises" done on DHSS notices about supplementary benefit, hardly a rich literary mine to quarry? Such forms have to be understood in the big, bad world, and if the English in them poses problems for people, this must be overcome.

Information retrieval is a skill demanded by employers. So some of the pupils have compiled their own directory of useful addresses in Edinburgh, combing reference books and contacting organizations to do so.

The school chose the 27 pupils in the original group because they had at one time shown some talent or initiative which by the age of 15 seemed to have disappeared. Why have the buried talents come to light again? The pupils are clear that it is because they are allowed to work at what they want. They have no fixed timetables, no teachers shouting at them, a common room of their own, and programmes aimed at influencing future employers.

This is no "sin bin", but is the evident success in terms of reinvigorating the pupils and in helping them find jobs a tribute to the separateness of the unit, with period bells for the rest of the school which can be ignored there, or is it a reflection of the dedicated teaching which will always win through?

There is no doubt that with two full-time staff for a small group of pupils the odds on success are shortened. Dr Thomas was able to persuade Mr G. E. Ferguson, the divisional education officer (who has given strong backing to the experiment), that she should have an extra member of staff to make up for the two promoted teachers who run the unit.

These teachers are themselves the kind whom every pupil in any part of a school would wish for. Mr Bob Mutter, whom Dr Thomas asked to take charge, was singled out for his ability at handling difficult pupils. Once an art teacher, he had gone into guidance and outdoor education, and he jollies along his sometimes lethargic charges with neither the carrot nor the big stick. He was allowed his choice of a colleague, and so his partnership with Mr Ken Ferguson makes for the kind of team-matching which is ideal in theory but rarely practised.

Many problems have come their way, especially in the early stages when they were dealing with a group which had by definition opted out of school life. They have tried to run a democracy, but one with leadership. When the pupils have decided themselves to lead, it has been unsettling, as on the occasion when they voted to expel one of their number for disruptive behaviour and would not be denied the sanction (the pupil had to return to an ordinary class).

Mr Mutter and Mr Ferguson survived the storms, and found the haven of pupils proudly returning from interviews with jobs in the bag, or in the case of one entrepreneur three jobs to choose from.

SCOPE – Student Centred Occupational Preparation Exercises (a name better left as an acronym) – had all the advantages of a nurtured experiment, advantages quickly spotted by other fourth-year pupils who would like to have abandoned their classes in the main Gillespie's building in favour of the unit's six rooms in an annexe whose grim Victorian aspect would daunt the stoutest spirit.

Next year there will be up to 30 successful candidates for the unit, though more will seek entry. What about the lessons to be learned for the rest of the school? I asked Dr Thomas if, having spotted pupils with abilities which have been allowed to wither in the secondary school, she did not feel that the success of the unit was an indictment of the ordinary curriculum.

Naturally, she didn't say Yes outright, but she thinks there are lessons to be learned, especially whether pupils might be treated in a more adult way. As it is, the school will extend its own work experience scheme, for which it is also noted, to embrace some of them.

One of the SCOPE pupil wrote graphically about initiative, self-motivation and teacher attitude: "The teachers don't tell you that they knoe everything and you are dum they say go and look it up or go and ask sumbody that is an expert and will tell us."

could draw on staff support for, for instance, writing a CV or honing their job interview skills and – as was made very plain – they would be treated like civilised adults. To considerable surprise, the rules these teenagers came up with were stricter than anything staff would have dared to impose. They even indignantly expelled one classmate whose antics proved incorrigible. They built canoes for Loch Tay; machine-tooled wooden signs they could sell; crafted jewellery; repaired bicycles; mastered the keeping of accounts and meticulous records. The improvement in their confidence and bearing was immediate. Exuberant and articulate, all but one of them had secured a job within weeks of leaving Gillespie's (one boy was offered three) and a professional woman wrote to Dr Thomas in May 1982 with signal enthusiasm –

> As the supervising social worker of one of your 4th Year pupils, Jackie _____, I am writing to express my appreciation for opportunities offered Jackie through SCOPE over the course of the last year. I am convinced that without the support and encouragement from this small group of staff and pupils Jackie would not have completed her secondary education successfully.
>
> Last year Jackie's attitude towards school was fairly negative: she could not cope with the large group of pupils and appeared to absorb little of the academic training. She was at risk of truanting persistently and subsequently being referred to a residential school. However, from the start of her attendance at SCOPE her attitude

Perhaps Dr Thomas's most inspired idea, SCOPE attracted national interest.

changed and she became enthusiastic about the job preparation courses and how she could usefully apply such skills in the future. This, I feel, is the result of being seen to be successful at something and also the individual guidance, care and attention from the staff. Jackie is now much more prepared to face the tough realities and demands of employment than she would otherwise have been.

I look forward to working together with the SCOPE project in the future and hope it will continue to provide for the needs of other teenagers like Jackie.

Dr Thomas besides insisted on a term of dedicated community service, one afternoon a week in the first term, from all Fifth Year pupils – working with disabled children, in old people's care-homes and so on – and in this had the support and contacts of Iona Cameron. The second, spring term of the session saw the same afternoon devoted to lectures – and not by municipal worthies or academic bores, but stimulating and even controversial addresses on hot, touchy topics. In my session, playwright John McGrath came to talk about the media and censorship. The nasal Judy Bury of the Brook Advisory Clinic banged on for a mortifying afternoon about sex. We visited, on another occasion, the Royal Observatory; we pondered a number of topics – private education; race and racism; how to bear yourself through a job interview; how we might vote, had we the vote, in the upcoming (1983) general election; how Scottish local government worked. Most memorably, consultant surgeon Keith Little, of the Royal Infirmary's Accident and Emergency Department, gave a lecture on road safety, with a great many slides (most in colour, from actual tragedies) of broken bodies, or bits of bodies, occasionally pausing to check on the latest strapping lad to faint with a profound sigh in his seat.

And on one matter Pat Thomas would brook no opposition: she insisted, from the moment she arrived, that all boys and girls would do the same practical subjects in junior secondary – Home Economics, Technical Drawing, Metalwork and so on. There was hysterical protest, but in this she would not be gainsaid; and though it fell to my lot to attend Home Economics for just a few weeks (under the cool and authoritative Miss Gray) I learned, for the first time and much to my surprise, and some curried eggs and tomato soup and pineapple upside-down cake and rather a neat rhubarb pie later, that I could actually cook. For that alone, I owe Dr Thomas much.

Opposite.
At Dr Thomas's decree, and from the start of her reign – despite uproar – boys and girls shared all practical subjects from the start of their secondary education. In the Scotland of 1975, this was sensational.

•   •   •

The Old Guard: Emily A.K. Ferguson, Deputy Head Teacher, retired in June 1980. Left to right: Alexander B. Dall (Principal Teacher of Geography), Dr Thomas, Miss Ferguson, Catherine H. Lambert (Principal Teacher of PE), Jean C. McIntyre (Principal Teacher of History) and Alexander R. MacKenzie (Principal Teacher of Physics). A spinster all her days, and a teacher of Biology, Miss Ferguson once distributed to her class a lengthy, detailed and illustrated paper on the reproductive system of rabbits, concluding with three agonised words – 'Similar in humans'.

An old generation of teachers began slowly to fade from the scene. Thomas Sommerville retired as Head of Music in 1977; Emily Ferguson in 1980; John S. Hay in 1981, Moira Burnard and Alexander Dall and Murdo Duncan in 1982; Anne Cuthbert in 1983. Bright, engaging young staff grew to the fore – Kenneth Ferguson, Paul Hutchison, Tom Johnson, Hamish McDougall, Colin Nisbet, Paul Raffaelli, Lyn Rodie, Hamish Thom, Douglas Young.

Accommodation remained a frustration, and took up much discussion at the monthly School Council – comprised of senior teachers from both Gillespie's and its feeder-primaries, community representatives, parent representatives, the local district and regional councillors, the school captains and, of course, Dr Thomas. It was responsible not just for affairs at the High School but also for overseeing the best interests of the primary schools.

They fought successfully to end the summer-letting exclusively of the High School premises to groups of overseas students, who often left them in filthy condition just two or three days before the start of the autumn term and, to the caterwauling of Lauderdale Street, the students besides 'kept apparently unrestrained discos till the early hours of the morning'. Other local schools at last had to share this burden. The School Council won its campaign for a pelican crossing on Bruntsfield Place, just south of Leamington Terrace and easing the safe to and fro with the Darroch Annexe; and lobbied against imprudent adjustments of the catchment area proposed in 1976. Dr Thomas had also to see off enthusiasm for the wholesale censorship of school library books. And by February 1977, the fabric of the High School – scarcely a decade old – was evidently failing –

> Dr Thomas reported that the general internal state of the school was poor. The school had not been decorated since it had been opened … Settlement cracks in the plaster had been replastered but had not been repainted. The whole school was very shabby in appearance … Dr Thomas had recently expressed concern about the safety of the floor in one third-storey classroom in Bruntsfield House. Cracks were appearing round the side of the ceiling in the second floor room. Someone did visit the school but did not discuss the situation with either the Head Teacher or the Janitor. The ceiling was reported as being safe after a single test which consisted of standing on a desk and pushing a hand up on the ceiling! … Dr Thomas reported that for some time there had been structural defects in the classroom block. This was causing cracks to appear and the walls at the ends of the building are not vertical. Gaps have appeared round some window frames which are becoming distorted. The only report that Dr Thomas has was that it 'was not as bad as expected'. The school has now been informed that holes are to be made in several classroom walls to examine the situation further.
>
> Dr Thomas wrote to the Architect's Department asking for a written report on the state of the building and proposed work to be done in the future. The only response, so far, has been a telephone call from a Mr Dice when he stated that there was no need to worry as the building was safe and that further tests were to be made. He indicated that further information would not be forthcoming …

After all, she was only a woman. An ongoing worry was pupil safety in the vicinity of the service entrance to the High School on Warrender Park Road; pupils were forbidden to use it, but had to cross it, as oil-tankers, refuse lorries and so on bumbled in and out. Yet even exacting appropriate warning signs from Lothian Regional Council took inordinately long. By June, the Architect's Department had been asked still more firmly to carry out repairs to

> Holes in stairwell plaster, music area
> Swimming pool curtains
> Leak in gym hall roof
> Fallen ceiling tiles in Science block
> Cracking and bulging brickwork and blockwork
> Plaster cracks throughout . . .

And, to cap everything, there was a plague of mice in the school kitchens. The internal telephone system was repeatedly repaired, and repeatedly broke down. The city fathers, by autumn, had been pleased to allow the (limited) use of the Meadows for school games, thus reducing dependence on (and the two-mile trek to) deplorable facilities at Kirkbrae, not even on a direct bus route. In October 1977, the School Council enthusiastically supported Dr Thomas's eagerness to secure entry to the International Baccalaureate for Gillespie's pupils – though this was one of very few of her dreams, decades ahead of her times (as usual) that she would not accomplish. (She had, though, successfully introduced University of London A-level courses for senior pupils; Dr Thomas never greatly rated the Scottish Certificate of Sixth Year Studies. Gillespie's students are still presented for A-level Art today.)

Heating at the Annexe was a concern, especially in the hard winters of the time; on occasion classroom temperatures were a shivery 47 °F. The whole building needed to be rewired – and, of course, there was no money. The proposed Munn and Dunning reforms were explained in great detail by Dr Thomas; no one could have foreseen it would be the mid-1980s before they were finally implemented and the O-Grade consigned to history. Truancy remained a serious problem; the proposals of the Pack Report were considered. There was a fraught discussion of sex education in 1978. 'Dr Thomas presented us with a programme of the work being done in Health and Social Education in the Secondary School and spoke of the difficulties of dealing with the teenagers and again the danger that warnings might be tantamount to an encouragement to experiment. She explained that the Guidance staff dealt with small groups, and that they would be with the same children for four years, which provided continuity. Certain aspects of health were brought into the general curriculum by the PE, Home Economics and Biology Departments. The emphasis in the Senior School was on discussion, and a special effort was made to see that the boys were not neglected.'

But even this three-year span of School Council discussion gives a keen glimpse of the extraordinary pressures with which Dr Thomas had to contend. From 1981 it was strengthened by an enthusiastic Free Church minister, Rev. Fergus MacDonald – his five children attended Gillespie's; and another parent, an ambitious advocate and the local Regional councillor, Alistair Darling, who would go on to great things. From 1988 it was replaced by a School Board, dealing only with High School concerns.

Dr Thomas's brisk, clear, uncompromising style of writing is evident in this bold proposal – heartily endorsed by the School Council; characteristically strewn with blunt block-capitals and emphatic underlinings – published in November 1978:

DRAFT PROPOSALS
THE FUTURE DEVELOPMENT OF
JAMES GILLESPIE'S HIGH SCHOOL

TOP PRIORITY
To contain the school on one site and to discontinue the use of the Annexe at the earliest possible time.

PRESENT SITUATION

A. Annexe.
(a) Art Department – completely housed in the Annexe – all pupils taking Art travel to the Annexe – this includes all S.1 and S.2 pupils.
(b) Technical Department – as for Art.
(c) Remedial Department – based in the Annexe – staff travel to the Annexe but extraction is difficult.
(d) Drama – based in the Annexe but lessons also in the Main Building.
(e) Second Year Pupils – most classes are in the Annexe – pupils travel to the main building for Physical Education, Home Economics, Social Education and Music – otherwise staff travel to the Annexe to teach S.2.

B. Dining Rooms (shared with primary school).

(a) Two storey block with one large kitchen area and four classroom-sized dining rooms – one at each corner – on each floor.

(b) The design and layout does not permit a cafeteria-type service – food is dished up by the pupils on the tables, i.e. 'family service' – this can lead to 'distribution' arguments among the pupils.

(c) Pupils NEVER have a CHOICE OF MENU – possibly the only school in Lothian without any choice of menu.

(d) Poor dining facilities have led to an alarming fall in the number of pupils taking school meals – as a result pupils buy food at shops in the vicinity of the school and are outwith the school grounds at lunch-time.

(e) Adequate supervision of eight dining rooms is difficult.

(f) A social event is impossible, e.g. Burns Supper, as each individual room is too small to hold a full gathering.

C. Main Building.

THERE ARE NO ROOMS IN THE MAIN BUILDING WHICH COULD BE CONVERTED INTO USE BY THE TECHNICAL AND ART DEPARTMENTS. Several factors influence this, namely noise of machinery, space for workshop/craft areas and storage facilities.

PROPOSALS FOR PHASE ONE

A. Build a new dining area and kitchens

Plans are already available – the building could proceed without interfering with either the present High School or Primary School facilities. (1974 Project XQ – No. 3.)

B. Convert the ground floor of present dining area to accommodate technical and remedial departments

(a) Kitchen Area – an open area for technical craft subjects.

(b) Two Dining Rooms – technical drawing rooms.

(c) Two Dining Rooms – remedial rooms.

(d) Storerooms/staffrooms – technical stores and technician's room.

C. Convert the first floor of present dining area to art and drama departments and a resource area.

(a) <u>Kitchen Area</u> – an open area for art-based crafts including pottery.
(b) <u>Two Dining Rooms</u> – Art rooms.
(c) <u>One Dining Room</u> – school resource centre.
(d) <u>One Dining Room</u> – Drama studio.
(e) <u>Storerooms/staffrooms</u> – Art/Drama storage rooms and preparation areas.

<u>COMMENTS ON PHASE ONE</u>

This work could commence at any time.

The school roll would stabilise at 800–850 (my estimate!). The statisticians fail to take account of parents who move into the area so that their children can attend Gillespie's, e.g. James Gillespie's Primary School has 62–85 pupils in all year groups.

The movement of pupils between the Annexe and the Main Building involves crossing a main road and is dangerous. All S.1 and S.2 pupils travel to the Annexe at least once a week (480 pupils). At least 180 middle school and senior pupils travel three times each week.

Time has to be allocated to staff to travel. This is the equivalent of 3.6 teachers – a wasted resource.

Pupils' timetables are distorted because of the many constraints imposed by the existence of the Annexe.

Many interdepartmental activities involving Art/Technical/Drama departments are not possible because of the split site.

If these phase one plans were put into operation the school could be contained on one site in August, 1981.

LONG TERM PROPOSALS – PHASE TWO (1984–85)
TRANSITION TO A COMMUNITY SCHOOL

In the not too distant future James Gillespie's <u>Primary</u> School is likely to find alternative accommodation.

1. <u>Either</u>
    (a) in a new building which might be built in the present grounds
    (b) in the present Boroughmuir Annexe when their roll falls enough for Boroughmuir High School to be contained in its main building or in a new school.

2. The present primary school grounds and buildings would then become available and used as suggested below:-
    (a) A games hall and complex could be built,
    (b) A music area with practice rooms could be built,
    (c) Part of the present primary school could be used for social areas for senior pupils, etc.
    (d) Community accommodation could be built on the primary grounds.
    (e) There would still be room for some playing field areas.

3. The area lacks facilities for young people.

4. The school is already well used in the evenings.

The <u>gradual</u> transition of the school to a community school would ensure its success.

I hope you will find those proposals of interest and that they will provide a basis for further discussions at an early date.

P. THOMAS,
Head Teacher.
8.11.78

Nearly four decades later, in 2014 – and when Gillespie's was once again forced to use the Darroch Annexe – her successor successfully used this pamphlet to gain desperately needed extra teachers from the City Council.

In 1978, of course, Dr Thomas's proposals got nowhere – and, from 1980 and the controversial Parents' Charter, granting the (but slightly qualified) right to send your child to a school outwith your catchment area, Gillespie's attracted youngsters in droves and the roll did not fall nearly as fast as forecast. At last, under a more sympathetic Regional Council administration, and other political changes – the Edinburgh Central and Edinburgh South seats both fell to Labour in 1987, elevating Alistair Darling and Nigel Griffiths to Parliament – extension of the 1966 school was finally granted, with renovation of Bruntsfield House and the erection of a new James Gillespie's Primary School also approved. But there would be no return to the 'School on the Links'. When, by the early 1990s, it was at last no longer required by Boroughmuir, it was acquired by the University of Edinburgh and converted to student flats.

Dr Thomas's robust, clear writing skills hugely advanced the interests of her school and, often, members of staff. When, in August 1988, a job-scenting piano tutor dared to suggest to her superiors on Torphichen Street that Tom Laing-Reilly, who had joined the Music Department in 1982 and was besides an internationally regarded organist, rather shirked his duties, Patricia Thomas was incandescent –

> I was extremely angry about the insinuations about Mr Laing-Reilly, who is an excellent, most conscientious and concerned teacher. During school time he is solely involved in school business. He also gives us much time outwith school.
>
> At present he is with the school full-time – of this 0.6 is allocated to instructing and 0.4 to class teaching. Mr Laing-Reilly is a most talented keyboard specialist and is the only member of the Music department with the ability to accompany some of the more difficult pieces selected by pupils for examination purposes.
>
> Over the past session the Music department has only had available two of their three rooms – although alternative rooms were available they did not have a piano. The department co-operated fully by taking larger classes on many occasions so that some staff time became available. In order to make use of this time Mr Laing-Reilly used this extra time to give more piano lessons. These extra lessons have been discontinued.
>
> I might also add that Mr Laing-Reilly has frequently given up non-teaching time and time at lunchtime to be with pupils. The demand for instrumental teaching greatly exceeds the available instruction time for all instruments.

In Gillespie's the number of pupils taking certificate courses is extremely high. In the practical examinations nearly all the pieces need to be accompanied and Mr Laing-Reilly is the teacher usually used. At these times the 'extra' classes mentioned in the last two paragraphs will stop – and this may be the source of complaint . . .

'This high level of uptake in Music is very demanding on the staff,' she concluded silkily, 'and I would be delighted to have some extra piano instruction in the school.'

But year upon year of such doughty communication – from a woman, at that, correcting error, scolding slander, clarifying confusion, putting down the pompous and the incompetent or evasive; the relentless block-capitals, the emphatic underlinings – inevitably made Dr Thomas her foes; and as a communication style within the school – she much preferred memoranda and round-robins to personal conversation – it increasingly grated, especially on younger members of staff schooled in less deferential times, and the more as society wearied generally through the 1980s of another bossy English lady. If you make close study of the 1990/91 HMIE report on the school, internal concerns about managerial ways are clearly hinted.

'The Liaison Committee informs me that some members of staff feel "obliged" to attend these [in-service training] meetings because they feel that failure to do so would receive an adverse comment on any reference,' had stormed a typically unflinching Head Teacher's communiqué, to all staff, on 17 November 1978. 'This is completely and utterly without founda-tion. At the same time, I would expect staff attending any such in-service courses to note this on any application forms they completed . . . Staff are reminded that pupils should not be on the grass areas, including the grass between the Science Department and the driveway. The Liaison Committee feel that while some staff enforced this rule, others did not.' As for S.2 pupil absence for Outdoor Education, 'Since the liaison meeting this matter has been investigated. It has been confirmed that each pupil has ONE AFTERNOON OF OUTDOOR EDUCATION EACH SESSION. Parents sign consent forms. This is not excessive and will continue. P. THOMAS.'

•   •   •

*Opposite.
Informal school life,
as snapped for Snuff,
1984.*

By April 1990, Dr Thomas's enlarged school was slowly taking shape. Bruntsfield House had been extensively renovated and many of the upper rooms rearranged; three on the top floor, for instance, were knocked

Out and About

together to make one large bright classroom. The school library was redec-
orated and, for the first time, carpeted, and – regrettably – the original tables
and chairs were discarded. A big new games hall was under construction
on the east elevation of the main block and a new, 1988 extension bridged
to the upper floors of the dining block, creating new rooms for Art, Drama,
Commercial Subjects and the Social Sciences. The vacated rooms in the
single-storey Thirlestane block could then be converted for Technical classes
– and all this would finally allow departure from the Darroch Annexe.

There were other leavings. Jean McIntyre in 1986, for instance, to be
succeeded by the chilly charm of Alan Wilson. The gruff but kindly Mrs
Domanska had now stepped down. And, with the expected demise of the
Annexe, the school would be forced to shed one Assistant Head Teacher.
On the basis of last-hired-first-fired, that should have been Stewart
McDougall, but Iona Cameron gracefully took the opportunity to retire
instead, early – she was still only fifty-five – and on attractive terms. Her
speech at the leaving-do is still fondly recalled for its deftness of wit, under-
statement and diplomacy; she besides, that year, presented the prizes. Her
post was filled internally, on a continuing short-term AHT basis, by Colin
Dalrymple. Catherine Lambert at last quit in 1989, for what would prove
forlornly short retirement, and his former colleagues reeled in April 1988
when Allan Leslie – a hugely popular personality, who had in 1984 become
AHT of Boroughmuir, his old school – died suddenly of awful medical
mishap, still only in his mid-forties. Only one member of staff, the quiet
and respected Robert Galt, Principal Teacher of Biology, now survived from
the selective girls-only era. And another tragedy was imminent: by June
1991, gaunt in Dr Thomas's last staff photograph, Stewart McDougall was
gravely ill. He died on 16 August, as school returned only the following
morning; the victim of aggressive lung cancer. Just forty-five years old, he
left a young family.

The Conservative Government of the day had, in Scotland, become of
late very keen on encouraging schools (and especially good, popular
schools) to 'opt out' of local authority control, be run by parent-elected
boards and be directly funded by the Scottish Office. The appropriate legis-
lation took effect on 1 April 1990 and it was in this context – and as the
school continued to mend after the late industrial unrest – that Patricia
Thomas granted an interview to James Mitchell of the *Scottish Educational
Journal*.

Don't mention Jean Brodie or Marcia Blaine's to Pat Thomas. Being
Head Teacher of a large six-year comprehensive is a big enough

challenge without resurrecting the ghosts of popular fiction.

Dr Thomas has been Head of James Gillespie's High School since 1976 [*sic*] and admits that a significant part of her time has been spent dispelling the image created by Muriel Spark in *The Prime of Miss Jean Brodie*.

Yes, Gillespie's was the model for the fictional Marcia Blaine's; yes, Muriel Spark was a former pupil. But, 'we don't mention her. That image is so anti what we are trying to do now.'

Not all of the blame, though, can be laid at the door of the novelist. Until 1973, Gillespie's was most commonly known as a grant-aided girls-only school.

Like many examples of that sector, it took a considerable time to throw off the past and become accepted into the comprehensive, co-educational system. Inevitably, traditions endured.

Dr Thomas says of the change, 'The former pupils' association disowned themselves – they didn't want to know. But I don't pander to them.'

Nowadays, Gillespie's could be regarded as a model local authority secondary. Lothian Region saw fit to invest £3 million last year in an extensive building and refurbishment programme. And parental demand for places is such that, since 1985, the roll has been 'capped' by the council at 1100.

School EIS representative Colin Dalrymple, who is also secretary of the union's Edinburgh local association, says: 'To some extent, there is a perception by parents that they can get a private education for their children here without paying the fees.'

Dr Thomas takes a less hard-bitten approach. '(Our popularity) seems to come from parents who have spoken to other parents with children who are happy here. In addition, we do have a good record for results – but I say happy first.'

The school prospectus states, in block capitals, that 'the pursuit of excellence at all levels of study and ability is a major objective.' Yet it also makes clear that Gillespie's main function is to provide a wide variety of all experiences for learning.

For Dr Thomas, education is not just about academic achievement, but also social and personal development. 'I don't think you can achieve academic excellence unless the school staff are content and unless the pupils find school acceptable and are happy. Without those things, you can't get any academic success.'

It appears to be a view which is endorsed by the parents, given

Gillespie's roll numbers. There is, however, a problem ineluctably associated with popularity – class sizes.

The Head concedes that this does present difficulties, particularly in S.1. 'We are capped at 198 pupils, which very nearly divides into six classes at the maximum of 33 pupils. But I want to make it into seven next year.'

Dr Thomas is enough of a realist to accept that the much-cherished maximum of twenty pupils per class is unlikely to be achieved, if only for reasons of space and accommodation. But she feels a figure of 25 or 26 would produce significant improvements.

'Because education is so pupil-centred now, that would give the staff more time and more direct contact with the class as individuals.'

Colin Dalrymple points out that the huge recent increase in assessment also places a strain on a teacher with a 33-strong class.

Class sizes are not the only problem associated with success. The spectre of opting-out has often been attached to schools with proven academic records, situated in middle-class catchment areas. Gillespie's fits that bill.

Earlier this year, the extreme right of the Tory party – in the form of [Michael] Forsyth apparatchik, Peter Clarke – chose to float the possibility of opting-out for the school, along with Edinburgh counterparts Broughton High and the Royal High. His move brought an indignant response.

'The six parent members of our Board were elected on a platform of remaining within the state sector, and they took umbrage at this suggestion,' says Dr Thomas.

Mr Dalrymple adds that the unions locally suspect that the supposed parental interest was 'simply manufactured' and the Head was openly critical of political pressure groups in an internal newsletter.

'This is not the way to go about things. Trying to bring about change by pressure is just not on,' she says.

In a sense, though, the incident helped cement the already good relationship between the Board and the school. Dr Thomas describes the new body as 'very supportive, without wanting to interfere unduly'.

And the Board have already made some progress in working on the school's behalf. Gillespie's have a long-standing grouse about being separated by two miles from their playing-field, where facilities are described as 'very poor'. After hearing a deputation of board members, the Region's Education Committee called for a report on the situation by education director David Semple.

Perhaps one of Gillespie's most impressive achievements in recent times is its success in racial integration. Some 12 per cent of the school's roll could be described as from an ethnic minority – the list includes Chinese, Indian, Colombian, Brazilian, Norwegian, Icelandic, Canadian, French and German.

That figure gives the school the highest number of 'ethnic' pupils in Edinburgh, though Drummond Community High has a higher percentage.

Dr Thomas says: 'We have just about every nationality here – it's a super mix. We are trying to give the pupils a breadth of experience, and this aspect can only be to the good.'

Although Gillespie's do not practice positive discrimination, a racial equality does seem to exist. Indeed, the current deputy head boy, elected by his peers, is of Chinese origin.

The spirit of egalitarianism can be found elsewhere. It was significant that my interview with Dr Thomas included Colin Dalrymple, in a three-way conversation. And the Head was mostly in agreement with the union rep on current national issues. Both are EIS members.

Inevitably, Standard Grade featured prominently in the discussion. Dr Thomas is 'not happy that everything is as it ought to be', particularly at Credit level in the social subjects.

'There is such a variation in the material, and it has been so slow coming out. Some of the work needs revising for use in particular schools. Its success very much depends on the individual teacher – the good teacher will change things to suit.'

On head teachers' pay, a slight difference of opinion crept in. No surprise there, you might say. Dr Thomas feels a salary increase should be paid, given the extra workload and responsibilities endured by heads in recent times.

But she adds, 'Extra money by itself is not enough, because unless we get additional staff to help – then you might die rich.' Mr Dalrymple concurs, believing that increased staff is the most important way to help heads.

Appraisal brought considerable unanimity from the two interviewees. Dr Thomas says: 'So long as it's positive, and there are resources to do something about identified needs, it's fine. If not, you will simply end up with frustrated teachers. We also need a very thorough training programme for both appraisers and appraisees, and the whole thing must be linked to staff development.'

But on the possibility of local financial management, conflict emerged. Mr Dalrymple stuck loyalty to union policy of resisting it, while Dr Thomas would be prepared to try a scheme which brought financial benefit to the school, if support staff were provided. She would not, however, be happy to include decisions on staffing resources within her remit.

Most of the above issues are still some way away. For the moment, Gillespie's is using a current innovation, senior teachers – three in post, and two about to be appointed – to develop a 'whole curriculum' approach to education.

Each has a cross-curricular responsibility, with the intention of reinforcing links between departments, and making subjects more relevant for the pupils.

But Dr Thomas says; 'The most difficult thing is to allow them enough time to do the job they are supposed to do.' Sounds familiar . . .

•   •   •

On Friday, 15 March 1991, at two in the afternoon, there was a brief and elegant official opening ceremony for the new facilities. The platform party in the school hall included the guest of honour, Nigel Griffiths MP; Mrs Griffiths; Councillor Eric Milligan – Convener of Lothian Regional Council; and David Semple, Director of Education. There were appropriate remarks by Angus Wallace, Chairman of the School Board, and Elizabeth Maginnis, Chairman of the Education Committee. Fr Paul Rennie, of St Michael and All Saints Episcopal Church in Tollcross, school chaplain, offered a prayer of dedication, and pupils in the school's Jazz Ensemble diverted the assembled guests with 'Li'l Darling' and 'Killer Jo'. The Head Teacher finally gave an assured vote of thanks. Small groups then enjoyed conducted tours, before joining her for a finger buffet. It was a sweet, final triumph.

Dr Patricia Thomas retired, rather reluctantly, three months later at the end of the session – along with Robert Galt, an emphatic ending of an era. Not a trace of resentment or self-pity appears in her foreword, that June of 1991, to what besides would prove the last issue of *Snuff*. 'Change is always with us,' she said, 'especially in our personal life. More than half the

A relaxed moment in her Bruntsfield House study, March 1990. Though austere and shy, Pat Thomas cared passionately about her school and especially its poorest and most disadvantaged pupils. 'I think her greatest strength was planning and managing,' a colleague remembers. 'This masked a more caring side ... although few staff got close to her, I do not know of any former colleagues who did not respect her and the type of school she ran.'

sorrow and pain at the end of a pleasant episode in one's life is caused by a fear of a less happy future. The end of one stage will always coincide with the beginning of another and should be a time for looking forward with hope as well as reflecting with thankfulness on the past.'

In a long and extraordinarily busy retirement Dr Thomas has been true to her word. She has doughtily continued to be vigorous, to study, to serve – both as secretary of her local residents' association and for some years as a governor of St George's School for Girls, caring for youngsters with learning difficulties, and, an example to many to never stop studying, in her ninetieth year she is a pillar of the Edinburgh branch of the University of the Third Age, leading classes in sewing, homecraft and 'armchair travel', sitting in many others, enjoying its regular luncheons and, besides, frequent sessions of bridge.

CHAPTER NINE

'You can teach till you're blue in the face'

1991–2012

It is just after half past eight on a Friday morning early in November 2012 – a soft, autumnal one – and for the first time in nearly thirty years I walk to school, as I last walked it in June 1984, and by the same route, then in my maroon blazer and for the last time. In fact, I have left too early, striding up Morningside Road and in by Church Hill; journeys always seem longer, more arduous, more fraught when we are boys – and I have to kill time on Whitehouse Loan before, at five to nine, I slip timidly in by the great wooden doors in the high stone wall and trot down the avenue with the primary school on one side and the Spylaw science block – condemned, now, like the rest of the cheap 1966 erection – on the other.

At least I have the right tie on. By the stone arch I pause, a sign catching my eye. The little gated enclosure on my right is, now, the Alison Laidlaw Memorial Garden, honouring a life well lived from 1909 to 2007, surely the last who could remember watching a Zeppelin float balefully over Marchmont. I learn, later, this gentle memorial – a place of retreat – is maintained by gentler pupils under the warm supervision of Hamish McDougall.

The playground, if one could ever call it that, is already deserted; the buildings about me now humming, ever so quietly, with murmured education. Bruntsfield House has not changed, nor the great flight of steps up to the clock tower and the central campus. The clock is still not working; it is, apparently and for always, ten to two. The cedars and pines are much bigger than I remember; but, of course, they have had twenty-eight years for expansion.

The lobby has scarcely changed, save that the old janitor's lair at the lower level has gone and there is a new, glass-fronted reception box, where I explain my appointment and fill in a visitor's pass, clipping it on my lapel.

I amble about for a minute, taking stock – Mr Gillespie's benevolent bust still gazing down, May Andrew glowering hungrily as always from her portrait, the honours boards proclaiming successive Duxes and Head Girls – but the cabinets full of trophies have gone. There are wall-displays by pupils, on bullying and Aids. Finally, I sit down, faintly intimidated, as if I were past my time, from another age, and had no business to be here, and leaf through the latest school newsletter.

But there has been that strange recurring dream, of late – discomfiting; of being suddenly summoned back to school, told that because of an administrative error I never actually passed my Highers, that my entire adult life since has been, really, illegal. And thus, in my late forties, unaccountably clad in that long-lost blazer, I in my sleep toil anew amidst young people over thirty years my junior, no one finding my presence at all remarkable – finally, one day, awaking, I snapped. A tour of the old place might slay this weird nightmare; and, besides, the new Head Teacher – actually, the latest new Head Teacher, the third since Patricia Thomas – is a Hebridean; and one might as well see the gaff one last time before the bulldozers move in. So I had emailed: there was another excuse, besides, for the school has appealed for former pupils to form an Alumni Choir for this year's special Christmas Concert . . . but there is movement through the door, and instinctively I jump to my feet, almost expecting Stewart McDougall himself to materialise in authoritative scorn.

'Good morning, Headmaster,' I gabble. 'I'm John MacLeod …'

'Good morning,' says Donald J. Macdonald BSc DipEd SQH MBA pleasantly, with a level stare. 'Would you be more comfortable, John, if we speak in Gaelic, or do you prefer English?'

The school's new commander – taking office only that January – is very different from what I had expected. Erect as an officer, just under six feet tall, dignified as a bishop, Macdonald oozes gravitas; even – if you pushed it – a potential for menace. He is immaculately dressed; navy suit, neat tie, a stylish waistcoat. He looks much younger than his fifty-two years, with hair at once fair and grey, wide-set eyes of the palest blue making cool assessment behind square steel-framed glasses. He has – as I shall learn, over many months ahead, he almost invariably has, just as Miss McIver did – a folder under his arm, suggesting great business in hand, and a way of bracing his shoulders when about to unleash a speech, a decree, or a rebuke. He is, I will learn, kind, wise, intensely observant, in tune with his times and often very, very funny – but he is a man, first and foremost, of authority; and, of course, a native of North Uist. The folk of Tir an Eòrna are a maddeningly sorted lot.

Born in Stornoway, in July 1960, raised first in busy Lochmaddy and

then, from 1969, the quiet township of Blashaval ('my parents were worried
we would lose our Gaelic'), Mr Macdonald passed through Portree High
School, his contemporaries there including that eminent Free Churchman,
Rev. David Meredith, and film and television director Douglas Mackinnon.
Macdonald undertook teacher training at Moray House after graduating
from the University of Edinburgh with a degree in Physics. He drifted into
teaching on learning, he insists, that there was an acute shortage of science
teachers in Hawaii. 'And I still haven't got to Hawaii,' he observes wryly,
many years later.

Donald J. Macdonald has spent his entire career, launched in 1982, in a
succession of Lothian piles – Teacher of Physics and Sciences at Firrhill
High School; Assistant Principal Teacher of Sciences at Beeslack High
School in Penicuik; Principal Teacher of Physics and then Assistant Head
Teacher at Portobello High School; Deputy Head Teacher at Knox Academy
in Haddington; and finally Head Teacher at Liberton High School, before
his recent elevation. He has a reputation as a new broom, a troubleshooter,
a canny and determined Mr Fixit, as the *Evening News* reported in
November 2011 –

> An award-winning Head Teacher who turned around the fortunes
> of a city school has been appointed to the long-vacant top post at
> one of the city's best secondaries.
>
> Donald Macdonald is moving from his current post as Head of
> Liberton High to take up the position at James Gillespie's.
>
> Education bosses had to advertise the 'very prestigious position'
> at the Marchmont school three times before finally appointing Mr
> Macdonald, who will start in January.
>
> Parents at Gillespie's had written to education director Gillian
> Tee over their concerns in the delay in recruiting a new Head
> Teacher to replace Alex Wallace, who retired at the start of the
> summer holidays. They said it was causing 'disruption' and 'demor-
> alising' staff.
>
> Mr Macdonald is credited with turning around the fortunes of
> Liberton after taking up the post six years ago.
>
> When he first started, just seven students went on to university
> and school inspectors rated pupils' overall attainment as 'unsatis-
> factory'.
>
> Last year the number going on to university rose to 52 and the
> school was praised by inspectors for its outstanding educational
> improvement.

Wide-set eyes and an air of danger – Donald J. Macdonald has commanded Gillespie's since January 2012. Astute, engaging, highly experienced, a son of North Uist . . . and on no account to be messed with. (Andrew Digance)

Mr Macdonald took a tough line on bullying and discipline, excluding badly-behaved pupils who refused to change their ways. He also brought back uniform in an effort to give pupils more pride and help improve behaviour.

Inspectors said the changes resulted in the biggest improvement they had witnessed in a Scottish school.

Last March, Mr Macdonald was among 40 'outstanding' Head Teachers invited to Downing Street to meet Gordon Brown as a way of recognising their good work.

City education leader Councillor Marilyne MacLaren said: 'James Gillespie's have a great new recruit in Donald Macdonald.'

I assure him I am rather more confident in English, and we embark on a smooth tour of the central building. What was our cheerful Sixth Year common room is now a Guidance and careers-advice unit. Youngsters still bounce and splash around the swimming pool, but a framed copy of the Declaration of Arbroath no longer hangs by the staffroom door. The library these days is carpeted, the old fixtures gone; here, Sixth Year students take one look at us and peck suddenly at laptops.

No one wears uniform – that went with Dr Thomas, apparently, though a simplified version (white shirt or blouse, dark trousers or skirt and the school tie) is still worn for concerts and other public functions. 'I brought it back at Liberton,' says Mr MacDonald, 'shirts and ties; blazers for the prefects, and when I first came here I thought, "Well, this'll have to change," but now I am beginning to wonder . . .'

The hall has scarcely altered, though the tiered seating at the rear has long gone and the once ruby-red stage curtains are faded. The parquet flooring is very worn. I ask the Head Teacher how many of the 1966 buildings are to come down.

'The lot,' he says briskly. 'The fabric is in very poor condition. The buildings are, well, tired – and they're simply not suitable for modern teaching methods, which require much more flexible space; "hub" areas and so on.'

He sweeps a hand at the distant hall ceiling. 'On a *good* day, a day of moderate rain, we only need six buckets to catch the leaks when it rains . . .'

We pause at the gym, sticking our heads in. A girl has just completed some sort of elaborate somersault. 'Gemma,' enthuses the young male teacher, 'you showed control, poise, perfect execution .' He wheels on her watching classmates. 'What do you think? Any comments . . .?'

It strikes me in that instant that this is an easier, less fraught teaching environment – at least in PE – than I remember, and Donald Macdonald agrees. 'Well, we realised at last that if you don't involve pupils in your teaching – invite their opinions on each other's performance, and so on – you're wasting an important resource.'

He pauses.

'And, of course, when you and I were at school, things were very different. You were dealing with teachers who could physically attack you . . .'

We explore the new upstairs classrooms Dr Thomas finally won in 1991 – art, history and so on. We do not trouble the class in Music Room 2, though do cross the bridge and creep apologetically by the boys and girls in Music Room 1, where I am introduced to their ebullient teacher, Mrs Deirdre O'Brien, née Furie.

Scarcely any staff now survive from my era – just Hamish McDougall, in the Biology Department, and John Swinburne, Principal Teacher of History since a dismal turn of events at the end of the century. Douglas Burke retired in 2002, and Marianne Harkness soon after – who, over two decades earlier, on an elusive answer I gave in my Higher English prelim interpretation exercise, had dashed in bold red pen, '1/2 mark deducted for hedging your bets'. Gillespie's has never respected dithering.

Tom Johnson quit the chalkface in 2005; Tony Merriman in 2008.

Duncan MacLeod, Modern Languages, Ian Watson, of the PE Department, Mrs Young (née Stobbie) and Sandra Evans stepped down only in 2011. I ask about Thomas Laing-Reilly, but the name means nothing to Mr Macdonald. (I learn subsequently and with sadness of Mr Laing-Reilly's sudden death in November 2010, still a tutor at the school and for some years previously Principal Teacher of Music. Well I remember his patient piano coaching through my last session at school; the dry humour and the green blazer. The Christmas Concert in December 2010, at St Cuthbert's – where he was the cherished organist – was dedicated to his memory; and Laing-Reilly's wonderful album, *Adeste Fideles: Organ Music for Christmas*, is well worth buying.)

The Head Teacher's office is as majestic as ever, if rather less elegantly

The genial Douglas Burke at his 2002 retirement bash. Back row, left to right, Tony Merriman, Bruce Munro, Colin Finlayson, Alex Wallace. Front: Sally Westerman and Mr Burke.

furnished. Here Mr Macdonald apologises; he must place me in the hands of Mrs Janis Croll for the rest of my tour, but we will meet in an hour or so for a 'wee strupag', a cup of tea and something to nibble.

Janis Croll is an Acting Deputy Head Teacher – rather confusingly, like most state schools these days, that actually means Assistant Head Teacher. Gillespie's by late 2012 has four, including her for the duration of the rebuild, of these DHTs. There is no longer a Deputy Head Teacher in the true sense – a fearsome second-in-command, in charge of running the pupils while the Head Teacher runs the school. Mrs Croll is handsome, authoritative, bristly – and herself a Gillespie girl, leaving in 1975, not far behind Edi Stark and Elaine Anderson in that tragic class of 1973. Better still, considering her coming and important mission, she teaches Technical Studies and is a qualified architect.

We talk about the extraordinary shock to Gillespie's when it went co-educational and comprehensive at such short notice, as Janis Croll entered senior school. 'Oh, teachers did leave. Loads left. *Loads* . . . most of them were quite old, and had never taught boys in their entire career.' We chuckle over those we had shared, in our respective Gillespie's careers – Hugh Davidson, Mr Hay, Mrs Domanska ('Yes, she was rather gruff, wasn't she?') and Miss Jean McIntyre. She tells me, too, that in the girls-only days the belt was never used. 'Oh, no. Ladies didn't hit ladies. It was worse than that. They spoke to you. Said really mean, *horrible* things, tore you off a strip . . .'

We pass the boys' changing room, redolent of memory. 'I can't let you in there,' says Mrs Croll, quite properly. We waft, at once visitors and ghosts, authority and guest, around Spylaw and Warrender. They have scarcely changed – the old science benches; surviving, rolling rubber blackboards. But the corridors now seem cramped, dark; the decoration poor and peeling, skirting boards battered and upper floors ominously spongy. These are buildings old before their time, not fit for modern purpose, doomed to die.

The atmosphere is subtly different, though, from the 1980s. The young-sters are quieter, and seem happier. Come the morning interval, and there is not the old jostling, scrapping, de'il tak' the hindmaist Darwinian rush for exits. They talk, rather than shriek. Many, of course, instantly flick on their smartphones. (There are signs by all the entrances now ordering that mobile telephones be switched off during class; forbidding headgear indoors, save the culturally prescribed.) You are struck, too, how boys mingle with girls, chatting as equals; in our time, without even thinking about it, and at least till Fourth Year, we tended to hang apart.

For the first time in my life I am admitted to the staffroom. There is an

Gillespie Girls enjoying school dinner in elegant style, 1959.

ongoing weekly baking competition and relaxed, cheerful faculty hand out cake and buns and fruitloaf. The tea is good. The Head Teacher joins us. Mr Macdonald cheerfully announces my presence and compliments me for wearing the old school tie. Everyone is very kind. Departing, a little overwhelmed, I thank him warmly for my experience today; he eyes me in a thoughtful sort of way.

A week or two later, I have an email from him: might I drop in on such-and-such an afternoon? He has a proposal . . .

Days later, I am again in his office, around the big conference table, enjoying more tea and ginger biscuits. Mr Macdonald explains about the James Gillespie's Trust, their plans to mark the opening of the rebuilt campus in four years' time – and asks if I might consider writing this book. I assent on the spot.

•   •   •

Colin Finlayson
(seventh from left,
front row) with his
staff, around 1996.
Some familiar faces
are still in harness.

Colin Finlayson MA (Hons) Dip Ed succeeded Dr Thomas as Head Teacher of James Gillespie's High School in August 1991. It was practically a coronation, the Education Department and certain local councillors being determined on his installation and her departure from the earliest point. They had, after all, just closed his school down. He besides had the immediate emergency of Stewart McDougall's death, and quickly appointed Alex Wallace as a new Assistant Head Teacher – and, as events proved, later Deputy Head and, finally, in October 2003, his (acting) successor. Wallace was not, though, confirmed as Head Teacher till July 2005, and might just have been pipped by Donald Macdonald, six years early. He also applied for the position but was offered the headship of Liberton High School four days before candidates for Gillespie's were to be assessed. He hesitated momentarily before accepting that difficult brief.

'I felt it wouldn't be fair to Liberton to keep them hanging till I saw how the Gillespie's interview went – if I hadn't got Gillespie's then I'd have begun at Liberton on the wrong foot – and it would have been a bit hard for Alex if I had got Gillespie's then . . . he'd been deputy for long enough, Acting Head Teacher for nearly two years.'

Finlayson and Wallace worked so closely together – there was growing emphasis, by the 1990s, on collegiate and consultative school leadership – that the two decades from 1991 to 2011 can broadly be regarded as one continuous head-teachership. It was a reign of the same values and emphases and priorities, the exuberant, outgoing if somewhat divisive Wallace balancing the quieter, more thoughtful style of Finlayson, with like determination that no child should feel marginalised or unvalued within the school community – and a certain desire to strip Gillespie's of the last baggage of, as they insisted, its selective and 'privileged' past.

It was not so much conscious iconoclasm as generational changing of the guard; an almost casual (but sudden) break with yore and anything that hinted of a private school with venerable honours. School uniform *redux* was now but for high days. Blazers, prefects, prize-giving and the old house system were discarded. Founder's Day had, in any event, lapsed from 1984. So had the school magazine, till two last-gasp issues of *Snuff* in 1990 and 1991. There would now be no more till senior pupils launched *The Spark* late in 2013. Even the word 'pupils' fell from favour from 1991; suddenly, James Gillespie's High School belonged to 'students'.

Senior management besides came up with a wordy 'mission statement', for all intents and purposes a new motto: 'We respect and care for each other and value the diversity which exists among people.' This was by the mid-1990s prominent in a long mural by the ramp through the school hall – and not just in English, but in Urdu, Arabic and Cantonese, and besides images of assorted pupils of varied ethnicity. This, Finlayson recalled in January 2013, 'was one of our first efforts to change the physical culture of the school into one which reflected diversity and equality. The mural was actually real physical profiles of students at the time taken from photographs and projected onto the wall so they could be painted. They were really chuffed! Liz Radcliffe, who was one of our art teachers, created them . . . I regularly talked about the profiles and the statement in assemblies as a means of bringing to life their meaning and articulating them into the consciousness of the students and staff. Another of these physical changes was the removal of the bust of James Gillespie from a plinth in the music room to the high-level display in the entrance hall – which Colin Greenham, Head Janitor, created.' The bust was always in the foyer in my own time; it had probably been briefly removed to Music Room 1 when, in 1990, pressures on space were such that all Dr Thomas could afford for a Sixth Year Common Room – of sorts – was that same entrance hall, and no doubt wisely feared for the Merchant of Spylaw's health and well-being.

That said, it is worth reminding ourselves that by 1990 Dr Thomas had clear racial awareness and multi-cultural policies in conspicuous place; and that her prospectus drafted for a final session, preserved in the Gillespie's archives, also began with multi-lingual greetings reflecting the school's broader ethnic base. Her successors invented little but shouted it far louder; might have talked up the ossification they inherited. What they certainly delivered was a distinctly happier working environment for teachers after strained, unhappy years from the mid 1980s.

There was, though, one important reform – a much more powerful and

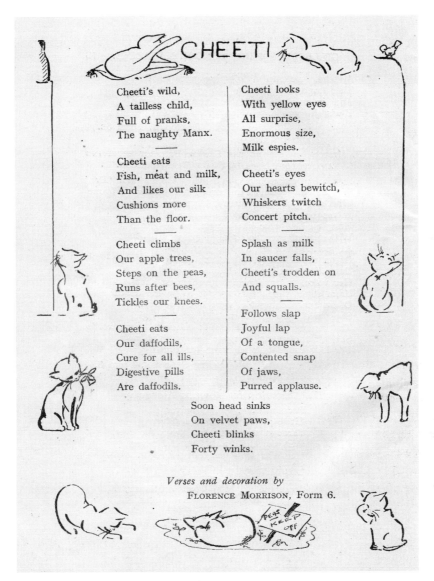

CHEETI

Cheeti's wild,
A tailless child,
Full of pranks,
The naughty Manx.

———

Cheeti eats
Fish, meat and milk,
And likes our silk
Cushions more
Than the floor.

———

Cheeti climbs
Our apple trees,
Steps on the peas,
Runs after bees,
Tickles our knees.

———

Cheeti eats
Our daffodils,
Cure for all ills,
Digestive pills
Are daffodils.

Cheeti looks
With yellow eyes
All surprise,
Enormous size,
Milk espies.

———

Cheeti's eyes
Our hearts bewitch,
Whiskers twitch
Concert pitch.

———

Splash as milk
In saucer falls,
Cheeti's trodden on
And squalls.

———

Follows slap
Joyful lap
Of a tongue,
Contented snap
Of jaws,
Purred applause.

Soon head sinks
On velvet paws,
Cheeti blinks
Forty winks.

Verses and decoration by
FLORENCE MORRISON, Form 6.

Senior pupils have in recent years launched a lively review, *The Spark*. They do not, these days, write about fluffy little kittens. From the school magazine, 1944.

influential role for the parent body. Though Dr Thomas had established a Parent–Teacher Association, she kept mums and dads firmly in their place. Under Finlayson and Wallace, though, they proved a resource mightily to be deployed and through (especially) the new Parent Council, Gillespie families now had a powerful platform – and were not afraid to use it in vigorous support of senior management, lobbying of the Education Department, and so on.

One notable offshoot, too, was the creation of the James Gillespie's

Trust, which 'aims to support the school and foster strong links between the school, the community and the alumni. The Trust wishes to harness the tremendous goodwill that is felt for James Gillespie's High School to support the work of the school through various educational schemes and community projects.' The Trust also contributes to good causes and pupil initiatives, its website noting – among those for the 2005–06 school session – '£250 was awarded to Callum Skinner, who competes in track-cycling at a national level. The award will pay for travel to his training weekends and competitions and for various pieces of equipment for his bike. He hopes his success will lead him to the Olympics! Good luck from the Trust, Callum!' It was some investment: Skinner returned a decade later from Rio de Janeiro as an Olympic champion. By 2007 they had established the 'Living Stories' project – a priceless oral-history programme, run by senior students with appropriate support and which has created a splendid archive of recorded interviews with dozens of former pupils. A still more tangible memorial was in 2008 also shaped –

The Alison Laidlaw Memorial Garden Project

In memory of a very special Former Pupil and Former Teacher 1909–2007.

The Garden was opened on Friday June 20th by the son of the only remaining living relative of Miss Laidlaw, her cousin in Canada.

A small phial of Miss Laidlaw's ashes was placed in the garden, just before the opening ceremony.

It was a lovely sunny day and over eighty former pupils attended the opening, preceded by lunch and followed by a concert by current pupils and tea.

We were delighted to have so many former pupils attend and re-visit the school, some for the first time in many years. The garden remains open in term time and can be visited by former pupils.

We are grateful to the Trustees of the Laidlaw-Hall Trust for their generous donation towards this project; the funds originated from Miss Laidlaw's estate.

We are also grateful to Miss Laidlaw's cousin in Canada and her family, for their generous donation and to those of you who have, or may wish to give, a donation.

In Miss Laidlaw's name, we thank you for your generosity.

We felt a garden was the most fitting memorial to Miss Laidlaw. She loved the outdoors and her modern holistic attitude to education is reflected in the concept. She would not have wanted a brass plaque: we can imagine her saying "someone would only have to clean it!" The garden is designed for the use of the current pupils and staff and is open to visitors and former pupils. We have plans to open this part of the campus to the public, in the future.

The Garden design is by Marion Rodger, a parent at the school. She donated her time and expertise to the Trust.

The garden has been created within the ruined walls of an ancient salt store at the front of Bruntsfield House, near to the 'famous' archway.

Current pupils at the school are helping with the restoration and planting.

The garden is a project in process and the opening marks the completion of Stage One: further work will be continuing on its design and upkeep in the context of this part of the school campus.

•   •   •

Born in Edinburgh in 1943, Colin Finlayson was, of course, not just the first man to captain Gillespie's in over half a century, but, too, the first native of the city in still longer – and a man of modest background who, in youth, he felt strongly and feels still, had been badly let down by the education system.

Finlayson is a humble, unassuming and very fine man; tall, with luxuriant hair even in his eighth decade and a rather becoming little beard. On occasion, he could be magnificent. His address at the funeral for Ian Nicol – the much-loved, long-serving PE and Guidance teacher, recently snatched by Peter Galloway to become an AHT at Trinity Academy, only to succumb to stress-related illness and take his own life in February 1996 – transformed what could have been the grimmest occasion into something most moving, worthwhile. The Head Teacher besides went to great pastoral length to support and console the shaken school community, and arrange appropriate rites for distraught pupils.

'I think the sad tragedy has been handled, by the school, very sensitively and with great dignity. The response from the staff and pupils has been immense in our shared grief and we have all been given the opportunity to pay our last respects in a way we will remember,' Tom Johnson wrote his Head Teacher. 'I would like to thank you for the very moving oration at Ian's funeral yesterday,' says a note from Anne Inglis, School Librarian. 'I can only guess at how difficult such a speech is to prepare, but even worse to deliver. Speaking personally, I found the other descriptions of Ian's life to be fairly anonymous. The spiritual evaluation of his death left me unmoved. Your humorous and full account of Ian confirmed what we have all lost. I am sure that it was a great comfort to his family.'

Colin Finlayson came up the hard way. He had never passed the 'qually', leaving school in 1958 with no Lowers or Highers. At seventeen, though, he began attending a local church, became a Christian, found himself active in various useful organisations and applied himself to private study. At twenty-five he entered the University of Edinburgh and, after graduation, the teaching profession. He enlarged on all this, near retirement, when Edi Stark asked him cheekily if he felt he 'fitted in' with his formidable predecessors –

> I don't suppose I do feel the same. Frankly, going back two or three head teachers, the perception of many people is that head teachers of Gillespie's have been fairly austere and very strict people. My own background is very working-class – my father was a plumber and my mother was a cleaner – and I left school when I was fifteen, and the school system – I was obviously able, but the school system at that time failed me. I failed within – or it failed me. Probably one of the two. And I think that has marked the way I felt about educating children all the way through.

Nor had he any time for the 'crème de la crème' mentality.

> There's certainly a lot of former pupils who will always see Gillespie's in that light. But I think I would reject the whole philosophy of that. I think the good part of the philosophy, if you like, was that it gave youngsters a sense of self-esteem – that it built them up and raised their expectations that you could achieve things. I think we still have that, but it applies to all children rather than a 'crème de la crème'. And I think one of the bad things about that philosophy is that it created in other people a view that some people are better than other people, and I think what I feel most pleased about is the fact that, though not really focused that much on academic attainment, academic attainment has improved despite that. I think what we've focused on is creating a learning-environment for our youngsters in which they feel valued and secured, where individuals are valued and where cultures are valued. And we've done a lot on improving learning and teaching. But I think it's the combination of that and

the ethos of the school that has changed academic attainment.

I think it would be true of people outside the school who are not parents that Gillespie's is still a bit like a private school. I think most of our parents would not recognise that picture and would think we're a good comprehensive school.

As for 'Fidelis et Fortis' – 'Mottos like that, I don't think they fit in with the modern world.'

At times one wondered if the new regime was deliberately out to tease: old Gillespie girls turning up for a bicentennial 'Afternoon Tea' event on 27 September 2003 were startled to be treated to 'a string quartet, tabla, clarsach ensemble, a Spanish dancer, Chinese fusion, break-dancing and hip-hop . . .'

Certainly Finlayson and Wallace were determined to celebrate positively the variety of beliefs, traditions and ethnicities in the school community; to stifle chauvinism, bigotry and prejudice of any kind. On occasion, though, it must have felt (as Archbishop Fulton Sheene joked of hearing nuns' confessions) as if you were being stoned to death with popcorn. There survives, amusingly, in the school archives a draft questionnaire for pupils, 'How equal do opportunities feel at Gillespie's?', dotted with trite cartoons of Arabs and Eskimos and so on. It was filed away with the tart comment, 'Colin, I spoke to Dave and recommended the removal of cultural stereotypes! Alex.'

By 2001, workshops on equality were held for S1 pupils. The Parent Information booklet for the 2002/2003 session bears still another epigram on its cover – 'A welcoming and secure environment in which individuals can realise their potential in a climate of mutual respect.' More, the mantra is reprinted at the foot of every page following in the 52-page publication; and there is still a third mission statement inside –

James Gillespie's High School has, for many years, welcomed students from different countries and cultures. Our school is a multiracial one, where we value all our students equally, believing that school is a reflection of society itself and that good relationships within the school can help promote harmony outside in the wider community. We have many years' experience in multicultural education and are able to give specialised help to those with language problems. We encourage all parents to come and discuss areas of difficulty, language or otherwise, with us, believing that education must involve parents as well as students.

This is reprinted over two pages following in Gaelic, French, German, Spanish, Urdu, Punjabi and Cantonese. On page 6, we meet

Our school values

This school, as a community, will provide a welcoming and secure learning environment in which individuals can fully realise their potential in a climate of mutual respect.

We are committed to ensuring that the James Gillespie's High School community is one in which:

- We trust and respect each individual.
- We respect and care for each other and value the diversity which exists among people.
- Students develop responsibility for themselves and a sense of self-worth, which is strong in success or failure.
- There is a commitment to education as a lifelong experience.
- There are high and realistic expectations of success.
- Learning experiences fully meet the learning needs of all people.
- There are stimulating learning experiences of the highest quality.
- There is a positive attitude to progress, change and improvement.
- All members develop an awareness of their social responsibilities.
- All members have opportunities to work towards improving the environment, both locally and globally.

On page 7 we are finally told the school's address, contact information and the name of the Head Teacher.

Both Finlayson and Wallace were, inevitably, stamped by their own experience. Wallace, among the first of more radically trained teachers to emerge from colleges in the early 1970s, was a warm-hearted Fife lad, born in 1949, attending St Andrew's High School in Kirkcaldy and entering the teaching profession with a degree in Geography and Modern Studies. He taught first in Kirkcaldy's Balwearie High School and, just six months into the profession and still a probationer, became Assistant Principal Teacher of Guidance. He then served at Edinburgh's Craigroyston High School as Principal Teacher of Learning Resources – one of the city's more robust academies and where the youngsters could have joyously taught 'the hard cases down the Annexe' a thing or two. Like many of his contemporaries in that position, Alex Wallace boldly developed an unconventional, very informal and even buddy-buddy pedagogic style – an egalitarian approach, a way of high-fives, banter and nicknames. His new position was the first of its kind in Scotland – 'I introduced Thinking Skills, Cognitive Skills etc., with an emphasis on how to learn rather than what to learn.' After secondment to Lothian Region's Education Department to train teachers in 'Student-Centred Learning' he, too, came to Gillespie's, late in 1991, as Assistant Head Teacher of Teaching and Learning and in the late McDougall's stead. Wallace was later promoted to the deputy headship, on the departure of Jack Hamilton (who had succeeded the gifted Alan Waugh in 1992) and by then had long rejoiced in the nickname of 'Waldo'.

Colin Finlayson had come to Gillespie's, months before Wallace, after three years in the still more desperate environment of Ainslie Park High School, covering some of the most notorious schemes in Edinburgh (including West Pilton, shortly to be immortalised in Irvine Welsh's *Trainspotting* and the subsequent 1996 black comedy of a film adaptation.) In an interview with *Scottish Child*, late in 1990, we gain a good glimpse of his philosophy –

I felt that the school needed to look at its *value* system. I want a system in our school that puts the young person right at the centre. By that I mean I would like to develop in the children a trust that the staff do genuinely care about them . . .

But you don't change it by issuing circulars or revising the curriculum, however important these things may be. The most crucial skill the staff of any school have to learn is being able to *listen* to children, as well as to talk to them. You learn to listen by wanting to hear what the other person has to say – that's the change in attitude that is required. And of course there are other obvious ways in which you make sure you hear more – like being around in the corridors and open spaces more when the pupils are moving around. Being *available* to children . . .

I think we have to acknowledge that a lot of the children we teach actually do not know how to behave in a whole number of situations. Once you look at the problem from that angle, you can see that it's not so much a 'discipline' problem as a 'learning' problem. So the answer lies not in the mechanisms of punishment but in those of education – learning greater self-control, better social skills and so on. That's what we've set up – using a range of different behavioural techniques.

The other side of the coin is that if we expect young people to behave more politely to us, we have to do the same for them. I don't expect the staff to shout at their pupils . . .

If I've not talked much so far about the classroom and subjects and exams, it's not because I don't think they're important. I think they are vital but you can teach until you're blue in the face – if you're teaching children who don't enjoy working, don't enjoy learning, you have small hope of really reaching them. It's all part of the overall theme that you feel better about yourself if you do better, work harder. Everyone can make something of themselves, not just the lucky few. That's what we want to get across. But if we're going to make it sound convincing we have to overcome our own resistances, as well as the resistance of a culture of non-achievement.

Ainslie Park closed in 1991, despite a ferocious campaign to keep it open and in which Colin Finlayson played his part deftly and well, fighting hard to save it without crossing any line and embarrassing his employers.

He has spoken well of his Gillespie's predecessor. 'I think I only met Pat Thomas twice – she seemed a fairly formal and reserved character. However, I think she was pretty highly regarded as a very good administrator with some innovative ideas . . . Once on an in-service course prior to my appointment where she gave a very good presentation about the JGHS use of senior teachers. I attended one Board of Management meeting which she chaired before I took up post (the last one before Stewart McDougall died) and then she graciously disappeared and was not present from my appointment.'

It was Alex Wallace, Colin Finlayson says with quiet pride, who in 2000 came up with 'Diversecity,' an annual celebration of the joyous *smörgåsbord* of Gillespie's cultures and traditions, with projects or exercises as well as performance and the occasional feast. Their colleague Marie Chetty – she taught Drama and Media Studies – helped with its early organisation, and as a 2008 School Review by Edinburgh City Council's Education, Children and Families sub-committee observed,

> The manner in which the school welcomed and celebrated diversity and addressed discrimination was considered by the review team to be sector-leading. An outstanding example of this was recognised nationally by the award of substantial Lottery funding for the work done as part of the Diversecity project. Pupils took part in a sponsored walk organised around the One Scotland–Many Cultures theme which encouraged them to illustrate and celebrate their diverse cultural backgrounds.

A 2009 mural celebrating the school's links with South Africa. (Ann Henderson)

This of course built on the school's long-established tolerance – and Dr Thomas herself, in her last years, had reinforced it in detailed policy – but Diversecity became a show-stopping event in the Gillespie's calendar and has been widely studied by other schools and local authorities. Alex Wallace besides, from 2003, fostered what is now a cherished relationship between James Gillespie's High School and friends in post-apartheid South Africa, as that same School Review noted: 'As part of its enterprise and citizenship programme, the school had developed links with Zwelibanzi High School, Ulmazi Township in Durban. Pupils at James Gillespie's High School had organised and participated in a range of activities to raise funds which had been used to provide the African school with a wide range of resources. Examples include raising money to build a library and create a sports field. Currently, S1 and S2 pupils are raising money every week to fund a soup-kitchen feeding over 120 children every day and S3 and S4 pupils raise money to pay for a sports coach. Every year 30–40 S6 pupils along with 5–6 members of staff visit the school to work with the children and teachers … Global citizenship issues were given a very high profile through the link with Zwelibanzi High School.'

The Zwelibanzi bond in the years since has only strengthened, the project winning praise from such luminaries as pop artist Annie Lennox and Archbishop Desmond Tutu. And if all this sounds like a soggy, ongoing tale of group-hugs, hands-across-the-sea and all-must-have-prizes, Colin Finlayson's point to Edi Stark nevertheless stands: without undue focus on academic success, the school grew even more successful anyway. As a sharp writer for *The Scotsman* observed on 16 September 2003 –

> In May 2002, Her Majesty's Inspectors gave Gillespie's a glowing report, with the ethos of the school coming in for particular praise. The report said: 'Cultural, ethnic, religious and linguistic diversity was recognised, valued and celebrated. The school had taken a number of steps to ensure that pupils were valued equally and treated fairly. Pupils and staff were proud of the school. Relationships between teachers and pupils were very positive and morale was high.'
>
> The HMIs can say what they like, but equally telling is how parents vote with their feet. There is a waiting list of 80–90 children hoping to enrol. As the catchment area zigzags to include parts of Bruntsfield, Tollcross, Marchmont and the High Street, the intake is largely middle-class.
>
> The school's Higher results last year were the 13th-highest in Scotland, and Gillespie's is, with good reason, a magnet school.

It should be noted firmly that Finlayson made special efforts for the one group neglected by Dr Thomas – the cleverest pupils. 'The Additional Learning Opportunity (ALO) was one of the really good curricular innovations of our time,' he recalls, 'aimed at developing the intellectual challenge of the most able students in JGHS. We provided it for a number of years – aimed at the most able students, but self-selected, where we withdrew them from the curriculum in S3 for a day a month and did whole-day alternative activities on themes such as writing and art, often bringing in external leaders. Alex and I led this as a way of motivating the most able – it was a highly successful experience.

'Alex and I had a great partnership,' Finlayson says, 'and he often said that my real gift in terms of leadership was enabling others to be creative and develop their vision of how to lead the school forward.' Wallace, ebullient, charismatic, of toothy grin and luscious wit, was hugely popular with the youngsters. Delivering a few remarks at the 2012 Christmas Concert in the Usher Hall, over a year after his retirement, a very former pupil mentioned the three sometime Head Teachers still living and, as he named 'Mr Alex Wallace . . .' the galleries echoed from this tremendous,

spontaneous roar from the massed choir behind him, whooping and whistling and applauding. For half a minute he could say no more: it was the children, dozens and dozens of them, ecstatic at the very mention of their old hero.

Some staff were more ambivalent. 'I got downright enraged at the cult rally masquerading as Alex Wallace's farewell gala evening,' recalls one former teacher, 'when he more or less claimed that it was entirely due to his efforts that Gillespie's was no longer an elitist establishment and that his initiatives had ensured that the less able or culturally different students were only now able to flourish. The audience received this gleefully and he left the stage to the chant of "Waldo, Waldo". I quietly left and reflected on the many initiatives which my colleagues from the Dr Thomas era had pioneered, with the aim of making the world a fairer place but without a

Gillespie's teachers, old and new, at Napier University's Craighouse campus for the Sixth Year leavers' party, June 2002. Though the school culture was now much less formal, academic attainment continued to climb.

fanfare of self-promotion . . .' But the two had never got on, and Wallace, after two decades and with big, substantive achievements, and whose early months at Gillespie's had not been very pleasant, was entitled to a little glory.

We should not overlook one notable accomplishment of Colin Finlayson's: he moved quickly when a large chunk of garden-ground on Thirlestane Road, once part of the policies of St Margaret's Convent, was sold for housing development. It was but one block south of Gillespie's. As part of their planning consent, though, the concern had to allow some of the land to be used for local recreational purpose: Finlayson negotiated warmly and long, secured an extraordinarily generous deal, and the upshot was that at long last Gillespie's won some safe, walled and useful outdoor sports ground within ready walking distance of the school.

He besides with extraordinary delicacy, in March 2003, negotiated the passions raging within the Gillespie's community about the invasion of Iraq –

> A number of organizations are encouraging school students to attend anti-war demonstrations during school time. Whilst we recognize that many children and adults have strong convictions about the war, the school has conveyed a clear line to all students about absenting themselves from school. We cannot give permission for any young person to absent themselves from school for political purposes. It is also not acceptable for a parent to write to school seeking to authorize the absence since the law is clear that it is the responsibility of parents to ensure their children attend school. We are also concerned for the safety of children who leave school. All absences related to anti-war demonstrations will therefore be recorded as truancy from school. This does not indicate the school is adopting a pro-war or anti-war stance. It would be improper for us to do so. Our responsibility and duty is to record attendance, to encourage students to be responsible learners, and to keep you informed. These are difficult times for all of us and feelings are running high. We are urging restraint and calm, considered responses in line with our school ethos and value statements.

A group of banner-waving 'James Gillespie's High School' students was nevertheless photographed at a vast STOP THE WAR event in Edinburgh.

And, after years when she had been all but *persona non grata*, channels of communication were somehow quietly established with an eminent former pupil. In March 1997, Dame Muriel Spark travelled to London to accept the David Cohen British Literature Prize – effectively for lifetime achievement, bestowed previously only on V.S. Naipaul and Harold Pinter – and with a fat cheque for £30,000 and another £10,000 for the good cause of her choice.

Characteristically – almost eighty – she bought herself a new Alfa Romeo. And, to widespread surprise, gave that £10,000 to James Gillespie's High School.

And late in January 2003, launching the school's bicentenary celebrations, Colin Finlayson boldly booked out the entire Lyceum Theatre for the opening night of Siobhan Redmond's revival of *The Prime of Miss Jean Brodie* – the sign, surely, now of an institution at peace with its past.

•   •   •

There were, in all this period, but two minor trials and a squalid tragedy. The first was the witless decision by the city fathers not to buy the site of an obsolete electricity substation, within the school grounds by the White-house Loan wall, when the land came on the market at very short notice. By the time City Council officials had moved – with all the vigour of a frozen sloth – it had been snapped up to build national offices for the charity Children First. There was hair-tearing vexation in Finlayson's Bruntsfield House study; real anger from neighbours and the wider school community. It was not that they had no respect for Children First, or that the completed structure – on the Whitehouse Loan side, towards the southwest corner – was particularly unattractive; but it limited still further any options in the future for extending or rebuilding the school itself.

The second, in 2005, was the substantial revision – the first in over thirty years – of the James Gillespie's High School catchment area. There was still more terrific fuss – these things are not just about sentiment or inconvenience; they affect property values – but the changes were implacably made. The catchment area shifted eastwards and a little north. Bruntsfield Primary (and all the lush and gracious villas of its catchment) now fed into Boroughmuir High School: Gillespie's gained the Sciennes, Preston Street and Royal Mile Primary Schools as feeder-primaries. There were new little pockets of serious social deprivation and, as of natural course, Gillespie's dipped – on ill-analysed unpasteurised data – in the sort of examination league tables beloved of headline-writers and right-wing politicians

We might besides note that Gaelic-medium education had begun in a special unit at Tollcross Primary School as long ago as 1988, and inevitably – it being a feeder-primary for Gillespie's – demand steadily built for

Gaelic-medium classes there. By 2002, Gaelic was at last taught as a language in Gillespie's, both for the traditional Higher (for native speakers) and the alternative Higher course for Gaelic learners. As the Tollcross project slowly but steadily prospered, parental desire grew for a free-standing school and the redundant Bonnington Primary School would finally open for this purpose on 16 August 2013, rebranded Bun-sgoil Taobh na Pàirce. Gillespie's, for the time being, is its reception-secondary, and Donald Macdonald's own fluent Gaelic was perhaps a factor in his appointment.

And there broke, sorely, the only serious scandal in the school's history. In May 2000 Alan Wilson, Principal Teacher of History, suspended since February 1999, was convicted at Edinburgh Sheriff Court of eight charges of sexual assault, on three Gillespie's boys, and subsequently sentenced to eighteen months in prison. In ghastly postscript, in March 2004 his body was found in the city's Merchiston Gardens – in six bits. Ian Sutherland, 33 – they had met in jail; he had not the least connection with the school – was subsequently convicted of Wilson's murder.

'It seems to me,' Colin Finlayson reflected quietly in February 2015, 'that the Alan Wilson story is *not* a part of the school story, but part of the human tragedy . . . sin . . . how brilliant, inspirational people can destroy themselves and others.

'No doubt there are other dark episodes in the history – like the pupil who threatened to firebomb the school a number of times, causing chaos for days – but perhaps the focus of the history should be about how a school community, with a very diverse human population with all the innate weaknesses we have, creates a culture and ethos that strongly promotes positive behaviour and achievement and manages to deal helpfully (mainly) with the frailty of human beings.'

On leaving for higher things in October 2003, Finlayson told staff, pupils and parents, 'My years at James Gillespie's have been a great privilege for me, working with the staff, parents and the fantastic young people who pass through our school.

'Gillespie's has a long and proud academic tradition. In recent years we have been able to extend that tradition by developing an ethos that is in tune with modern society. It is a different tradition from the Gillespie's of history. But, tradition needs to be continually updated so that it is appropriate for the children of today. Her Majesty's Inspectorate described the Gillespie's of 2002 as having "a culture which promotes high levels of attainment and mutual respect and understanding between pupils from diverse cultures". We could not, I think, ask for more.'

Alex Wallace in turn declared, 'Our bicentenary year has been an exciting one for all of us . . . I am, I hope, known to the young people and parents of our school since I have been Assistant Head Teacher and Deputy Head Teacher over the past 12 years. I am delighted to be taking over as the Head Teacher, and there is nowhere else I would rather be.

'Gillespie's is a wonderful school to work in as Colin's quote from the HMI indicates. I look forward to consolidating the excellent reputation of the school and I have a number of ideas for further developing our high levels of achievement. I would like to publicly thank Colin for his excellent leadership throughout his time here. I promise you that I will give my all to ensuring that JGHS carries onwards and upwards.'

•   •   •

The work went on. But Wallace's eight years in immediate, genial charge were exasperatingly dominated by one issue – the school's infernal, failing, disintegrating buildings. As early as 2002, that same HMIE report – piling praise on staff and teachers – had besides noted a lack of classrooms, inadequate science facilities, incessant 'difficulties' with the antiquated and grossly inefficient heating-plant and leaking roofs. Her Majesty's Inspectorate still, politely, described the state of the campus as 'fair'. By 2008, it was positively debauched, as Sue Leonard related in an article that May for the *Times Educational Supplement Scotland* –

Ceiling tiles are missing, sections of carpet are being held together by gaffer tape, chunks of stonework have been devoured by damp and netting has been placed around loose brickwork to stop it falling on to the playground below. Welcome to James Gillespie's High, one of Scotland's top academic state schools.

With poor ventilation and uneven paving stones, broken doors, smelly toilets and missing roofing, James Gillespie's would look more at home in eastern Europe than it does in Edinburgh's affluent south side. Parents have jokingly described its down-at-heel appearance as 'shabby chic', but the joke is beginning to wear as thin as the ageing flooring which has become a potential hazard. None of the teachers is laughing; they are fed up and morale is low.

An emergency meeting was held by the School Board in March, following a damning report into the condition of the buildings. It concluded that they were 'increasingly proving no longer fit for purpose'. Most of the roofs, windows, external doors, sanitary and shower facilities, electrical systems, heating plant and ceilings are reaching the end of their serviceable life. And that's official.

Less than a mile away, across the Meadows, the grass is definitely greener for pupils and staff at St Thomas of Aquin's High. Opened in 2002, the £14m school – voted Britain's best new civic building that year – is from another world: the 21st century.

Inside its smart sandstone walls lies an impressive building set on four floors with a lift for disabled students, classrooms that are 65 square metres, a dedicated support-for-learning area, interactive whiteboards in each classroom, social areas and one large, impressive entrance. This modern edifice rose from the ashes of old Victorian school buildings which were condemned 10 years ago and pulled down after the then-janitor put his foot through a staircase.

Even after five years, St Thomas's looks fresh, clean and welcoming. Staff and pupils at the Catholic school, the last in Edinburgh to be built before the public-private partnership, were heavily involved in its design. The teachers, who all have laptops, love it and so do the pupils who got everything their predecessors put on their wish-list, except a swimming pool, a Burger King in the canteen and a pool table in the Sixth Form common room.

Stephen Phee, the Head Teacher, is justifiably proud of this award-winning construction, but it is the vision and values of a school that make it successful, he says, not nice buildings: 'Ethos is stronger than bricks and mortar. The fact that the school is beautiful is the icing on the cake for us.'

This tale of two schools is a tale of the haves and have-nots of an education system which is trying very hard to improve the school estate across Scotland. The Scottish Executive has funded Scotland's biggest ever school building programme, aiming to have 300 schools revamped or rebuilt by 2009.

Across the country, sod is being cut and new buildings are going up. South Lanarkshire Council boasts one of the biggest UK education PPP programmes, which involves private companies building and maintaining new schools and leasing them to the local authority for a period of around 30 years. With a capital value of £319 million invested in its 19 secondary schools, and its 124 primaries being updated in an £850 million modernisation programme financed through a different method, they are being transformed to meet the needs of a 21st-century learning environment. By 2010, one third of Edinburgh's pupils will be taught in brand new or significantly refurbished school buildings. Twenty new schools have opened since 2002.

However, at Braes High in Falkirk, a post-occupancy evaluation raised a range of issues including lack of storage, too few staff toilets, ventilation and the size of the staff car park. The 1,200-pupil secondary school, which opened in 2000, was part of the council's first PPP project.

No school will be perfect for everyone but the new come a lot closer than the old.

Edinburgh City has acknowledged that further investment is required in its schools and is developing proposals to replace five, including James Gillespie's. The others are St Crispin's, Portobello High, St John's Primary and Boroughmuir High, another of Scotland's leading state schools.

The council has already written to the Scottish Executive asking for the proposals to be considered for any future funding packages. But that's not fast enough for pupils and teachers in schools like Gillespie's who are left to wait their turn in the queue.

The survey, which was commissioned by Edinburgh City Council and led to the School Board's emergency meeting on March 26, said the condition of the buildings was having an 'adverse impact on the operation of the school' and that it needed ideally to be rebuilt. In the meantime, £1m is being spent on urgent repair work, money that the school was due to get for improvements in 2009–10.

After the elections last year, decisions about the future funding of schools are on hold until the new administration has found its feet. If money is forthcoming, it is likely to be around five years before the new-builds will be open for business.

There has been unprecedented investment in school buildings across the country but councils are trying to make up for a backlog of under-investment. That offers little comfort to parents and pupils of James Gillespie's, where buckets and mops are essential equipment and a new £500,000 heating system put in last August only began to work in February. 'Children should not have to acclimatise to this,' says Alex Wallace, the head. 'Virtually everything is past its sell-by date. I'm embarrassed at what parents think.'

He is disappointed that his bright students are not learning in a better environment. 'It's not that we can't provide an appropriate curriculum or a range of experiences. Students are missing out.'

What is remarkable is that despite all this, James Gillespie's is still a very good school. The league tables show that the state of the buildings has done nothing to affect high attainment levels. Pupils are active in many extra-curricular activities as well as their academic work, and their sense of community has resulted in them raising £10,000 to help pupils in other parts of the world. They have also collected £4,000 for their own school.

A trip around James Gillespie's reinforces the view that a school is more than the sum of its buildings. The pupils are happy. The atmosphere is warm and friendly and there is respect for Mr Wallace, who chats with pupils as they make their way to classes. He obviously enjoys this aspect of his job.

A cynical look at school routine, against the backdrop of Spylaw eerily loosed in space. It was flattened in all its matchless ignobility in May 2015. From *Snuff*, 1981.

A GUIDE TO BREAKS IN J.G.H.S.

Arriving at school: I am always six minutes late, no matter when I set out. (Ten minutes late on Mondays).

First Break: Crawl into playground after having slept for the first two periods, stand and die slowly of hypothermia until the bell rings.

Almost interesting note: a strange school custom! All the pupils rush out of the school buildings in a great rush, realise how cold it is and then charge back in again?!!

Lunch Break: At the sound of the bell resounding through the school most pupils react on instinct; they plunge their hands into their pockets, fumble for a ticket and charge to the lunch halls. This seems strange to the few pupils who insist on walking and retaining some dignity.

Queue/scrummage: To gain access to your dinner you must take your place in the lunch queue/scrummage, then, if you want to eat you must push with all your might until you reach the door and are pushed through (I personally prefer to wait for half-an-hour for my lunch).

Eating school meals: To perform this simple but dangerous operation you require a fork, plate, a jack hammer and finally a cast-iron stomach to digest the stuff (I recommend the salad).

Post-lunch life: Much the same as the first break, only with less activity.

Third break: This is often spent travelling to and from the Annexe and is done at a steady crawl. This is the one time when you may think the list of truly stunning philosophical thoughts made on this route almost nil, but when compared with the truly stunning philosophical thoughts thought elsewhere, this is quite something.

Going home: This must be performed with the utmost caution as there are many motorists in the service of the Government who will gladly drop the school roll by a few souls.

DUE TO THE RELATIVE CHEAPNESS OF MAFIA HIT MEN THE AUTHOR HAS DECIDED TO REMAIN ANON. (HE WEARS A BLACK DONKEY JACKET).

Unfortunately, much of his time is taken up with building issues.

He's tired of talking about the poor state of his school rather than teaching and learning, and he's anxious that parents don't worry. 'I am concerned that the parents might read the press reports and feel they are not going to get as good an education in Gillespie's,' says Mr Wallace.

'You do not get a better education in a new building. A good school is not a good building, but a good school like Gillespie's deserves a good building.'

Pressure on Edinburgh City Council, and indeed the Scottish Government, grew inexorable, and late in 2009 the axe finally fell: James Gillespie's High School would be comprehensively rebuilt. But how? The multi-agency Edinburgh Urban Design Panel – including representatives from Architecture + Design Scotland, Historic Scotland, the Cockburn Association, JM Architects and even Lothian and Borders Police – wrestled with the practicalities at a meeting in August 2010.

Lindsay Glasgow, Asset Planning Manager for the City Council's Children and Families Department, briefed (in the jargon of the New Labour age) that the project would be part of the 'Wave 3 Schools Programme. The brief for the new school is being developed by the exploration of current and future pedagogies set by the Curriculum for Excellence to identify the best teaching model in the new school. It is envisaged that a planning application will be lodged at the beginning of next year, start on site is scheduled for 2012 with a completion date of 2015. It was also explained that several building failures on the campus have informed the decision that the existing school buildings should be demolished.'

That raised one immediate priority – to secure agreement with Historic Scotland that the 1966 campus not be 'listed' before it could be humanely flattened. Bruntsfield House, of course – an A-listed building – would have to be treated with great respect, the new constructions complementing it. The restrictions of the site generally were a problem: would there be space for staff parking? Neighbours on Lauderdale Street would not appreciate undue 'overlook', so new structures could not be very high. Entry points, public access, the threat to mature trees . . . all were considered. Behind all this, of course – as the city fathers and the James Gillespie's High School community knew full well – was the biggest headache of all: how would the school continue to function while demolition and reconstruction took place?

Edinburgh's leaders finally agreed, in principle, to schedule the rebuild

An art class in the Darroch Annexe, 1978. Suddenly, in 2013, Gillespie's students would return.

in such a way that two-thirds of staff and pupils could use the campus at any given time – and to 'decant' the rest to that old friend of, at least, its most senior staff: the Darroch Annexe. Students for most PE lessons would, for the duration, be bussed to facilities at Meadowbank. And there was, besides, enormous input into the design and the project generally from pupils and their parents, who over many months were consulted intensively by Alex Wallace and his senior management team. Pupils were even consulted on appropriate adaptation of the Darroch building, winning almost all their demands save for 'a few pet goats'. Wallace himself toiled on the detail of everything and to sacrificial degree – as, in retirement, he continues to spend himself in his Jabulani Project, a charity bringing young

Scots and South Africans together and to great good works in that far country.

In January 2012, detailed plans were finally unveiled for a £42 million redevelopment of the entire campus, including still better buildings for James Gillespie's Primary School and the associated Nursery School. £34 million of that would fund the construction of three new High School buildings: a main classroom teaching block, parallel to Lauderdale Street (which would be completed first); a Sports block, with games hall and swimming pool, in the southeast corner where the janitor's house and Warrender currently stood; and an Expressive Arts block, including a 300-seat theatre, roughly where the Spylaw Science block sat. The historic avenue and arches would of course be retained and Bruntsfield House would again be refurbished. The entire 1966 campus, including the additions of 1990, would – by stages – be flattened, though as much of the rubble as possible would somehow be incorporated in the foundations or material of the new buildings. The *Evening News* on 20 January enthused –

A new school has been given the green light as part of a £42 million campus project – despite householders' concerns about the 'brutal' impact of the new buildings.

The new James Gillespie's High School in Edinburgh, due to open in 2015, will be the first school to be built around the principles of Scotland's new education curriculum.

It will feature open spaces to encourage collaborative working between different classes and specially-designed 'learning gardens'.

However, earlier this month the *Evening News* reported how neighbours of the high school had launched a petition against the impact of the new buildings, with the main objections focusing on the 'over-dominance' of a new pool and sports building at the school's Lauderdale Street campus.

Residents in the neighbouring Thirlestane Road and Spottis-woode Road fear it will intrude on their privacy, while noise and artificial lighting will also have a negative impact.

The City Council said the school, which will be built on the site of the present James Gillespie's High, had been designed to comple-ment the Curriculum for Excellence. The school, which is being part-funded by the Scottish Government, is part of a larger campus development which is expected to include an extension to a nursery and improvements to James Gillespie's Primary.

The school will include a number of open spaces where pupils

Pupils and parents joked of 'shabby chic', but in 2009 the Warrender teaching-block – with the rest of the tired, failing and obsolete 1966 fabric – was finally condemned. (Andrew Digance)

studying different subjects will be able to take part in cross-curriculum learning.

There will also be covered 'learning gardens', as well as 'collaborative research spaces', presentation areas and an 'innovation hub' for teachers and pupils to collaborate.

Head Teacher Donald Macdonald said: 'I am looking forward to leading our school community through this rebuilding programme and, in a few years, taking ownership of what will be a first-class educational facility that is ideally suited to achieving the aspirations of a Curriculum for Excellence.'

City education leader Councillor Marilyne MacLaren added: 'I am absolutely thrilled that this exciting project has finally been given the planning go-ahead.

'The new High School will provide a modern and inspiring environment, with a number of pioneering design features that I think will lead the way for contemporary school buildings throughout Scotland. We progressively developed the plans based on feedback we received from the community to make sure that the new school reflects the positive characteristics of the surrounding area.'

Finance, funding and multi-agency supervision of the rebuild was of eye-watering complexity. (As, indeed, was 'Curriculum for Excellence', the latest top-down reinvention of Scottish secondary education and which has imposed untold extra work on teachers, still enduring a protracted pay freeze in the austerity economics of our day.)

'This is a school for 1,150 pupils,' advises the dedicated Edinburgh City Council web page for the project. 'It is being built in stages on its current site to offer separate buildings for general teaching, sport and performing arts. The school sits in the grounds of Bruntsfield House, which is a Grade A-listed building. This historic building is being refurbished as part of the project so that the school can continue to use it . . . this project is being delivered in partnership with Hub South East Scotland Limited. It is part-funded by the Scottish Government through the 'Schools for the Future Programme' that is managed by the Scottish Futures Trust . . . Main contractor is Morrison Construction. Architects are JM Architects.'

JM Architects had not merely to design the building, they declared, but ingeniously work out a twelve-stage decant programme that would as far as possible minimise disruption for the school's 1,150 children and 104 staff. (In this the City Council was quite mistaken: the 'decant' would be the responsibility of Donald J. Macdonald and managed in fine detail by Janis Croll, who executed it with assiduous aplomb and was more than a match for any architect or engineer unwise enough to gainsay her.)

And the Scottish Government would directly foot much of the bill, 'supporting £20 million of the cost of the new school with funding from its £1.25 billion Scotland's Schools for the Future programme under which 67 new schools are planned. Deputy First Minister Nicola Sturgeon said: "In Scotland we are building many new schools, and refurbishing still more to provide an excellent learning environment for staff and pupils. Investment in infrastructure projects, such as the new James Gillespie's High School, not only supports jobs and apprenticeships locally, but it also helps the wider Scottish economy."'

Despite warnings, given the growing popularity of Bun-sgoil Taobh na Pàirce, the powers-that-be declined – against intense parental pressure and agitation by the School Council – to ease the school roll upwards to 1,350 pupils; the roll was firmly capped at 1,150 and the new premises designed to the last desk on that basis. There is still a noisy anti-Gaelic lobby in Edinburgh and by the spring of 2016 this malicious myopia would cause acute embarrassment.

In the event, preliminary demolition works – removal, for instance, of the covered walkways – did not begin till June 2013, the security fencing fast arising around the central complex from session's end. The janitor's house was fast obliterated, so that a temporary classroom block – including dining rooms – could go up that summer. And, on an afternoon in November, as staff and pupils watched from the higher windows of Warrender and with a stir of emotions, the first excavators bit hungrily into what had been the school library. The hall, the pool, the gym and the old dining centre inexorably followed it into one enormous mound of smashed concrete, tangled metal and broken brick.

Many bitterly regret the blithe demolition of the 1966 Clock Tower – long a local landmark and a useful meeting-point for the school community; quite outwith the footprint of the three new buildings – and, to dry cackles, flattening it proved very difficult, for it proved to be of almost solid concrete. Attempts on social media to organise a final vigil, as it was brought down in a matter of wrecking-ball moments, were fast abandoned; it was, instead, determinedly gnawed to death over many days. The great bronze hands – and the plaque the Queen Mother had forty-seven years earlier unveiled – were saved, for some future imaginative purpose. Many had worried about asbestos, but in the event the astute professionals found it only in the great concrete plant-holders that had long sat on the concourse between the main foyer, Warrender and the library.

And thus, as the relentless tap-tap-tapping of serious concrete-breaking began, I went back to school after all . . .

CHAPTER TEN

'The place where I was
first understood'

Glimpses, encounters, snapshots . . .

Friday, 14 December 2012: pleasant, uniformed students selling tickets in the foyer, the school hall given over to a joyous 'Concert, Ceilidh and Cakes' night. The brilliant Mairi Campbell sings; the school's own Mr Brice and his 'Auld Reekie' band have our toes tapping; and there are indeed 'cakes – more cakes than you could toss a caber at!! – as well as tea, coffee and drinks!' I sit quietly in a corner in the hall where once I sat my Highers, where, once, gloriously, Miss Lambert's chair collapsed beneath her at our prize-giving; where the late Stewart McDougall used to convene us for Sixth Year registration. Again and again I eerily confound a glimpsed, contemporary pupil for one of my own peers, decades ago – and then remember that Alan, or Sinclair, or Colin, or Eva, or Allyson are today fortysomethings long scattered to all points of the compass; that this is not 1983; that, in under a year, this memory-laden space will be but dust

Tuesday, 18 December 2012: the 2012 Christmas Concert, home in its traditional venue of the Usher Hall, sponsored generously by Morrison Construction. The glossy colour programme includes a potted history of James Gillespie's High School and photographs of the day the Queen Mother opened these premises now condemned. The rising choir-stalls, behind the stage, are filled with a vast host of children – not just from Gillespie's, but all the feeder-primaries, immaculate in school tie and white shirt. The standard of performance is extraordinarily high – the Chamber Choir, assorted orchestras and ensembles, a delightful Gaelic Choir and the new, brilliantly baudacious James Gillespie's High School Pipe Band – shortly to boast their own exclusive tartan. And, with the backing of the pupils' string orchestra, two dozen of us gnarled old alumni belt out, rather wistfully, 'Fidelis et Fortis'.

Members of the
school pipe-band
regaling visitors
outside Bruntsfield
House, June 2013.
(Ann Henderson)

Afterwards, over drinks and nibbles, a very big man of vaguely familiar features bears down on us veterans of the late Seventies and early Eighties. 'I am Hamish McDougall,' he beams. 'I am the last teacher standing from your era!' He has been serving at Gillespie's since October 1977, will retire early in 2015, and return for fair stretches of supply teaching till the spring of 2016.

June 2013: a gorgeous, blazing summer Saturday, and a reunion event with a difference – our final goodbye to the old buildings. These occasions tend to be low-key and timid. With the aid of social media, though (and an exuberant plug by Grant Stott on Forth 1) this one is enormous, with not just hundreds of former pupils but dozens of staff present and historic – Douglas Burke, Sandra Evans, and Tom Johnson; Peter Galloway CBE – honoured for long and distinguished service as Head Teacher of Trinity Academy; Roddy Gray, the eccentric Chemistry master; Ian Watson, and still more...

'I shouldn't be here, you know,' confides my old classmate Mark Munro, these days high in the BBC, as we tour our old haunts of Warrender.

'Why?'

'Well, actually, because I'm banned for life,' says Mark, who is famous for *Mrs Brown's Boys*.

In August 1984, just after school returned from the holidays and we, the retiring Sixth Year, had gone for ever, he and Mark Dickinson had armed themselves with vast water pistols, donned balaclavas, stormed Spylaw and 'assassinated' Mr Gray – before fleeing the premises, pursued hotly by a puffing Mr Merriman, as pupils lined every window to cheer them on.

Munro made a clean getaway; Dickinson was collared. Mr Merriman did his best to impress upon him the dribbling irresponsibility and entire depravity of their conduct – less than convincingly, Tony Merriman again and again dissolving in helpless giggles – and epistles were duly sent to their respective homes, prohibiting them from the school campus for the rest of their days.

'Don't worry,' I assure my old schoolfellow, 'I won't tell.'

We duly bump into Mr Gray and he joins us, unknowing and innocent, for a photograph.

And then, still as dangerous and almost as tall, back down in the doomed school hall – tables are heavy with maroon-and-yellow cupcakes – we espy Dr Thomas (rather shockingly, in trousers; atypically affable, even giggly) and she deigns to pose with us too, and then with Mr Wallace and Mr Macdonald – both in loud Bermuda shorts – before asking if we might direct her to Douglas Burke. Wielding a stick with delicate ease, Dr Thomas, eighty-five, negotiates a flight of steps to find him and other teaching veterans by Hamish McDougall's *al fresco* and most informal bar, and there we knock back tumblers of Pimms and lemonade – former pupils, retired staff, hailing our noble queen, all supporting middle-age from either end . . .

For the rest of the afternoon, Pat Thomas holds court in the library, a small and respectful queue forming now and then.

October 2013, and Mr Macdonald wants to show me round the Annexe, in renewed JGHS service and largely for the use of the senior pupils, who after just a few weeks have taken avidly to its collegiate atmosphere and enjoy all the cafés and sandwich bars nearby. It has been much modernised internally. But as we step within these austere and lofty walls my stomach lurches and I feel myself pale, and sort of crumple, momentarily overwhelmed by negative memory . . . Donald Macdonald notices it too, and later – I gather – describes it to others, as an instance of how a bad school experience can haunt children far into their subsequent lives.

December 2013, and once more a handful of former pupils are back in Music Room 1, by its handsome chimney-piece and the same old grand piano, as Deirdre O'Brien warms us up for renewed Christmas Concert performance. 'Fish and chips and Irn Bru', we carol, relaxing those vocal-chords, 'fish and chips and Irn Bru, fish and chips and Irn Bru and salt and *sauce!*' Our *coup de theatre* proper is Harold Darke's ethereal arrangement of 'In The Bleak Midwinter' and – beaten to it in 1982 – I am, this time, picked out for the third-verse tenor solo; an undemanding decision for Mrs O'Brien as I am the only tenor there . . .

January 2014, and I find myself in school most afternoons, always neatly dressed and with my Gillespie's tie, signing myself in as 'School Historian', touching base briefly with Mr Macdonald for a 'wee strupag', and then working in a little room in the bowels of Bruntsfield House, the print-room in my time and, probably, the wine cellar of yore, now serving as a 'Support for Pupils' room and the door then still bearing the name of 'Mrs S. Evans' – and that is apt, for when I was first deposited in Gillespie's, down among the hard cases of the Annexe in April 1980, it was into her 2R1 History class I was first dropped, before most curious classmate eyes, by Mr Burke.

The near-entire archive is here, in this chamber, for my pleasure and in big plastic storage boxes – items of past school apparel, including several of the infamous little hats; school badges; folders of documents; assorted books (including two large Bibles); two or three sets of the school magazine; great ring-binders of photographs; assorted ephemera, long-preserved autograph books, even a tawse. There is that invaluable 'oral history' – the CDs of 'Living History' interviews recorded with former pupils several years ago; assorted cassette tapes; and Miss Lambert's person-ally maintained album of sports teams, each characteristically welded down with lashings of thick glue.

The period bell goes; the piano plays somewhere overhead; pupils move about in giggly shuffle – little, it seems, has changed since my last studies in this building three decades ago, or those lunch-hours hiding in some music practice-room with a book; but then you remember the sheet-steel fencing now quite enclosing what is now a building site, and all the while there is the roar and rumble of great machines, hewing the old rubble up for recycling as concrete founds . . .

It is still midwinter, dusky and chill as I head up the avenue after four or five hours of toil, the bare trees hissing a little in raw wind off the Forth. There is always something eerie about a school at night; something that haunts, something infinitely wistful, like the way the exuberant voices in a

The boys' football team, 1920. It is hard viewing such old pictures of poised children in the morning of life, knowing each of them must be long dead.

playground full of children – wherever you are in the land – have always, in combination, the same timeless and universal accent.

•　　•　　•

We all have our ghosts. I think often, through those weeks of intense research, about the old teachers remorselessly passing away. Jean Clark and Mairi Macdonald, in 2008; Jean McIntyre and Robert Galt, in 2012; Emily Ferguson, last year; Moira Burnard, in 2014 – but I am old enough, too, to have outlived a depressing number of classmates. Willie Bell, who died behind the wheel of an Army truck; Alan McMurray, the 'dreaded traffic cop', as he laughingly described himself on Friends Reunited, mown down by a speeding van in Broxburn, in February 2006, while attending the scene of an accident; little Andrew Hart, a 13-year-old team-mate for the Schools Challenge Quiz when I was in Sixth Year, and who passed away very young indeed; Moray Fotheringham, who was never well; the gifted Rupert Ford,

eminent scientist in the field of 'dynamical meteorology and oceanography',
lost to diabetic coma in the spring of 2001 – just thirty-two years old . . .

As the rest of us near or pass fifty, we are thus reminded that age is a
privilege; one not everyone is granted. Indeed, some never really live in the
first place. If there are two awful tensions in *The Pride of Miss Jean Brodie*,
it is the sense of terrible desperation we glimpse – just glimpse – in the
histrionic, manipulative Miss Brodie herself; but also the suggestion that,
for some in her special 'set', these brief years in her classroom really will be
the best and brightest they will ever know –

> These were the days that Mary McGregor, on looking back, found
> to be the happiest days of her life.
>
> Sandy Stranger had a feeling at the time that they were supposed
> to be the happiest days of her life, and on her tenth birthday she said
> so to her best friend Jenny Gray who had been asked to tea at Sandy's
> house. The speciality of the feast was pineapple cubes with cream,
> and the speciality of the day was that they were left to themselves.
> To Sandy the unfamiliar pineapple had the authentic taste and
> appearance of happiness and she focused her small eyes closely on
> the pale gold cubes before she scooped them up in her spoon, and
> she thought the sharp taste on her tongue was that of a special
> happiness, which was nothing to do with eating, and was different
> from the happiness of play that one enjoyed unawares. Both girls
> saved the cream to the last, then ate it in spoonfuls.
>
> 'Little girls, you are going to be the crème de la crème,' said
> Sandy, and Jenny spluttered her cream into her handkerchief.
>
> 'You know,' Sandy said, 'these are supposed to be the happiest
> days of our lives.'
>
> 'Yes, they are always saying that,' Jenny said. 'They say, make the
> most of your schooldays because you never know what lies ahead
> of you . . .'

Each of us, living and dead, takes something of this extraordinary school
away with us, sometimes touching on that which Gillespie's has left behind
at subsequent life-changing crisis.

'A few years ago,' wrote Muriel Spark, in an August 1962 essay for the
New Statesman,

> I was obliged to spend some weeks in the North British Hotel in
> Edinburgh, isolated and saddened by many things, while my father's

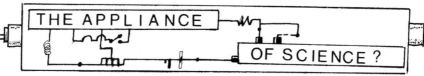

THE APPLIANCE OF SCIENCE ?

Over the past few years science has been subject to adverse criticism by the general public. Chemicals are now substances found only in poisons, and the mention of the word "nuclear" immediately conjurs up images of destruction. Professor Dobad appears in many cartoons, to be defeated by an artistic mouse with a flair for the unconventional. All very well, but what has he ever invented or discovered to make this world a better place in which to live?

Regrettably this polarisation of views has become commonplace. The arts are hailed by many people as the heroes of the piece, defeating all the "nasty" inventions of scientists. What we fail to realise is that if there is something of value to be discovered then surely that is all to the good. To whatever use it is put that is not the ultimate responsibility of the scientist. Surely when a scientist discovers something which could be put to good use it is his responsibility to brief government and industry as effectively as possible on the implications of this discovery. It is for the men of state and business to decide for themselves if and how the findings should be used to the benefit of mankind. Politicians are not scientists and scientists are not politicians. It is reasonable to expect the two to be able to work in a co-operative manner.

But the problem is more deep-rooted. It is not the fault of politicians per se, but rather something implanted in our culture. We expect scientists to be aware of the arts, but we do not expect artists (i e., in the wider sense, non-scientists) to have even the most basic grounding in science. Many scientists are extremely musical, and enjoy a good production of Shakespeare as much as anyone, but artists are not expected to follow developments in energy production or medical techniques.

Science is to many, a mystery, yet it has permitted them to enjoy a much easier lifestyle than they would otherwise have had. As science has contributed much, surely it is only right that everyone should be expected to respect it and at least be familiar with its most elementary concepts. This barrier between arts and sciences, "goodies" and "baddies" – heaven and hell almost – would be best broken down by artists coming out of their own cocoons and developing their own "fuller person". The "full" person must surely know at least enough science as not to be totally perplexed by it.

It would be incorrect to say that there are no mysteries in science, but what we know should not be beyond the comprehension of the average playwright or poet. But instead we have a most unfortunate divide forming in our society. If in the course of conversation you happen to say that "Maths was never my strong point" this serious deficiency is laughed off and you are accepted. But if, on the other hand, you "could never really understand literature" what a cardinal failing!

I leave you with a quotation from the former Energy Minister, Tony Benn:

"We, as a nation, take a perverse pride in our innumeracy; yet we would be ashamed to be called illiterate".

This, I believe, sums up the attitude of many people – it is a recipe for a potentially dangerous misunderstanding. It must be corrected.

RUPERT FORD, 5th Year

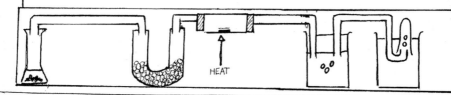

HEAT

last illness ran its course in the Royal Infirmary. It was necessary for me to be within call. I do not like the public rooms and plushy lounges of hotels anywhere in the world, I do not sit in them; and least of all in one's native city is it spiritually becoming to sit in the lounges of big hotels . . .

Edinburgh is the place that I, a constitutional exile, am essentially exiled from. I spent the first eighteen years of my life, during the 1920s and 1930s there. It was Edinburgh that bred within me the conditions of exiledom; and what have I been doing since then but moving from exile into exile? It has ceased to be a fate, it has become a calling.

My frequent visits to Edinburgh for a few weeks at a time throughout the years have been the visits of an exile in heart and mind – cautious, affectionate, critical. It is a place where I could not hope to be understood. The only sons and daughters of Edinburgh with whom I can find a common understanding are exiles like myself. By exiles I do not mean Edinburgh-born members of Caledonian Societies. I do not consort in fellowship with the Edinburgh natives. I do not consort in fellowship with the Edinburgh natives abroad merely on the Edinburgh basis. It is precisely the Caledonian Society aspect of Edinburgh which cannot accommodate me as an adult person.

Nevertheless, it is the place where I was first understood. James Gillespie's Girls' School, set in solid state among the green Meadows, showed an energetic faith in my literary life. I was the school's Poet and Dreamer, with appropriate perquisites and concessions. I took this for granted, and have never quite since accustomed myself to the world's indifference to art and the process of art, and to the special needs of the artist.

I have started the preceding paragraph with the word 'nevertheless' and am reminded how my whole education, in and out of school, seemed even then to pivot around this word. I was aware of its frequent use. My teachers used it a great deal. All grades of society constructed sentences bridged by 'nevertheless'. It would need a scientific study to ascertain whether the word was truly employed more frequently in Edinburgh at the time than anywhere else. It is my own instinct to associate the word, as the core of a thought-pattern, with Edinburgh particularly. I can see the lips of tough elderly women in musquash coats taking tea at MacVittie's, enunciating this word of final justification, I can see the exact gesture of head and chin and gleam of the eye that accompanied it. The sound was roughly 'niverthelace' and the emphasis was a heartfelt one. I believe myself to be fairly indoctrinated by the habit of thought which calls for this word. In fact I approve of the ceremonious accumulation of weather forecasts and barometer-readings that pronounce for a fine day, before letting rip on the statement: 'Nevertheless, it's raining.' I find that much of my literary composition is based on the nevertheless idea. I act upon it. It was on the nevertheless principle that I turned Catholic . . .

Most Edinburgh-born people, of my generation at least, must have been brought up with a sense of civic superiority. We were definitely given to understand that we were citizens of no mean city. In time, and with experience of other cities, one would have discovered the beautiful uniqueness of Edinburgh for oneself as the visitors do. But the physical features of the place surely had an effect as special as themselves on the outlook of the people. The Castle Rock is something, rising up as it does from prehistory between the formal grace of the New Town and the noble network of the Old. To have a great primitive black crag rising up in the middle of populated streets of commerce, stately squares and winding closes, is like the statement of an unmitigated fact preceded by 'nevertheless'. In my time the society existing around it generally regarded the government and bureaucracy of Whitehall as just a bit ridiculous. The influence of a place varies according to the individual. I imbibed, through no particular mentor, but just by breathing the informed air of the place, its haughty and remote anarchism. I can never now suffer from a shattered faith in politics and politicians, because I never had any.

When the shrill telephone in my hotel room woke me at four in the morning, and a nurse told me that my father was dead, I noticed, with that particular disconnected concentration of the fuddled mind, that the Rock and its Castle loomed as usual in the early light. I noted this, as if one might have expected otherwise.

And, though many might find another way of articulating such sentiment, there is – for most former pupils, and from memories silly or dark or humdrum as much as more inspirational recollection – that sense of being defined, lifelong, by the Gillespie's experience, as Liz Roberts put it deliciously to Edi Stark in 2003.

'Well, I think it's a little core inside of you that you touch for confidence

– it's like your lucky stone, you know – "I was chosen. I was one of the *crème de la crème*, wasn't I?" To go to Gillespie's was the pinnacle of achievement – I wanted to go there more than anything. I mean, it was Hogwarts, it was Mallory Towers, it was the Chalet School – it was every school that any girl in Edinburgh wanted to get to. Because you had to *pass* for Gillespie's. It wasn't enough to pass the Qualifying, or the 11-plus – you also had to do the Gillespie's exam.'

'Did you feel as if you belonged right from the very beginning?'

'Yes, because you had the uniform. The uniform instantly transformed you from an ordinary Edinburgh girl into a Gillespie Girl. Hideous, of course – maroon and yellow – and green dresses in the summer, which showed every mark and every crease – yes, it was probably the most hideous, but the most enviable and desirable uniform. I think sleeves were sometimes rolled up – just as in *The Prime of Miss Jean Brodie*, we were asked if we were thinking of doing a washing. Gillespie's was all rules – my goodness, there were rules about everything. Hairnets for gym, and for hockey – it was great fun at Meggetland playing hockey with your hairnet on . . .

'We had those amazing concerts in the Usher Hall,' Liz Roberts added, 'and I was the dramatic one – I spouted; and did Scottish poetry and things like that – then Maggie's lot,' and she nodded to one of her younger school pals, 'would get up in these little chitons, you know, little Greek thingies, tunics, and wave chiffon scarves in the air. And that was entertainment in 1955!'

She paused.

'It belongs to some of the magic that's Edinburgh for me now . . . a safe world where everyone went home for tea, and had their tea at half past five, and listened to the Home Service, and sat round coal fires – I think it's called nostalgia.'

Such fondness for the past, selective girls-only era – in a long-gone and very different Scotland – may seem strange to a new generation. But it is widespread among 'Gillespie Girls', it is as intense as it is unfeigned, and it must ever be respected. For thousands, even now, the 'School on the Links' is as cherished a place in memory as Loch Tay excursions are to us.

•   •   •

Inevitably, through intense bursts of work through lengthy Edinburgh trips over three years, I am at Gillespie's a great deal and see much of Donald J. Macdonald. There is always a wee strupag and sometimes, too, we brave a

school dinner together – and the fare is surprisingly good, the youngsters surprisingly quiet, engaging and friendly. Much of teenage social discourse these days, of course, amounts to knots of children chuckling over something on a smartphone.

It is fascinating to watch him headmastering. He has a smile for everyone he meets and a word, especially, for each Gaelic-medium student. Mr Macdonald happily takes occasional classes himself, in Gaelic or Physics as need arises, and relishes that more protracted contact. And those large Minch-grey eyes miss nothing. We pass one child snapping another with his mobile-phone camera. 'You'll get his permission before you post it online, won't you? Splendid . . . thank you very much . . . Some youngsters these days are at risk of abduction from an estranged ex-husband or whatever,' he murmurs in an aside, 'so photographs on the internet can be an issue . . . Excuse me, but would you put that in the bin for me? Thank you . . .' he says to a girl passing by a drifting crisp packet. If a 'toy-fight' breaks out in our vicinity – boys scrapping genially like puppies, rolling on the ground – he always gently investigates, satisfying himself that the rough-housing is consensual.

Donald Macdonald comes from a line of teachers. 'My aunt always used to say that things went downhill when the black gowns went out . . .' 'Do you have a black gown?' 'Yes, I wear it for special occasions – like the afternoon we organised a quidditch match; or last August, when I and others of the staff volunteered for the Ice Bucket Challenge.'

One tries to envisage May Andrew or Dr Thomas rejoicing in buckets of cold water being poured over them in the name of charity before hooting schoolchildren, but the mental picture is elusive.

'I remember once, one morning, as a boy, skiving school,' he says. 'Home on Uist, a beautiful summer's day, I had things I wanted to do . . . And just before ten in the morning this character came, he ran the local taxi, and he said, "Here, Donald, your mother sent me to take you to school."'

He looks reflective.

'And she never said anything. I wasn't blasted at all. But I knew that things were tight with us, and the fare for that taxi must have come out of her budget for the week; and that was how seriously she took our schooling. I never did it again.'

Head Teachers do not sit around their office all day engaged in light reading, with perhaps the occasional royal progress around the campus. Macdonald has a great many meetings with senior management. He has to stay on top of prodigious correspondence – most of it, these days, by email, and without any sort of secretary or personal assistant. There is no gatekeeper to protect him from interruption. As the 'responsible officer of the school' he is immediately summoned – and legally responsible – when there is a situation of true gravity. Twice, when I have been on the premises, the wee strupag or the quick lunch of cheesy panini has had to be thrown over because, variously, staff sought an 'intervention' with a girl whom they feared was being abused at home, and Second Year boys were caught exchanging prohibited items in a Modern Languages class. A Head Teacher's day can bring all manner of excitement. In a previous position, it once fell to Mr Macdonald delicately to negotiate with police over a pupil who knew the location of a weapon used in a recent local robbery.

Such incidents, I should stress, are exceedingly rare. There are no prefects now, but there is a real-life campus policeman – a young local constable who appears regularly, befriends everyone, walks about a great deal and with whom Donald Macdonald works very closely. He regrets the new, post-2012 order that denies him a single, indubitable and ideally rather scary Deputy Head rather than three titular ones. 'I cannot always be here – meetings with officials, and so on – and I wish there was one colleague I could leave in undisputed, unambiguous charge of the place.'

Observant, affable, cultured – he is a devotee of Gaelic song, traditional music and good curry; always repeating some aphorism or anecdote from a weighty, recently read book – Mr Macdonald likes to quote his late father, who once declared some mutual acquaintance going in for the teaching profession would not prosper – for the youth had failed successfully to train a sheepdog. "You need the 'eye'," he said to me – I mind it fine – "and he hasn't got the eye at all . . ." And he was quite right. That fellow didn't cope with teaching at all. You'll remember teachers that screamed and shouted and belted all they liked, and you and the rest of the class just dancing on your desks – and others who never raised their voice, just needed to look at you, raise one eyebrow, and you were petrified.'

'The classroom? Oh, it's a *stage* – the best teachers are tremendous actors. And there are so many little tricks. I almost always dress like this' – he brushes a hand over his immaculate suit – 'because it gives you an edge, you know, over anyone more casually dressed. And the constant staff travel to the Annexe is a worry for them, because a teacher loses a big psychological advantage if the children are in the classroom before you.'

Donald Macdonald assuredly has the 'eye'. One story he likes to tell, from his days in Liberton, was when some pupils were caught up in some petty crime, hauled in by the local bobbies, and the school duly contacted. The boys were cocky, cheeky, insolent. Then one officer thought – aloud – of sending them 'back to the High School for Macdonald to deal with'. At that point, the lads became very, very co-operative – far more terrified of their Head Teacher than of Lothian and Borders Police.

I have only once had the full-on Macdonald treatment when (without his permission) I took a valued book away one night to study at my leisure. When I was in the next day he suddenly asked to see it and I had to confess its abstraction. The shoulders stiffened. The jaw tensed. And he looked at me with eyes of fire and declared with wrought-iron menace – 'As far as you and I are concerned, that volume never left this office . . .'

It is a Friday evening in December 2014 and we are back at the Darroch Annexe for a night of festive drama – a production of *Lady Audley's Secret* by senior students and (as a play within a play) a most concise adaptation, by Leon Garfield and starring rather younger pupils, of *A Midsummer Night's Dream*.

Macdonald and I sit in state in the centre of the back row. The hall –
Miss Clark's drama classroom, in my time – is thronged with parents. 'Just
remember,' a master says to us by way of introduction, 'that *Lady Audley's
Secret* is a melodrama; and the difference between a melodrama and a
pantomime is that a melodrama is *funny*.'

It is an extraordinarily accomplished performance – the Shakespeare
earnest, even moving, and not in the least hammy; the melodrama milked
for every last laugh and shudder by the declamatory Stephan Robertson –
to say nothing of the sparkling Harriet Phillips, the assured Andrew
Haddaway, the poised and exuberant Molly Doran and (a talent of extraordinary power) Kai Stuart, who steals every scene he is in – and may yet be
an SNP politician near you.

Mr Macdonald has news to share afterwards: senior pupils have been
voting in recent days on the names of the three new campus buildings. The
results are intriguing. The main teaching block will be Malala, after that
inspirational young woman from Pakistan; the Sports block is to be named
Liddell, after Eric Liddell ('his niece went to Gillespie's') and the Expressive
Arts building is to be called Spark, which would have pleased her greatly.

'J.K. Rowling was in strong contention early on,' says the Gillespie's
Head Teacher, 'but the kids say they went right off her during the
independence referendum.' (Harry Potter's creator had noisily given a vast
donation to the campaign for a No vote.) Tennis champion Andy Murray
was also a strong contender, but pupils decided gravely not to risk naming
a building after anyone still living, lest there be a subsequent scandal. The
sainted Malala Yousafzai was an evident exception.

•   •   •

In January 2015, to much punching of the air, *Tatler* magazine listed James
Gillespie's High School among its pick of the best state secondary schools
in Britain – and the only one from Scotland.

This is the alma mater of Muriel Spark, who based Miss Jean Brodie
on one of her teachers at James Gillespie's. Then it was just girls;
now the school is Edinburgh's pre-eminent co-ed comprehensive.
There is a waiting list for entry but the catchment area is far-
reaching, which echoes the diverse student body. Thanks to a cash
injection from the Scottish government, the school is in the midst
of a huge rebuild, so it's a bit chaotic at the moment but the facilities,
due to be finished in 2016, will be worth the wait. We hear wonderful

things about the learning-support department. Ditto head Donald Macdonald, who received high praise for his work at previous posting Liberton High School and an invitation to Downing Street.

November 2015, too, saw the results of a long consultation with the wider Gillespie's community on school uniform. An unambiguous majority of children, parents and even staff opposed its reintroduction, and it will be at least eight years before the school revisits the issue. It was a 'positive decision for positive reasons', said Cath Downie, who chaired the Parent Council. 'I think the whole school community has been consulted and this is the decision that's been reached. The current situation works quite well. I think it just makes for a relaxed atmosphere of respect. It's not a sort of "them and us" thing. We are all part of this community. I think the concerns that parents have before their kids are at the school – "Is it going

Pupils gathered for Founder's Day, February 1982. The guest of honour was broadcaster Neville Garden. The last Founder's Day was held in 1984, but it is to be revived in 2017.

to be this big fashion competition?" and things like that – there is absolutely none of that.'

And, in December, we exulted anew when the school was again crowned with laurels, as *The Scotsman* reported –

James Gillespie's High has been named Scottish State School of the Year 2015.

The Marchmont school has been awarded the prestigious title by the *Sunday Times* Schools Guide, seen as the definitive list of the best primaries and secondaries in the UK.

Although it was not ranked at the top of the exam results league table – a title held by Jordanhill School in Glasgow – James Gillespie's was considered to be the best overall state school in Scotland.

It moved up eight places in the league table to rank seventh – the school's best ever position.

Last year, 78 per cent of its leavers gained five or more National 5s (or equivalent) at grades A–C, while 59 per cent left with a minimum of five good Highers.

And 26 per cent gained at least two Advanced Higher at grade C or above, bettered by just three other schools.

All of these academic achievements were obtained during a period of upheaval for both staff and pupils whilst a massive redevelopment of the school was carried out. Head Teacher Donald Macdonald said: 'It's been a challenging time for us but these results were achieved whilst we were in the middle of a building site so it's quite remarkable.

'Exam results would be a main factor [in being named Scottish State School of the Year] but also they look at the other achievements of the school.

'Having said that, these things go hand in hand – schools who do well academically are full of youngsters who are really busy with music, sport or Duke of Edinburgh.'

Since 2013, Gillespie's – the only Scottish high school to get a mention in *Tatler* magazine's 2015 list of top UK state secondaries – has operated in two campuses, with senior pupils walking almost a mile between them for classes.

Earlier this year, Gillespie's opened its new teaching block, known as the Malala Building, as part of a £42.8 million redevelopment of the Marchmont campus.

From the school magazine, 1938.

* * * *

GILLESPIE'S IN 2038,

when all children are taught by television in their own homes, and Gillespie's has fallen into sad disuse.

(with apologies to Mr Alfred Noyes.)

Gillespie's in the moonlight, is anyone awake?
Trim and tunicked shadows are here for old time's sake,
Shadows of bygone girls, kept in once again,
Dreaming of impositions by irate teacher-men.

Long-dead girls are here again, gliding down the stairs,
Now greeting an old acquaintance, shedding all anxious cares
Shouting as they used to shout, faint (?) and far away,
In the classrooms, in Gillespie's about the break of day.

Gallant gay Gillespie's has welcomed once again
All the joyous school-girls who long since dropped the pen,
Latin, French, and Maths., forgotten ages past,
Hockey, cricket, tennis, games, for ever gone at last.

Gallant gay Gillespie's is throbbing as of yore,
To shouts of happy laughter, and light (?) footsteps galore,
For all the girls are here again, shades from far away,
In the classrooms, in Gillespie's, about the break of day.

Cleaners, O cleaners, sweep away the dust,
Dust the dingy rooms again, banish all the must,
For Gillespie girls are here again, in Gillespie's, long since
    dead,
And the corridors are shining with Yellow and with Red.

Lowly First and haughty Sixth are singing shrill and loud,
Each feeling that of this their school, they should be justly
    proud,
The dead are coming back again, the years are rolled away,
In the classrooms, in Gillespie's, about the break of day.

KATHERINE RAMSAY, Form 2 A.

Pupils decided to name the teaching block in honour of Nobel Peace Prize winner Malala Yousafzai, who survived being shot in the head by a Taliban gunman in Pakistan in 2012. She was targeted because of her work promoting girls' education.

The new facility houses the main teaching area and features 57 classroom spaces with full-height glazing to maximise daylight and views.

Next August, the sports department – to be named the Eric

Liddell Building – will welcome pupils, with its 25-metre swimming pool, gym and full-size basketball court.

The new performing arts building with its 300-seat theatre – which will be named after the school's most famous former pupil, Muriel Spark – will also open, completing the redevelopment.

James Gillespie's follows in the footsteps of Boroughmuir High, which was awarded the Scottish State School of the Year title in 2012. This year Boroughmuir ranked behind Gillespie's at number 13 in the league table.

Education leader Councillor Paul Godzik said: 'Congratulations to all the staff and pupils at James Gillespie's for achieving this award – the second time Edinburgh schools have received this accolade.

'It demonstrates the high quality education on offer to pupils in the Capital, reinforced with impressive exam results across the city.'

Busy new classroom, the Malala Building, September 2016. (Andrew Digance)

•   •   •

The Malala Building is a wonderful, almost theatrical structure, with an amazing sense of light, space and flow, and students took to it avidly on their return from the 2015 spring holidays.

'Running down the middle of the building,' enthused Pamela Tunnoch for STV News – she and I enjoy a joint tour, with Donald Macdonald, on the eve of its official opening – 'is a series of outdoor courtyards, social spaces and the "Forum" assembly which has a special panelled roof which carries sound, meaning the speaker can speak at conversational level yet still be heard by the room.' Tunnoch continued:

> Settling into the building, Head Teacher Donald Macdonald says the new light environment has created a calming environment for learning. 'The building is extraordinarily quiet,' he said. 'We find it is calmer as a result of that. The feeling of light and space that it affords is just wonderful. Eventually, when the grounds are landscaped, it will be lovely.
>
> 'We have half a dozen spaces where [pupils] can plug in their mobile phones, laptops and there is wifi,' Macdonald adds. 'Having just had exam leave with our seniors, most of them chose to come into school rather than staying home to study. I have never seen so many children come in which shows what they think about the building.'
>
> The first phase opened in August 2013 with the new nursery, two new classrooms and a gym at the James Gillespie's Primary and a new synthetic pitch for the high school.
>
> The opening of the Malala Building is the latest phase, with the Sports and Music buildings next on the construction list. Councillor Paul Godzik, Education Convener for the City of Edinburgh Council, was among those at the official opening. 'I know the staff and pupils are excited to be in the new teaching block which is really impressive,' he said.
>
> 'This is a modern, fit-for-purpose facility which is unique in Scotland with its courtyards and collaborative break-out areas and will deliver an unrivalled learning environment for pupils. Work is already underway on the sports and performing arts buildings which will be finished next year and give the James Gillespie's community a school they can rightly be proud of for many years to come.'
>
> The Malala Building is brimming with new technology with smart boards in every room and computer-controlled temperature

controls. There are also some nice quirks such as an outdoor terrace classroom, a science greenhouse and a block where pupils can show their creative talents and chalk on the pavement.

'We have a mix of mechanical ventilation, air conditioning and under floor heating,' Donald said. 'All are computer-generated and controlled. As soon as the room gets too stuffy, the ventilation automatically kicks in and keeps oxygen levels at a certain percentage.'

Even the classic school bell has been swapped as a trial in favour of synchronised clocks. 'To promote this feeling of quietness, we have done away with school bells as an experiment. Every room has a clock which is radio-controlled and they are all synchronised to the second. It promotes calmness and quietness so we don't have the cacophony bell going off.'

The entire project is due to be finished for the start of the 2016/17 school year and work to the A-listed Bruntsfield House at the centre of the campus is also undergoing a major refurbishment.

It is indeed a beautiful, flowing sort of space, with an extraordinary sense of light, the flexibility necessary for modern teaching and all the social nooks and plug-in points vital to the modern youngster. And the modern, best-practice unisex toilets for the pupils, disconcerting as that might sound, are far cleaner and safer and more readily supervised than past, dank arrangements. Malala already feels a very happy place.

•   •   •

Yet further wonders are wrought, in the months since, as the larger campus takes shape and staff and pupils take avidly to what has already been completed.

The Spark Building rises: Deirdre O'Brien, increasingly a Gillespie's institution, has been consulted closely and in detail as to its immaculate 300-seat theatre. The Eric Liddell Building – an ingenious construction, from the 'tanking' of its swimming-pool to the erection of the Sports Hall – is a spectacle in itself as one walks up Spottiswoode Road. New trees are planted in great number; more will be added during the October 2016 holidays. Nor is Bruntsfield House neglected. There is general and quiet refurbishment. Its old rooms emerge new and bright; the ceilings in the two first-floor state apartments are magnificently restored and decorated. You are tempted to regret Donald J. Macdonald's summer flitting from the fabled Head Teacher's study to an attractive (but, naturally, very modern) lair in the Malala Building. He does not. Yes, the old chamber had a degree of 'wow factor,' he concedes, 'but it is so wonderful being at the heart of things now, all my senior colleagues within two minutes' walk . . .'

By June 2016, the Morrison Construction team now toils internally to finish off the new blocks. There is some wistful banter, in the school community, at the recent and sad passing of Ronnie Corbett, taught eight decades back in James Gillespie's Boys' School. 'Are they no gonnae call it the Corbett Theatre noo?' cracks one young workman. Children mischievously suggest that the airy new school canteen (also in the Spark Building) should at least be dubbed The Fork Handles in the late comedian's honour. It is finally called Brodie's Café. There is also, now, through the long summer days, close attention to landscaping. A paved plaza is laid out in the central concourse, its sweeps of gentle steps a lovely homage to the late 1966 school. In a particularly imaginative touch, a beautiful roundel is laid in the paving before Bruntsfield House – the engraved slabs not just recording the school's name and the date of completion ('Anno MMXVI') but both mottos, 'Fidelis et Fortis' and 'We Value the Diversity that Exists'.

And thus a far older Gillespie's tradition meets in peace with the new, and among unexpected volunteers one August 2016 morning – staff return a day early to unpack and sort out stuff for shiny new facilities – is former pupil Damien Hoyland. For several hours the Scottish Rugby Union internationalist, 22, unassumingly carries boxes and sports equipment back and fore, defined to degree – as are we all – by this remarkable school.

There are advantages, – conscious privileges – in being such an old institution as Gillespie's, with deep folk-memory and proud roots and these days, thanks to Dame Muriel Spark, now one of the most famous schools in the world.

The very weight of the past of James Gillespie's High School – and the still more fabled past of the grounds wherein it stands – in themselves put much in perspective, as Donald Macdonald shrewdly makes clear in his warm speech of welcome to Alasdair Allan MSP, Minister of Education, Science and Lifelong Learning, at the opening of the Malala building on Wednesday, 3 June 2015 – and in the impressive Forum, with that magical acoustic ceiling –

A Mhinisteir, a mhnathan agus fhir uasail – fàilte gu Ard-sgoil Sheumais 'ic Ghilleasbuig, airson a' chloinn, na tidsearan, agus coimhearsnachd na sgoile gu lèir . . . Minister, Councillor Godzik, ladies and gentlemen, on behalf of the children, the teachers and the wider community, we welcome you to James Gillespie's High School.

For over two hundred years, and – at first – by the kindly bequest of an eccentric snuff-merchant whose name we yet bear, we have served this city, always in Bruntsfield and for half a century from this campus.

Gillespie's was the first free school in all Scotland; it has always been an enlightened, liberal and diverse one and, all over the world, our pupils have made a name for themselves, especially in the media, drama and the arts and in the caring professions. As a school we genuinely and passionately value the diversity of our community.

And the more so since, over forty years ago, we became a co-educational community comprehensive, serving children of all classes, backgrounds and degrees of ability and – thanks, especially, to our dedicated staff – with abiding and signal success.

With Edinburgh Castle, the Royal Mile, Edinburgh University and even the Scottish Parliament within our catchment area, we might even boast that we are Scotland's High School.

Certainly we would honour today the Scottish Government, Edinburgh City Council, Morrison Construction and all involved in the completion of this magnificent new building.

But I would like just now to thank all my staff, the boys and girls, and especially our near neighbours for their patience and good humour over the last two years through the inevitable disruption and noise of so large a project on so confined a site – and, on *their* behalf, thank our builders for working so hard to minimise such difficulties.

Gillespie's has occupied these grounds since 1966. History is all about us. Below our feet is a medieval ice-house. Victims of the Great Plague are buried within these walls.

On a knoll, a few yards away, King James IV watched his forces muster for Flodden and Charles Edward Stuart marched his Highland host into the capital, just two streets away.

And Bruntsfield House itself, still at the heart of our campus, was once burnt out by Henry VIII's brother-in-law.

History now turns a new page, under rulers far less . . . robust.

Throughout those past two years, staff, parents and pupils have worked incredibly hard to ensure that our school maintained its high levels of attainment and achievement. Understandably, many were concerned that a school operating across not just two but three distinct sites would lose something along the way. Parents were particularly concerned at the impact this might have on examination results. I am delighted to report that not only have we maintained the previous high standards but in most of the national priorities we have achieved record highs. I am especially proud of the collective efforts of so many in ensuring that our most vulnerable pupils and our lowest attaining have all performed at or beyond expected levels. I am certain that James Gillespie would have been most proud.

After the Minister has delivered himself of apt and fair words, the Head Teacher then gives a few heartfelt thanks of his own. 'To make a project of this magnitude happen a large number of people played a part. There are far too many to mention but there are a few I would like to acknowledge today. Firstly, Alex Wallace, my predecessor, who, working alongside an inspired design team which included Maggie Barlow and Kirstine Robinson from Space Strategies, listened to members of our school community in order to develop a school for the twenty-first century. Their vision was turned into reality by those that followed. This included Ian Alexander and Cian Phelan in the JM architectural team.

'We give thanks to Hub South East Scotland with Morrison Construction for building our school. We thank Thomas and Adamson, our project managers.

'This £40 million project, jointly funded by the Scottish Government and City of Edinburgh Council, happened because our Council and our Government worked together for the benefit of the people of this community. Representing the school, over the past three and a half years, I am delighted to acknowledge input from Janis Croll who has worked tirelessly at my side in order to ensure that the school's voice was heard when needed. And finally, I extend thanks and enormous praise to Billy McIntyre, the project sponsor, who was, on behalf of the City of Edinburgh Council, tasked with ensuring that the school was delivered on time and on budget. I have no doubt that, under Billy's continued stewardship, phase 2 will be completed on time and under budget for August 2016.'

Then Mr Macdonald turns more reflective.

'By October 2016 James Gillespie's High School will have been a free, area-based co-educational comprehensive for a full forty-three years. Ours has always been a broad outlook and we are proud besides to be in such a cosmopolitan part of Scotland's capital – noted for medicine, higher education, printing and publishing and newspapers and bookshops – for pupils of any creed, any background, any nationality.

'Our most famous former pupil, the late Muriel Spark – who attended in the 1930s – enjoyed, as she recorded, studying at the Gillespie's of her day alongside Catholic pupils, Hindu classmates, friends Jewish and Presbyterian and Episcopalian.

'And, at the time of writing, forty-seven official languages – that is, tongues for which there is at least one dictionary in print – are spoken in our school community. And, of course, we are the reception-secondary for Edinburgh's Gaelic-medium pupils.

'Our motto, for some fourscore years, has been Mr Gillespie's own – "Fidelis et Fortis" – "faithful and brave".

'We have since moved on from snuff. But our spirit abides. Our values, timeless as they are, adorn the walls and corridors of our new school.

'For we,' says Donald J. Macdonald, 'for all at and from James Gillespie's High School, celebrate the diversity that exists; the differences that are the things that make us individual; the things that make us human and special.

'And,' he concludes, 'as a school community, we make this journey together.'

The veil is lifted, the plaque exposed; the applause warm and sustained.

The Minister lingers for a minute or two, bright and brittle. Those of us in the know make purposefully straight for the staffroom. For there are scones.

the end.

Sources

This book, as agreed in discussions with Donald J. MacDonald the Head Teacher, the James Gillespie's Trust and Hugh Andrew of Birlinn Ltd back in 2013, had to be heavily illustrated, limited in length and an accessible read for interested teenage pupils – while nevertheless covering over two centuries of history. A heavily annotated, fully sourced text would have been inappropriate and very expensive, though I have tried to make plain on the page where I have found material or heard an anecdote.

The chief resource, of course, has been the Archives of James Gillespie's High School. The school owes a signal debt to the late Miss Jean C. McIntyre, and the happily preserved Anne Inglis, the school's former librarian, who first conscientiously collated all this material; and, too, to many former pupils and members of staff who have donated old magazines, jotters, assorted badges and ephemera and even items of uniform. It should be made plain that no sensitive pupil information or staff records are retained: one looks in vain for any juicy disciplinary material – though a Lochgelly school strap was quietly conserved.

The Archives are inevitably patchy. Hardly any material survives from before 1874, when the school moved into Gillespie's Hospital and became fee-paying and co-educational, and very little indeed before its ascension to the Warrender Park Crescent building in 1914. We do have admissions-records, leaving-records and head teachers' logs covering most of the twentieth century, but of all the school's commanders only Dr Thomas kept a conscious record for posterity of correspondence, school events, press-cuttings and so on, and these papers – filed with characteristic neatness in a succession of ring-binders – are so absorbing and detailed the period from 1975 to 1991 could easily support a book all its own.

There are two other complications. From the early 1990s, inevitably, records, pupil handbooks, photographs and so on became increasingly digital and, sadly, a great deal of material from recent decades has thus been lost. Schools should make a conscious effort of retaining hard-copy of interesting things or, at least, downloading photographs to hard format for future reference.

I had besides to work on this book amidst all the upheaval, from June 2013 onwards, of the demolition, decant and rebuild. The Archives themselves flitted here and there and for long periods could not be accessed. There were inevitable mishaps: material generously set aside for this book by Mr Macdonald from the 1991–2012 records in his own office – before everything else in them was sent for 2014 incineration – went blithely missing. (The boxful will probably turn up next year in an overlooked cupboard; happily, he had already given me a few interesting documents.) And a splendid album of photographs of Opening Day,

21 October 1966, was briefly sighted in 2014 and then in turn went walkabout. It turned up in a box left in the school offices in mysterious circumstances on 6 September 2016 – and just in time.

Such entertainment besides, there was nevertheless a wealth of material. The school magazine, launched around 1911, was a precious resource. The earliest number in the school's possession is for 1912 and thereafter the set is complete to and including 1984, save for the issues of 1976 and 1978. (The school would welcome the donation of copies.) The magazine was not published in 1916, 1917, 1918, or 1979; publication resumed in 1980 (with the new title of *Snuff*) but ceased after 1984, apart from brief reprise in 1990 and 1991. Examination pressures in the summer-term, these days, now make production of school magazines anywhere very difficult; *The Spark*, a literary and cultural review launched in 2013, is of a high standard, but not a classic school magazine-of-record. From 1968, the school magazine ceased to give detailed biographical tribute to departing staff and from 1977 no staff information is given at all.

Mention should also be made of the 'Living History' oral archive, a far-sighted venture by the James Gillespie's Trust and pegged loosely to bicentenary celebrations in 2003. Dozens of former pupils were interviewed in the early years of this century – largely by senior students – and these recordings have given me many wonderful stories and telling asides. Inevitably the material is almost all from the girls-only Corporation Grammar era, Alison Laidlaw being one of the very few then still alive who had left Gillespie's before it and Linda Urquhart and Susan Middleton (daughter of John S. Hay, once our Principal Teacher of Classics) among the handful interviewed who had attended, or at least finished attending, during the modern comprehensive period. These CD recordings, immaculately packaged, should one day be transcribed in full.

I made use of the following books in research of James Gillespie himself and the earliest years of the school:

Henry, Lord Cockburn, *Memorials of His Time*, T. N. Foulis, Edinburgh and London, 1856. There have been many modern editions of this classic posthumously published memoir.

John Kay, *Original Portraits and Character Etchings*, Edinburgh – three editions, 1838, 1842 and 1877. There have been modern reprints, most notably Birlinn Ltd's charming *Capital Caricatures* version in 2007.

Portrait of a Parish – A record of interesting people and places over the years in the Parish of Colinton, various contributors, MacRae and Patterson Ltd, Edinburgh, 1968.

David Shankie, *The Parish of Colinton – From an Early Period to the Present Day*, John Wilson, Edinburgh, 1902.

Daniel Wilson, *Memorials of Edinburgh in the Olden Times*, Thomas C. Jack, Edinburgh, 1896 edition.

Reference must also be made to two sadly unpublished but impressive little histories by two conscientious Gillespie's pupils – Elaine C. J. Cochrane, in 1953, and Kathryn Thompkins, in 1960 – held in the school Archives. They are of scrupulous accuracy and were of the greatest assistance.

And I should also make mention of Rachel Cooke, *Her Brilliant Career: Ten Extraordinary Women of the Fifties*, Virago, London, 2013 – affording many astute insights to possibilities (and pressures) for able young women of Dr Thomas's generation.

I found the following books most useful in the broader history of Scottish education in the nineteenth century:

R. D. Anderson, Margaret Harrison and Willis Marker, *Teaching the Teachers – The History of Jordanhill College of Education*, Edinburgh University Press, 1996.

Andrew L. Drummond and James Bulloch, *The Church in Victorian Scotland 1843–1874*, Saint Andrew's Press, Edinburgh, 1975. The second volume of a masterly trilogy.

T. C. Smout, *A Century of the Scottish People 1830–1950*, Collins Ltd, London, 1986.

The website of Moray House, now the Faculty of Education for the University of Edinburgh, also gives a splendid potted history of Scottish education: http://www.ed.ac.uk/ education/about-us/maps-estates-history/history

I have quoted, too, from the late Dame Muriel Spark, and her biographer:

Muriel Spark, *Curriculum Vitae – A Volume of Autobiography*, Constable Ltd, London, 1992. Her memories of Gillespie's had first appeared in the March 25 1991 number of *The New Yorker*, under the title 'Personal History – The School on the Links'.

Muriel Spark, 'What Images Return,' essay in the festschrift *Memoirs of a Modern Scotland*, ed. Karl Miller, Faber and Faber Ltd, London 1970. Originally published in the *New Statesman* on 10 August 1962, Spark gave the piece to this collection in honour of the late Hector MacIver (1910–1966), a brilliant Lewisman and English teacher, whose pupils at the Royal High School included the late Robin Cook, and whose friends included many other notable Scottish writers. George MacKay Brown, Hugh MacDiarmid, William McIlvanney, Sorley MacLean, and Tom Nairn were other distinguished contributors.

Muriel Spark, *The Prime of Miss Jean Brodie*, Macmillan Ltd, London, 1961.

Martin Stannard, *Muriel Spark – The Biography*, Weidenfeld and Nicolson Ltd, London, 2009.

And, finally, I found these volumes on Edinburgh of great value:

James Buchan, Capital of the Mind – How Edinburgh Changed the World, John Murray Ltd, London, 2003.

Malcolm Cant, *Marchmont in Edinburgh*, John Donald Publishers Ltd, Edinburgh, 1983.

Malcolm Cant, *Marchmont, Sciennes and the Grange* (Foreword by Ronnie Corbett OBE), Malcolm Cant Publications, Edinburgh, 2001.

Malcolm Cant, *Sciennes and the Grange* (Foreword by Professor David Daiches), John Donald Publishers Ltd, Edinburgh, 1990.

Malcolm Cant, *Villages of Edinburgh, An Illustrated Guide, Vol. 2 – Colinton, Gilmerton, Juniper Green, Liberton, Longstone & Slateford, Morningside and Swanston*, Malcolm Cant Publications, Edinburgh, 1999.

Alan Hamilton, *Essential Edinburgh*, André Deutsch Ltd, London, 1977.

Sandy Mullay, *The Illustrated History of Edinburgh's Suburbs*, Breedon Books Publishing, Derby, 2001.

Alasdair Roberts, *Crème de la Crème – Girls' Schools of Edinburgh*, Steve Savage Publishers Ltd, London, 2007.

Alasdair Roberts, *Ties that Bind – Boys' Schools of Edinburgh*, Steve Savage Publishers Ltd, London, 2009.

Charles J. Smith, *Historic South Edinburgh,* John Donald Publishers Ltd, Edinburgh, 2000. Originally published as four succeeding small volumes: 1978, 1979, 1986 and 1988 by Charles Skilton Ltd, Haddington.

Charles J. Smith, *South Edinburgh in Pictures,* Albyn Press Ltd, Haddington, 1989.

Waters Under the Bridge – Twentieth Century Tollcross, Fountainbridge, and the West Port, Tollcross Local History Project, Aberdeen University Press, 1990.

Postscript

This book was commissioned by the James Gillespie's Trust, a charitable trust which seeks to support the school in all its various activities. The Trustees are immensely grateful to John MacLeod, himself a former pupil of the school, for having so readily taken on the task of writing it and for no other reward than the satisfaction it has given him. The result will not disappoint anyone familiar with his work.

The book was commissioned with a view to publication to more or less coincide with the opening of the new school and the Trust also wishes to thank Hub South East Scotland, Galliford Try and Morrison Construction for sponsoring the book's production so generously. Thanks are also due to Birlinn Ltd and particularly to Hugh Andrew, without whose advice and guidance it would never have seen the light of day. Donald Macdonald, the current Head Teacher and, as such, a Trustee *ex officio*, has been endlessly helpful in ensuring the book reached publication, including liaising with John and avoiding encroachment by a committee on the author's freedom to tell the story as he sees it.

Finally, the following former pupils took the opportunity of supporting production of the book by pre-ordering it and paying to have their names and dates of attendance inserted. We are immensely grateful to them all.

The James Gillespie's Trust
August 2016

Diane Alexander, 1948–1961
Margaret Anderson, 1958–1964
Joyce J. M. Armstrong, 1944–1946
Marjorie Ashworth, 1946–1950
Elaine Allan Baillie, 1947–1959
Frances Elisabeth Baillie, 1942–1954
Carol Josephine Baillie, 1950–1963
Enid Bannatyne, 1957–1970
Christine Elizabeth Bashford, 1958–1964
Elizabeth Brooks, 1952–1965
Catherine Elizabeth Brown, 1933–1945
Elizabeth C. D. Browne, 1966–1978
Jane A. S. Burn, 1930–1934
Jessie F. D. Burn (not known)
Isobel N. Burn (not known)
Ann Doreen Cameron, 1956–1962
Anne P. Cantley, 1933–1946
Pamela Anne Connet, 1958–1963
Jenny Cowper, 1957–1970
Janet Darling, 1940–1953
Anne G. Davidson, 1941–1950
Janice Dewar, 1949–1962
Celia Dorothy Dickson, 1958–1963
Fiona F. Donaldson, 1967–1973
Jean F. Dulson, 1952–1964
Patricia Dunsmore, 1955–1968
Ruth Easton, 1977–1983
Agnes Gray Foley, 1949–1955
Edith M. Forrest, 1940–1955
Jean Fraser, 1939–1951
Christine Elizabeth Fraser, 1941–1953
Patricia Fraser, 1941–1953
Barbara Fraser, 1950–1963
Wendy J. B. Froud, 1958–1964
Lilias Catherine Galloway, 1944–1949
Moira Christina Gibson, 1938–1950
Laurie Gilzean, 1955–1968
Norma Hardy, 1954–1960
Helen Heatlie, 1961–1974
Marion Heyworth, 1964–1970
Una B. Hope, 1954–1967
Mary R. Hope, 1947–1960
Margaret Elizabeth Howieson, 1946–1952
Eileen Helen Johnston, 1950–1958
Patricia Margaret Johnston, 1954–1967
Marlyn Kay, 1963–1969
Marion Kean, 1960–1965
Margo Kemp, 1939–1946
Christine M. Kemp, 1934–1946

Mabel Keppy, 1949–1953
Doreen Kidd, 1943–1956
Ruth I. Kinnear, 1950–1954
Christine W. Kirkwood, 1943–1954
Rosalind Adelman Landy, 1942–1955
Patricia A. Lawson, 1951–1964
Margaret Lothian, 1947–1952
Malvina MacDonald, 1948–1954
Angela C. MacLean, 1965–1971
Elspeth M. MacLean, 1965–1971
Kirsteen A. MacLean, 1964–1969
Fiona M. MacLean, 1965–1971
Ruth D. Macmillan, 1931–1941
Catherine MacPherson, 1958–1964
Margaret E. H. D. Macpherson, 1932–1942
Shirley Manson, 1949–1951
Anne E. Martin, 1955–1967
Christine Matheson, 1936–1949
Joyce McCurrach, 1938–1950
Muriel Elizabeth McCurrach, 1935–1946
Aileen McDonald, 1943–1955
Anne McDougall, 1946–1959
Margaret Helen Dawson McGregor,
    1943–1956
Sheila Jane McIntosh, 1962–1968
Evelyn Ann McLauchlan, 1942–1947
Elizabeth M. Menzies, 1962–1975
Lynne Murray, 1969–1974
Wendy Nicholl, 1954–1960
Susan Nicholl, 1953–1966
Mary Brown Osler, 1940–1953
Tom Parnell, 1992–1998
Lucy Pearson, 1950–1956
Christine Penman, 1952–1957
Irene M. Philp, 1950–1956
Phyllis Graham Pozzi, 1945–1958
Joan Purdie, 1957–1963
Rachel Quinnell, 1927–1938
Sheila Rennilson, 1942–1955
Sylvia Richardson, 1958–1962
Margaret Richardson, 1930–1943
Elma Dorothy Robertson – 1941–1951
Margaret B. Robertson, 1940–1947
Sheila Mary Jean Scott, 1933–1945
Moray Simon, 1974–1980
Elaine Sinclair, 1969–1974
Evelyn A. W. Small, 1927–1938
Winnifred Smith, 1944–1957
Rosemary Soutar, 1955–1968

Patricia Taylor, 1944–1956
Anne Sutherland Taylor, 1951–1956
Helen Todd, 1948–1960
Marjory Tucker, 1960–1973
Christine Turner, 1966–1972
Mike Turner, 1975–1980
Linda Urquhart, 1964–1977
Joyce Vinestock, 1937–1946
Shirley Wade, 1971–1977
Eileen Waitt, 1937–1950
Audrey Watson, 1946–1951

Alexandra M. Whigham, 1948–1961
Patricia Williams, 1955–1961
Allison Wilson, 1952–1963
Jean H. Wishart, 1942–1951
Olga Wojtas, 1959–1972
Frances T. Woodward, 1925–1938
Margaret Wylie, 1934–1946
Ann McLeish Wylie, 1954–1966
Betty Wylie, 1931–1943
Elinor Wylie, 1931–1944

Some notable former pupils
of James Gillespie's Schools

Nicola Auld, actor and entertainer

Conrad Balatoni, professional footballer

John Burgess, jazz musician

Robert Cavanah [Scott], actor

Jane Charles, glass artist

Ronnie Corbett (1930–2016), comedian (completed education at Royal High School)

Gina Davidson, journalist and commentator

Henry Raeburn Dobson (1901–1985), portrait painter (completed education at George
    Watson's College)

Dorothy Dunnett, neé Halliday (1923–2001), popular novelist

Rupert Ford (1968–2001), scientist

Herbert Snell Gamley (1865–1928), sculptor

Irene Glass, Christian missionary to India and Pakistan

Iain Henderson, filmmaker; BAFTA Scotland award for Best New Talent, 2015

Craig Howieson, international table tennis player (bronze medallist, 2014
    Commonwealth Games, Glasgow)

Damien Hoyland, international Rugby Union player (capped for senior Scotland side, 2015)

Andy Irvine, international Rugby Union player (completed education at George Heriot's
    School)

Moira Jeffrey, journalist and commentator

Pat Kinch, international track cyclist; held world record speed for streamlined recumbent
    from 1990 to 1996

Ellen King (1909–1994), international swimmer; won two silver medals at 1928 Olympics,
    Amsterdam

John Leslie [Stott], television presenter

Viv Lumsden, journalist and broadcaster

Billy Lyall (1953–1989), musician and pop singer

Sam MacDonald, sculptor

Danny McGrath, film director

Finn McGrath, film director

Ben McPherson, television director and producer; crime novelist

Dorothy Minck (1918–2016), former pupil and long-serving teacher at Gillespie's,
    classmate of Muriel Spark

Dr Sam Mohiddin, cardiologist
Mark Munro, BBC production executive
Stephanie Rew, artist
Liz Roberts, writer and commentator
Toby Shippey, musician; member of world music fusion band, Salsa Celtica
Morag Siller (1970–2016), actor
Alastair Sim (1900–1976), actor
Callum Skinner, international track cyclist: gold medallist, Team Sprint, 2016 Olympic
    Games; silver medallist, Individual Sprint, 2016 Olympic Games, Rio de Janeiro.
Colin Skinner, saxophonist, leader of The Syd Lawrence Orchestra
Muriel Spark, neé Camberg (1918–2006), poet and novelist
Shirley Spear, chef, restaurateur, chairwoman of the Scottish Food Commission
Edi Stark, née Stewart, journalist and broadcaster
David Steel, politician (completed education at George Watson's College)
Dr Ewen Stewart, Chairman of the Royal College of General Practitioners Sex, Drugs and
    HIV Group
Grant Stott, broadcaster and entertainer
Dave Swanson, drummer, jazz/blues/easy-listening musician
Michael Thomson, actor
Linda Urquhart, businesswoman; first female chair of CBI Scotland
Stephen White, illustrator, cartoonist and graphic novelist
Christopher Wood, artist
George Wright, professional footballer

Dr Patricia Thomas would like to point out that pupils who studied at the former Darroch
Secondary School in subsequent periods of use as the James Gillespie's High School Annexe
– from 1975 to 1991, and from 2013 to the present – can truly say they went to the same
school as Sean Connery, actor, Hollywood star . . . and legend.

Index